Gettysburg College
June 29, 1989

For Stan,
a fellow enthusiast
of the Civil War

Jay Luvaas

With best wishes

Harold Nelson

Remains of Union Breastworks on Bolivar Heights (HWN).

The U.S. Army War College

Guide to the

Battle of Antietam

The Maryland Campaign of 1862

Edited by Dr. Jay Luvaas
and Col. Harold W. Nelson

South Mountain Press, Inc., Publishers
Carlisle, Pennsylvania
1987

ISBN *0-937339-01-6*

Published and Distributed by South Mountain Press, Inc.
Please address all inquiries to the publisher:

South Mountain Press, Inc.
37 West High Street, P.O. Box 306
Carlisle, PA 17013-0306
Telephone: (717) 245-2933

Maps drawn by Mark Pfoutz

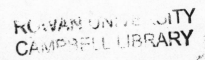

CONTENTS

MAPS

HOW TO USE THIS BOOK

If you were to arrive at Stop 1 east of South Mountain with the rising sun on a long summer day, you might move through all phases of this campaign before dark. But if travel schedules force such haste, you will probably have to spend long—and we hope pleasant—hours afterwards, expanding on initial impressions and unravelling complexities in a more careful reading of this *Guide*. It is difficult to absorb so much detail in what amounts to a forced march.

Should time permit, spend a full day enjoying South Mountain and Harpers Ferry. The battles fought there are integral parts of the campaign, the terrain is fascinating, and few students of the Civil War have worked out the tactical details of those battles as you can by using this book. If you are fortunate you may even come to appreciate the sentiments of G. M. Trevelyan, one of England's greatest historians, when he declared:

> The skilled game of identifying positions on a battlefield innocent of guides, where one must make out everything for oneself—best of all if no one has ever done it properly before—is almost the greatest of out-door intellectual pleasures.
>
> George Macaulay Trevelyan, *Clio, A Muse, and other Essays Literary and Pedestrian* (London: Longmans, Green and Co., 1913), p. 28.

If your travel schedule or specific interests take you to Antietam or Harpers Ferry before South Mountain, that causes no problem. Simply turn to the appropriate section of the *Guide* for the stops associated with the battle at hand. The first stop in each of these battle areas is easy to find if you follow the route laid out in the *Guide*.

Since this is not a *history* of the Maryland Campaign of 1862, some users may want to consult standard works on the Civil War or narrative histories of the campaign in conjunction with their visits to the sites. Time spent in reading—like time spent by the soldier in reconnaissance—is never wasted. People who visit battlefields with us report that their most productive study begins after they have stopped at key points, viewed the terrain, and shared the words and thoughts of participants—the approach you will experience by using this *Guide*.

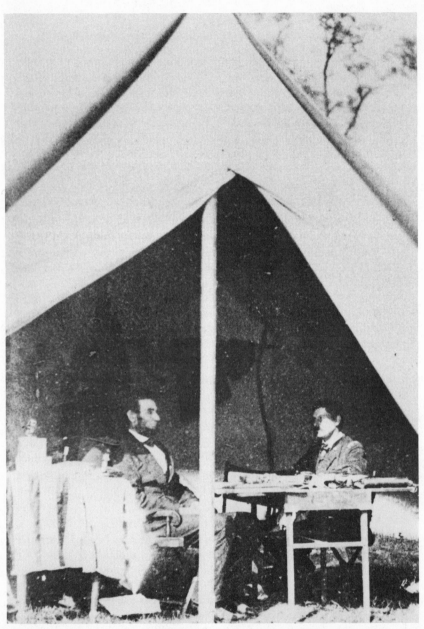

Lincoln and McClellan at Antietam. (USAMHI)

ACKNOWLEDGEMENTS

This book owes its existence to the support we have received from many people. Secretary Marsh began his Staff Rides for the Senior Army Leaders at Antietam and has continued to demonstrate the value of studying battlefields. The resulting enthusiasm for the method we pioneered in our *Guide to the Battle of Gettysburg* convinced us that this subsequent volume would be widely used within the Army and at the same time fill a need for the student of the Civil War.

Major General Thompson, as Commandant of the War College and Colonel David Hansen, Chairman of the Department of National Security and Strategy, gave us the local command environment needed to prepare the manuscript for publication while continuing our normal faculty duties. Roy Strong and the U.S. Army War College Foundation facilitated commercial publication. Our students and colleagues who accompanied us on our many trips to the battlefields helped us with their questions and insights. We are particularly indebted to three students: Hank Booth and Brian Flynn produced a painstaking analysis of the obscure Battle of South Mountain that served as an important departure point, and John Fuller's detailed study of Burnside's attack at Antietam contributed directly to our recreation of that phase of the battle. John Kallmann, our publisher, once again provided the creative insight required to unite text, maps, and photos into a cohesive volume while having the requisite patience to tolerate many last-minute discoveries and inevitable delays. Paula Murphy did all she could to reduce those delays, keeping the office on course and assisting in the production of manuscripts. Betty Otto, Paul Chiles, and other friends on the staff of the Antietam National Battlefield gave enthusiastic support at every step. We owe special thanks to our good friend and former colleague, Reg Shrader, for his admirable essay on Civil War logistics.

Above all others we thank our wives, Linda and Janet, true "Civil War Widows," who have tolerated increasingly numerous expeditions to these battlefields as we prepared this *Guide*, and to other fields in response to increased interest in Staff Rides throughout the Army. Even when at home, furloughed from the battlefields, we often seemed wed to word processors as we invested family time to fuse fresh insights and field notes into the finished text.

We enjoyed marching the Army of the Cussewago through an early draft of this tour in 1985. Their shrewd comments and good-natured gibes have sharpened our vision, and we thank them and all others who have enjoyed the battlefields with us.

Jay Luvaas
Harold Nelson

Army War College Antietam Tour, 10 June 1939, the last before the outbreak of war in Europe. Note the linen suits and pith helmets indicative of the influence of Central American duty in the 1930's. This would be one of the last staff rides of this era. Photo courtesy Antietam National Battlefield Park.

INTRODUCTION

Like the *Guide to the Battle of Gettysburg* that preceded it, this work is intended to serve two purposes. To those interested in the Maryland campaign of 1862 or the battles of South Mountain, Crampton's Gap, Harpers Ferry and Antietam, it should enable the reader to locate points—many of them unidentified by historical markers—where critical or fascinating events occurred that help explain *how* the battle was fought or *why* leaders on both sides acted as they did. To the soldier visiting these sites, this *Guide* may also help to raise broader questions about tactics, organization, leadership, unit cohesion, the use of terrain, and the application of principles that are fundamental to his profession. In either case this volume is intended to be enjoyed as a book as well as used for a self-guided tour on the field.

The book differs from its predecessor in one important respect: it deals with the campaign as well as individual battles, making it possible to view the campaign at the *Operational* as well as the tactical level. Civilian readers unfamiliar with the term "Operational level" should understand that whereas traditional campaign histories have dealt with *strategy* and *tactics*, modern U.S. army doctrine describes three rather than two broad divisions of military activity. *Strategy*—which used to be known as "policy" or "grand strategy", now refers to the employment of the armed forces of a nation to secure the objectives of national policy. *The operational level*, which first appeared in the campaigns of Napoleon and later was identified as "strategy" or "grand tactics" in most Civil War campaign histories, involves the employment of available military resources to attain strategic goals within a theater of war. Tactics remains the term for specific techniques used by smaller units to win battles and engagements which support operational objectives.

These categories seem arbitrary, for the lines separating the levels are often shifting or blurred. At corps and division level, for example, it is sometimes difficult to separate operations and tactics because both represent fighting levels within the context of a single campaign, while at the same time the operational level serves as the link between strategy and fighting battles. Our doctrine asserts that while the principles of war are appropriate to all three levels, "applying them involves a different perspective for each," and the best way for the modern soldier to broaden his own perspective on such matters is to study the interaction of the three levels throughout an historical campaign.

Students of the Civil War need understand only that what used to be called *strategy* in most military literature today would be regarded as *the Operational Level. Jackson's* celebrated Valley campaign as it is described in G.F.R. Henderson's classic, *Stonewall Jackson and the American Civil War*, is a superb example of the operational art, for it was planned and executed to implement *Lee's* strategy of keeping authorities in Washington from reinforcing McClellan's army before Richmond. Since the Maryland campaign also involves the use of large units in "sustained operations designed to defeat an enemy force in a specified space and time with simultaneous and sequential battles," with the "disposition of forces, selection of objectives, and actions taken to weaken or to outmaneuver the enemy" all setting the terms of the next battle, it too involved the operational level of war.[1]

The term "operational art" encompasses many of the important intellectual, technological, and organizational capabilities that we encounter in the Maryland Campaign. The central intellectual capability is the ability of the commander who conducts the campaign to "see" each engagement in terms of his larger purpose. How can he use battles to impose his will on the enemy? The generals who fought the Civil War tended to think in Napoleonic terms of a campaign of maneuver culminating in a single, decisive battle, many of them not fully appreciating how mass armies aided by railroads and telegraphs and supported by industrialized production bases made maneuver more complex—and battle less decisive. We see these forces at work in 1862, so we can learn from *Lee* and McClellan when we study their decisions as operational commanders.

[1] Department of the Army, *Field Manual No.* 100–5: *Operations* (Washington, 1982), ch. 2, p. 3.

The technological dimension addresses the ability of an army to capitalize on its own technological advantage while minimizing that of the enemy. We sometimes forget that there were "high tech" aspects of the Civil War such as pre-fabricated bridges, rifled artillery, repeater carbines, and signal communications that enabled these armies to move, shoot, and communicate better than armies of an earlier day. As this campaign clearly demonstrates, the presence of such potential technological advantage was not uniform in the two armies. Generally the Union had the advantage. If the student of the operational art should ask, "What did McClellan do to press the advantage of technology and what did *Lee* do to offset disadvantage," the answers might provide useful insights even though the specific technologies have changed.

The organizational aspects of the operational art flow from the size, duration, and complexity of modern battle. By 1862 the side that could organize massive logistics trains, instruct large numbers of recruits, process intelligence data from multiple sources, and treat thousands of casualties should have gained an edge over its opponent. Detailed study of each of these organizational specialties is therefore as important as careful study of the organization of the combatant arms. But here too the student of the operational art discovers the organizational superiority of one of the armies and then seeks to learn how – or if – that superiority was utilized as an advantage over the enemy.

In the final analysis, the operational art is entirely intellectual, for the organizational and technological advantages are meaningless unless the commander can capitalize on these superiorities with the same skill that he demonstrates in concentrating greater numbers or firepower upon the decisive point. This is what separates operational art from tactics, and what makes the Maryland Campaign such a fertile field for study.

At the tactical level, the visitor to Antietam will be struck by the difference in the way in which the two armies conducted the battle. *Lee* fought essentially one battle, moving guns and troops effectively from one sector to another, while McClellan may be considered to have waged three separate contests – the attacks of the I, XII and part of the II Corps across the Corn Field, the repeated efforts to break through the Bloody Lane, and finally Burnside's assault against the heights overlooking Sharpsburg.

Aside from differences in tactical ability and command style, this contrast between concentration and a dispersion of effort is in part explained by the way in which the contending forces were led and organized. In both respects the Army of Northern Virginia was the more effective military instrument.

Indeed, at Antietam McClellan did not command an "army" in the organic sense of the term. On 2 September 1862, following Pope's defeat at Second Bull Run, McClellan was placed in command of the fortifications of Washington and all troops available for the defense of the capital. The next day, anticipating a Confederate "raid" into Maryland or Pennsylvania, H. W. Halleck, General-in-Chief, ordered McClellan immediately to organize a movable army to meet the Confederates in the field. On the 4th McClellan sent Banks' corps from Pope's scattered Army of Virginia beyond the Washington defenses toward Rockville to keep a watchful eye on the Confederates, and on the 5th Pope was relieved and the armies of the Potomac and Virginia were consolidated under McClellan's command.

As these units took the field for active operations, Maj. Gen. Banks was left in command of the Washington defenses. Several days later President Lincoln directed that the three corps of the Army of Virginia be absorbed into the Army of the Potomac: Pope's First corps now became XI Corps, his Second corps was changed to XII Corps, and the Third corps was redesignated I Corps. Thus at Antietam McClellan commanded the II, V, and VI Corps of his original Army of the Potomac, I and XII Corps from the Army of Virginia, Burnside's IX Corps, which had conducted successful coastal operations off North Carolina and had fought Second Bull Run under Major General Jesse Reno (while Burnside commanded Pope's right wing), and the Kanawha Division, recently from West Virginia.

To make matters worse, half of McClellan's corps commanders had never before functioned at this level. Hooker, who had led a division during the Peninsular campaign, was placed in command of I Corps, and J.K.F. Mansfield, an engineer officer who never before had commanded large bodies of troops, was picked to command the XII Corps just two days before the battle of Antietam. To add to the confusion, on 14 September—the day the Union army forced the passes over South Mountain—McClellan placed Burnside, an old friend, in command of the Right Wing [there does not appear to have been a "Left" or a "Center"

Wing], comprising his own IX and Hooker's I Corps. Maj. Gen. Jesse L. Reno led the IX Corps in the fighting for Fox's Gap. When he was killed, the command was temporarily given to Brig. Gen. Jacob D. Cox. Cox, although not a professional soldier, had served effectively under McClellan in West Virginia the previous year, but his Kanawha Division was not organically a part of IX Corps. The following day Hooker's I Corps was "temporarily detached" from the Right Wing, but because Burnside exercised general command on the Union left at Antietam, Cox continued to lead IX Corps throughout the battle.

Moreover, two of McClellan's experienced corps commanders—Porter and Franklin—had been temporarily relieved of their commands until charges of disobedience in the Second Manassas campaign could be investigated by a court of inquiry, leading to a situation that prompted Halleck, the General-in-Chief, to complain of "the differences and ill-feeling among the generals" that embarrassed the administration and threatened to ruin the country, and caused Lincoln sadly to acknowledge that he had "only just now found out what military jealousy is."[2]

In contrast, the Confederate army at Antietam was far more cohesive and responsive. On 1 June, 1862, when *Lee* assumed command "of the armies of Eastern Virginia and North Carolina," he inherited a structure in which the division was the largest administrative and operational unit: no larger formal organization was possible under existing Confederate law. There could be, therefore, no such military body as a corps and no corresponding grade of lieutenant general. As early as 18 April *Lee's* predecessor, *Gen. Joseph E. Johnston*, had attempted to solve this command problem by dividing the Confederate forces in the Peninsula into three 'Wings' under major generals *J. B. Magruder, D. H. Hill* and *James Longstreet*, and on the eve of the Seven Days Battles *Lee* made *Longstreet* responsible for the "military movements and operations" of his own and *D. H. Hill's* division, while *Magruder* was to lead the divisions of *McLaws* and *D. R. Jones* along with his own. This practice of clustering two or more divisions under a senior division commander, especially when operating "in wooded country of confusing, bad roads" and with an inadequate staff, made it almost inevitable that the divisions would function as "dis-

[2] *O.R.*, XII, Part III, p. 813; Kenneth P. Williams, *Lincoln Finds A General* (New York: The Macmillan Company, 1949), I, 360.

tinct little armies." In only one of the Seven Days' battles had there been an instance where two divisions "had cooperated for the whole of a battle."[3]

Although *Lee* could not formally organize his army into two corps without enabling legislation, when the Army of Northern Virginia — which by this time it had come to be known — moved north, it operated as two distinct "commands" or "wings" under *Longstreet* and *Jackson* even though the two were not formally assigned to command corps until nearly three weeks after Antietam. In the weeks following the Seven Days battles, five of eleven division commanders (including two of the three wing commanders) had been transferred or shuffled off to other duties, leaving only *Longstreet* and *Stonewall Jackson* — who had led his own and *Ewell's* divisions plus a brigade of cavalry in his famous Valley campaign — with experience in controlling more than one division in active operations. In contrast to McClellan, who had been thwarted in his hope to delay forming army corps until he could pick commanders from men who had successfully led divisions in the field,[4] *Lee* was able to benefit from observing those who had demonstrated an ability to command at the corps level. And to replace the likes of *Holmes*, *Huger* and *Magruder*, who had commanded divisions in the Seven Days battles, *Lee* was now free to promote tested and aggressive leaders such as *Hood* and *R. H. Anderson. Wilcox.*

Thus in matters of command and control and in the forging of an instrument responsive to his audacious temperament, *Lee's* army enjoyed a decided advantage at Antietam. The fact that his army was organized into "commands" rather than formal corps, as the order of battle suggests, may help explain how Confederate divisions could be switched so easily from one flank to the other or plugged into a sector like the West Woods or the Sunken Road regardless of who commanded there. One cannot help but wonder, however, if the absence of a permanent corps organization and established chain of command may not also have been a factor in the decision to send two copies of *Lee's Special Orders, No. 191,*, outlining his operational plan for the Maryland campaign, to *D. H. Hill* — one from

[3] Douglas Southall Freeman, *Lee's Lieutenants: A Study in Command* (3 vols., New York: Charles Scribner's Sons, 1946), I, 670.

[4] *O.R.*, V, p. 13

army headquarters, and the other from *Jackson's* "Command." The copy from *Lee's* headquarters—the celebrated 'Lost Order' that was found by a Union soldier wrapped around three cigars and quickly relayed to McClellan—may well have been written by a staff officer under the mistaken impression that he was still dealing with "a distinct little army" under *Hill*.

There was another, more compelling reason why the Confederate army at Antietam was superior: as a tactical instrument it was better organized. While *Lee's* army lacked the symmetry that it later achieved, by the time Antietam was fought he had organized his infantry into two "commands" or "wings", giving *Longstreet* 5 divisions and *Jackson* 4. Except for the divisions of *Walker* and *Hood*, comprising two brigades each, and *Evans'* independent brigade, which apparently functioned part of the time as a provisional division when detached and augmented by one of *D. H. Hill's* brigades, Confederate divisions at Antietam contained from 4 to 6 brigades, each comprising from 4 to 6 regiments.

Initially most artillery batteries in both armies had been distributed unevenly among brigades, reflecting the way in which artillery had been organized in time of peace and used throughout the Mexican War. *Lee*, appreciating the weakness of this system, soon assembled these batteries into division artillery and reorganized the old Reserve Artillery into 5 battalion groups under a new Chief of Artillery, *Brig. Gen. W. N. Pendleton*. At Cedar Mountain and Second Bull Run the new artillery organization worked well, and by the time of Antietam *Lee* had introduced additional changes to place the artillery on a more effective footing. His new plan was to organize the artillery of each division into a battalion, commanded by the division chief of artillery, and to retain 3 battalions as a general reserve. He also intended to give each of his two 'commands' an additional battalion as a corps reserve, but by Antietam this had been accomplished only for *Longstreet*. The Order of Battle gives no reserve battalion to Jackson, whose chief of artillery apparently had to borrow guns from divisional artillery when needed and who was not even present on the field until evening. No matter: in this battle Jeb Stuart, commanding the Confederate cavalry, to all intent and purposes functioned as Jackson's chief of artillery, demonstrating once again the flexibility of Lee's command system.[5] Before the next battle was fought, *Jackson* had his reserve battalion.

Throughout the day the reserve battalions of artillery were switched from one sector to another: *Col. Stephen D. Lee's* battalion, for example, supported *Jackson's* infantry in the Corn Field, *D.H. Hill's* troops in the Sunken Road, and finally opposed Burnside's advance from its position near the present National Cemetery. If the Confederates at Antietam were unable constantly to enjoy massed artillery support, the cause lay not so much with organizational problems as with the superior numbers and weight of Union guns of position in battery on the heights across the Antietam.

Lee also was organized to make maximum use of his cavalry. The army he had inherited contained only ten regiments of cavalry organized into a single brigade under *Brig. Gen. J. E. B. Stuart*, for when *Jackson* marched from the Valley to join *Lee* near Richmond he left his cavalry behind "to follow as long as the enemy retreats."[6] After the Seven Days battles *Lee* reorganized his mounted arm into a division comprising three brigades with two batteries of horse artillery, commanded by *Jeb Stuart*, who meanwhile had received his second star. By the time of Antietam a third horse battery had joined the division. What ultimately became a cavalry corps was therefore a growth rather than a creation, and the most important part of this process was the experience that *Jeb Stuart* and his principal subordinates had acquired in leading large cavalry units in the field and in combined arms.

Whereas the Army of Northern Virginia already had developed an organization enabling cavalry and artillery to realize their capabilities, this was not the case with McClellan's forces. However admirable was the organization of the Army of the Potomac for administrative and training purposes, half of the Union troops at Antietam had but recently been grafted onto the Army of the Potomac, and McClellan's own policies greatly handicapped the tactical efficiency of cavalry and artillery and thus of his entire army.

Because his 'army' was an amalgam thrown together when *Lee* crossed the Potomac, McClellan's corps varied in strength and composition. The I, II and IX Corps were half again as large as the VI and the XII, which had only two instead of three divisions. The 35 new regiments ordered on 6 September to join their respective corps had not all arrived, and those

[5] Jennings Cropper Wise, *The Long Arm of Lee, or The History of the Artillery of the Army of Northern Virginia* (2 vols: Lynchburg, Virginia: J. P. Bell Company, Inc., 1915), I, 197-327 *passim*.

[6] *O.R.*, XII, Part III, p. 912.

that had were unevenly distributed. IX Corps assigned one new regiment to each brigade, whereas in II and XII Corps the inexperienced troops were concentrated. One brigade in French's division, II Corps, was put together entirely of new regiments, while half of the regiments in Williams' Division, XII Corps, "knew absolutely nothing of maneuvering" and were "without drill or discipline."[7]

There was an additional problem in that Pope and McClellan had originally organized their divisions along different lines with respect to artillery: in the two corps which later were absorbed into the Army of the Potomac (I and XII Corps), Pope had assigned all batteries to the corps, while McClellan preferred instead to assign three or four batteries to each division. Even here there were inequities: McClellan left the corps artillery organization intact when Pope's Second Corps became XII Corps, but he reorganized the artillery of the old Third (now I Corps), assigning all 10 batteries to the divisions. For reasons not apparent in the Order of Battle, Ricketts' division was given only two batteries, while each of Hooker's other divisions had 4. In IX Corps the three divisions had only five batteries among them, while the two brigades in the Kanawha Division had one battery apiece. And even though the artillery in Hooker's I Corps was now concentrated in the divisions, the experience of Battery B, Fourth U.S. Artillery, suggests that the original organization under McDowell wherein each brigade controlled its own battery had become an ingrained habit. Throughout the fight for the Corn Field (see below, pp. 143–44), the battery received its orders from the brigade commander, and the after-action report was submitted not to the chief of artillery, First Division, but to the assistant Adjutant-General of Gibbon's brigade.[8]

When McClellan first organized the Army of the Potomac he created an Artillery Reserve of 18 batteries, commanded by Col. Henry Hunt. This was a complete organization in itself, with its own commander, staff and supply departments, but Hunt's control was administrative in nature rather than tactical. Only when terrain permitted, as at Malvern Hill and Antietam, could the Artillery Reserve provide massed tactical support: its main function was to serve as a source for the replacement or reinforce-

[7] O.R., XIX, Part 1, pp. 169–80; Part II, p. 197; Milo M. Quaife, ed., *From the Cannon's Mouth: The Civil War Letters of General Alpheus S. Williams* (Detroit, Wayne State University Press, 1959), p. 125.

[8] O.R., XII, Part 3, pp. 250–57; XIX, Part 1, pp. 170–72 177–78, 229–31, 482.

ment of front-line batteries. Shortly before Antietam, Hunt, now a brigadier general, became McClellan's chief of artillery. Because his predecessor had exercised administrative responsibilities only, Hunt agreed to take the position only when McClellan conceded "the right to oversee field dispositions" whenever it seemed vital.[9]

Apparently it never seemed vital. Each division commander (and on occasion individual brigade commanders as well) retained control over his artillery. The "division artillery commander," who was always the senior battery commander in the division, was given administrative responsibilities but had no authority to make important tactical decisions. Military readers especially will appreciate the problems that arise when a captain ventures to disagree with a major general over how and where his guns should be employed. About one third of the Union batteries at Antietam were commanded by lieutenants, and, apart from the Artillery Reserve, there was only one field officer of artillery—a major—who served with the guns in any capacity. According to one battery commander, Hooker's artillery at Antietam never exploited some positions that enfiladed the Confederate line of battle simply because Hooker himself had not observed them, and because the original organization under Pope assigned a battery to each brigade and made no provision for division artillery, there was no officer between the corps commander and the battery captain responsible for the deployment of the guns.[10]

Even when the division commander—who rarely was an artilleryman—knew enough to position his batteries correctly, there was still the problem of massing the guns as Napoleon had done in so many battles. For as long as individual batteries served with brigades and divisions they were dependent upon the trains of these units, which usually were some distance in the rear, to resupply ammunition in battle. This meant that even had an infantry commander been willing to give up his guns for the sake of greater concentration elsewhere on the battlefield, it would have been difficult if not impossible to replenish ammunition chests unless the division trains happened to be handy. At best this caused unnecessary delay; at times it caused a necessary withdrawal, as at Chancellorsville, where the batteries at Hazel Grove "were crying out for ammunition"

[9] Edward G. Longacre, *The Man behind the Guns: A Biography of General Henry J. Hunt* (South Brunswick: A. S. Barnes and Company, 1977), p. 119.

[10] J. C. Tidball, "Artillery Service in the Rebellion," *Journal of the Military Service Institute* vol. XII (1891), pp. 964, 973.

while "there was an abundance of it with the division trains nearby, but the batteries could not obtain it."[11] This problem would not be fixed until Hooker reorganized his artillery prior to Gettysburg.

In the judgment of the foremost authority on the artillery of the Army of the Potomac, never before Antietam did the Army have

> so many batteries under its control, but there had been an appalling misuse of their fire, not by the artillerymen but by the infantry commanders who still controlled them. The basic fault . . . was . . . the lack of a higher echelon of tactical organization and command. That the Blue gunners had things on the battlefield virtually their own way despite gallant efforts by the Confederates in counter-battery fire, only points up the possibilities of what might have happened under a better command set-up. . . . Brigade and division commanders ordered their guns to fire, regardless of whether the positions enabled the batteries to accomplish anything, and . . . the battery commanders were obliged to obey these orders.[12]

Union cavalry was similarly handicapped by faulty organization. Nearly all Union armies had initially made the mistake of distributing cavalry among infantry units, leaving commanders of corps and divisions "to decide when, where, and how the cavalry regiments attached to their units were to function." Although Pope had organized his cavalry in the Army of the Mississippi into a separate division, when he came east to create the Army of Virginia he gave to each corps one cavalry brigade while reducing the companies or detachments of cavalry customarily on duty with division or brigade headquarters. In the Peninsula McClellan had distributed his cavalry among the corps except for one brigade designated the "Cavalry Reserve." At Antietam the Order of Battle shows a

---

[11] *Ibid.*, XIII, 301–2; Allan Nevins, ed., *A Diary of Battle: The Personal Journals of Colonel Charles S. Wainwright 1861–65* (New York, Harcourt, Brace and World, Inc., 1962), pp. 192–93.

[12] L. Van Loan Naisawald, *Grape and Canister: the Story of the Field Artillery of the Army of the Potomac, 1861–1865* (New York, Oxford University Press, 1960), p. 227.

cavalry division of 5 brigades commanded by Brig. Gen. Alfred Pleasonton, which would suggest that cavalry was evolving in the Army of the Potomac in much the same way as in the Army of Northern Virginia.[13]

But this is misleading. The twelve regiments in Pleasonton's division were divided into 5 brigades, four of them having but two regiments each, and his official report of the campaign makes it apparent that he used his cavalry in driblets and frequently assigned regiments to the different corps. Moreover each regiment had companies serving on escort and provost duty with the various corps, which diminished the strength of the Cavalry Division by 25 companies, or 17 percent. Pleasonton lacked both experience with large cavalry units and the ability to serve as the eyes and ears of the army, while McClellan, despite his pre-war studies of European cavalry, apparently did not know how to make good use of his mounted arm. According to Major General Wesley Merritt, one of the foremost Union cavalry leaders to emerge during the war, McClellan treated his cavalry regiments as

> . . . a corps of mounted orderlies and messengers whose horses served no higher purpose than to bear their riders on rapid trips for messenger duty, or enabled an orderly to keep pace with a fast riding subaltern, detached for duty, and too often for pleasure. The cavalry under him was decimated instead of being concentrated, and each corps, division, and even brigade commander, was supplied with a force of this expensive arm, which necessarily reduced the available force of cavalry proper.[14]

Because battles are fought by men and not by organizational tables, it should be understood that at the level of regiment and even of brigade, there was probably no appreciable or consistent difference between the two armies. At division level there was: *Lee's* command structure gave him greater flexibility in utilizing terrain and in reinforcing threatened sectors, and his artillery battalions probably gave Confederate divisions an edge whenever the guns could be screened. In the open the Confederate guns "could not cope with the superior weight, caliber, range, and number" of the Union guns across the Antietam. According to *D. H. Hill,* whenever

---

[13] Stephen Z. Starr, *The Union Cavalry in the Civil War: I. From Fort Sumter to Gettysburg, 1861–1863* (Baton Rouge: Louisiana State University Press, 1979), p. 289; *O.R.,* XI, Part II, pp. 24–37; XII, Part II, pp. 249–57; XIX, Part I, p. 180.

[14] Wesley Merritt, "Life and Services of General Philip St. George Cooke," *The Cavalry Journal,* vo. VIII (1895), p. 87; Starr, *Union Cavalry,* I, 313.

the Confederates "were made to reply to the Yankee guns" they were "smashed up or withdrawn before they could be effectively turned against massive columns of attack." *Hill* considered the artillery duel between the Washington artillery and Artillery Reserve posted on the high ground east of the Antietam on the 16th "the most melancholy farce in the war."[15]

At corps level and above the Confederates clearly had the best of it. *Jackson* and *Longstreet* had more experience at this level than half of their Union counterparts and were superior to all of them in tactical ability and a willingness to cooperate. They also had more artillery at their immediate disposal.

As long as *Lee* could enjoy this advantage his system of command, which was to rely upon principal subordinates once he had brought his troops to the right place and at the right time, would work. At Antietam it worked very well.

[15] *O.R.*, XIX, Part 1, p. 1026.

The U.S. Army War College

Guide to the

Battle of Antietam

The Maryland Campaign of 1862

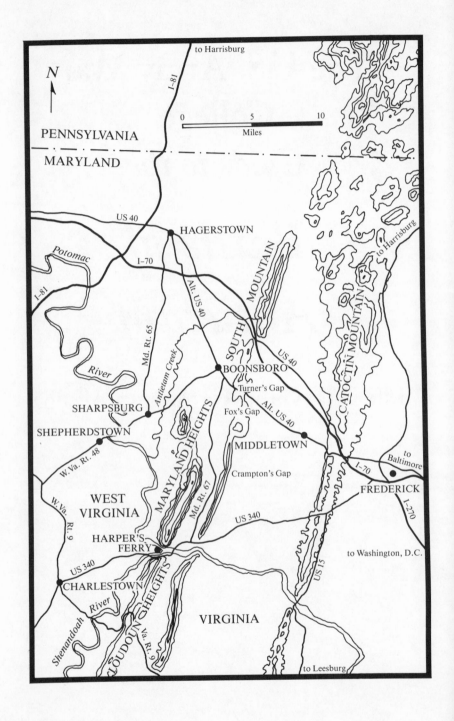

THE MARYLAND CAMPAIGN
4–19 September, 1862
THE ROAD TO SOUTH MOUNTAIN

*Report of General Robert E. Lee, CSA, Commanding
the Army of Northern Virginia*

The enemy having retired to the protection of the fortifications
around Washington . . . the army marched on September 3 toward
Leesburg. The armies of Generals McClellan and Pope had now been
brought back to the point from which they set out on the campaigns
of the spring and summer. . . . Northeastern Virginia was freed from
the presence of Federal soldiers up to the intrenchments of Washington, and soon after the arrival of the army at Leesburg information
was received that the [Federal] troops which had occupied Winchester had retired to Harper's Ferry and Martinsburg. The war was thus
transferred from the interior to the frontier, and the supplies of rich
and productive districts made accessible to our army.

To prolong a state of affairs in every way desirable, and not to
permit the season for active operations to pass without endeavoring
to inflict further injury upon the enemy, the best course appeared to
be the transfer of the army into Maryland. Although not properly
equipped for invasion, lacking much of the material of war, and
feeble in transportation, the troops poorly provided with clothing,
and thousands of them destitute of shoes, it was yet believed to be
strong enough to detain the enemy upon the northern frontier until
the approach of winter should render his advance into Virginia difficult, if not impracticable. The condition of Maryland encouraged the
belief that the presence of our army, however inferior to that of the
enemy, would induce the Washington Government to retain all its
available force to provide against contingencies, which its course
toward the people of that State gave it reason to apprehend. At the

same time it was hoped that military success might afford us an opportunity to aid the citizens of Maryland in any efforts they might be disposed to make to recover their liberties. The difficulties that surrounded them were fully appreciated, and we expected to derive more assistance in the attainment of our object from the just fears of the Washington Government than from any active demonstration on the part of the people, unless success should enable us to give them assurance of continued protection.

Influenced by these considerations, the army was put in motion, *D. H. Hill's* division, which had joined us on the 2d, being in advance, and between September 4 and 7 crossed the Potomac at the fords near Leesburg, and encamped in the vicinity of Fredericktown.

It was decided to cross the Potomac east of the Blue Ridge, in order, by threatening Washington and Baltimore, to cause the enemy to withdraw from the south bank, where his presence endangered our communications and the safety of those engaged in the removal of our wounded and the captured property from the late battle-fields. Having accomplished this result, it was proposed to move the army into Western Maryland, establish our communications with Richmond through the Valley of the Shenandoah, and, by threatening Pennsylvania, induce the enemy to follow, and thus draw him from his base of supplies.

It had been supposed that the advance upon Fredericktown would lead to the evacuation of Martinsburg and Harper's Ferry, thus opening the line of communication through the Valley. This not having occurred, it became necessary to dislodge the enemy from those positions before concentrating the army west of the mountains. To accomplish this with the least delay, *General Jackson* was directed to proceed with his command to Martinsburg, and, after driving the enemy from that place, to move down the south side of the Potomac upon Harper's Ferry. *General McLaws*, with his own and *R. H. Anderson's* division, was ordered to seize Maryland Heights, on the north side of the Potomac, opposite Harper's Ferry, and *Brigadier-General Walker* to take possession of Loudoun Heights, on the east side of the Shenandoah, where it unites with the Potomac. These several commands were directed, after reducing Harper's Ferry and clearing the Valley of the enemy, to join the rest of the army at Boonsborough or Hagerstown.

The march of these troops began on the 10th, and at the same time the remainder of *Longstreet's* command and the division of *D. H. Hill* crossed the South Mountain and moved toward Boonsborough.

General Stuart, with the cavalry, remained east of the mountains, to observe the enemy and retard his advance.

A report having been received that a federal force was approaching Hagerstown from the direction of Chambersburg, *Longstreet* continued his march to the former place, in order to secure the road leading thence to Williamsport, and also to prevent the removal of stores which were said to be in Hagerstown. He arrived at that place on the 11th, *General Hill* halting near Boonsborough to prevent the enemy at Harper's Ferry from escaping through Pleasant Valley, and at the same time to support the cavalry. The advance of the Federal Army was so slow at the time we left Fredericktown as to justify the belief that the reduction of Harper's Ferry would be accomplished and our troops concentrated before they would be called upon to meet it. In that event, it had not been intended to oppose its passage through the South Mountains, as it was desired to engage it as far as possible from its base. [*The War of the Rebellion: a Compilation of the Official Records of the Union and Confederate Armies* (129 vols., Washington: Government Printing Office, 1887), vol. XIX, Part 1, pp. 144–45. All citations from the *Official Records* will refer to Part 1 unless otherwise indicated.]

Report of Maj. Gen. George B. McClellan, USA, Commanding Army of the Potomac

Upon the unfortunate issue of that [Second Bull Run] campaign, I received an intimation from the General-in-Chief that my services were desired for the purpose of arranging for the defense of the capital. . . . On the 2d of September the formal order of the War Department placed me in command of the fortifications of Washington 'and of all the troops for the defense of the capital.' On the 1st . . . I had been instructed that I had nothing to do with the troops engaged in active operations under General Pope, but that my command was limited to the immediate garrison of Washington. On the next day, however, I was verbally instructed by the President and the General-in-Chief to assume command of General Pope's troops (including my own Army of the Potomac) as soon as they approached the vicinity of Washington; to go out and meet them, and to post them as I deemed best to repulse the enemy and insure the safety of the city. . . .

The various garrisons were at once strengthened and put in order, and the troops were disposed to cover all the approaches to the city, and so as to be readily thrown upon threatened points. New defenses were thrown up where deemed necessary. A few days only had elapsed before comparative security was felt with regard to our ability to resist any attack upon the city. The disappearance of the enemy from the front of Washington and their passage into Maryland enlarged the sphere of operations, and made an active campaign necessary to cover Baltimore, prevent the invasion of Pennsylvania, and drive them out of Maryland. . . .

Having made the necessary arrangements for the defense of the city in the new conditions of things, I pushed forward the First and Ninth Corps, under Generals Reno and Hooker, forming the right wing under General Burnside, to . . . New Market and Frederick. The Second and Twelfth Corps, under Generals Sumner and Williams, on the 6th were moved . . . to Rockville; thence . . . on Frederick, the Twelfth Corps moving by a lateral road between Urbana and New Market, thus maintaining the communication between the center and right wing, as well as covering the direct route from Frederick to Washington. The Sixth Corps, under General Franklin, was moved to Darnestown on the 6th . . . thence, on Buckeystown, covering the road from the mouth of the Monocacy to Rockville, and being in position to connect with and support the center should it have been necessary (as was supposed) to force the line of the Monocacy. Couch's division was thrown forward to Offut's Cross-Roads and Poolesville by the river road, thus covering that approach, watching the fords of the Potomac, and ultimately following and supporting the Sixth Corps.

The object of these movements was to feel the enemy—to compel him to develop his intentions—at the same time that the troops were in position readily to cover Baltimore or Washington, to attack him should he hold the line of the Monocacy, or to follow him into Pennsylvania if necessary.

On the 12th a portion of the right wing entered Frederick, after a brisk skirmish at the outskirts of the city and in its streets. On the 13th the main bodies of the right wing and center passed through Frederick. In this city the manifestations of Union feeling were abundant and gratifying. The troops received the most enthusiastic welcome at the hands of the inhabitants. On the 13th the advance, consisting of Pleasonton's cavalry and horse artillery, after some skirmishing cleared the main passage over the Catoctin Hills, leaving no serious obstruction to the movement of the main body until the base of the South Mountain was reached.

While at Frederick, on the 13th, I obtained reliable information of the movements and intentions of the enemy, which made it clear that it was necessary to force the passage of the South Mountain range and gain possession of Boonsborough and Rohrersville before any relief could be afforded to Harper's Ferry.

On the morning of the 13th I received a verbal message from Colonel Miles, commanding at Harper's Ferry, informing me that on the preceding afternoon the Maryland Heights had been abandoned, after repelling an attack by the rebels, and the whole force was concentrated at Harper's Ferry, the Maryland, Loudoun, and Bolivar Heights being all in possession of the enemy. The messenger stated that there was no apparent reason for the abandonment of the Maryland Heights, and that, though Colonel Miles asked for assistance, he said he could hold out certainly two days. I directed him to make his way back, if possible, with the information that I was rapidly approaching and would undoubtedly relieve the place. By three other couriers I sent the same message, with the order to hold out to the last. . . . I should here state that on the 12th I was directed to assume command of the garrison at Harper's Ferry, but this order reached me after all communication with the garrison was cut off. Before I left Washington . . . I recommended to the proper authorities that the garrison of Harper's Ferry should be withdrawn, via Hagerstown, to aid in covering the Cumberland Valley, or that, taking up the pontoon bridge and obstructing the railroad bridge, it should fall back to the Maryland Heights and then hold its own to the last. . . . It was not deemed proper to adopt either of these suggestions, and when the subject was left to my discretion it was too late to do anything except to try to relieve the garrison.

I directed artillery to be frequently fired by our advance guards, as a signal to the garrison that relief was at hand. This was done, and I learn that our firing was distinctly heard at Harper's Ferry, and that they were thus made aware that we were approaching rapidly. It was confidently expected that this place could hold out until we had carried the mountains and were in a position to make a detachment for its relief. The left, therefore, was ordered to move through Jefferson to the South Mountains, at Crampton's Pass, in front of Burkittsville, while the center and right moved upon . . . Turner's Pass, in front of Middletown. During these movements I had not imposed long marches on the columns. The absolute necessity of refitting and giving some little rest to troops worn down by previous long-continued marching and severe fighting, together with the uncertainty as to the actual position, strength, and intentions of the enemy, rendered it incumbent upon me to move slowly and cautiously until the headquarters reached Urbana, where I first obtained reliable information that the enemy's object was to move upon Harper's Ferry and the Cumberland Valley, and not upon Baltimore, Washington, or Gettysburg. . . .

The South Mountain range near Turner's Pass averages perhaps 1,000 feet in height, and forms a strong natural military barrier. The practicable passes are not numerous and are readily defensible, the gaps abounding in fine positions. Turner's Pass is the more prominent, being that by which the National Road crosses the mountains. It was necessarily indicated as the route of advance of our main army.

The carrying of Crampton's Pass, some 5 or 6 miles below, was also important to furnish the means of reaching the flank of the enemy, and having, as a lateral movement, direct relations to the attack on the principal pass, while it at the same time presented the most direct practicable route for the relief of Harper's Ferry. [*O.R.*, XIX, Part I, pp. 24–27.]

Special Orders,   Hdqrs. Army of Northern Virginia,
No. 191   September 9, 1862.

I. The citizens of Fredericktown being unwilling, while overrun by members of this army, to open their stores, in order to give them confidence, and to secure to officers and men purchasing supplies for benefit of this command, all officers and men of this army are strictly prohibited from visiting Fredericktown except on business, in which case they will bear evidence of this in writing from division commanders. The provost-marshal in Fredericktown will see that his guard rigidly enforces this order.

II. *Major Taylor* will proceed to Leesburg, Va., and arrange for transportation of the sick and those unable to walk to Winchester, securing the transportation of the country for this purpose. The route between this and Culpeper Court-House east of the mountains being unsafe will no longer be traveled. Those on the way to this army already across the river will move up promptly; all others will proceed to Winchester collectively and under command of officers, at which point, being the general depot of this army, its movements will be known and instructions given by commanding officer regulating further movements.

III. The army will resume its march tomorrow, taking the Hagerstown road. *General Jackson's* command will form the advance, and, after passing Middletown, with such portion as he may select, take the route toward Sharpsburg, cross the Potomac at the most convenient point, and by Friday morning take possession of the Baltimore and Ohio Railroad, capture such of the enemy as may be at Martinsburg, and intercept such as may attempt to escape from Harper's Ferry.

IV. *General Longstreet's* command will pursue the main road as far as Boonsborough, where it will halt, with the reserve, supply, and baggage trains of the army.

V. *General McLaws*, with his own division and that of *General R. H. Anderson*, will follow *General Longstreet*. On reaching Middletown he will take the route to Harper's Ferry, and by Friday morning possess himself of the Maryland Heights and endeavor to capture the enemy at Harper's Ferry and vicinity.

VI. *General Walker*, with his division, after accomplishing the object in which he is now engaged, will cross the Potomac at Cheek's Ford, ascend its right bank to Lovettsville, take possession of Loudoun Heights, if practicable, by Friday morning, Keys' Ford on his left, and the road between the end of the mountain and the Potomac on his right. He will, as far as practicable, co-operate with *Generals McLaws* and *Jackson*, in intercepting the retreat of the enemy.

VII. *General D. H. Hill's* division will form the rear guard of the army, pursuing the road taken by the main body. The reserve artillery, ordnance, and supply trains, etc., will precede General Hill.

VIII. *General Stuart* will detach a squadron of cavalry to accompany the commands of *Generals Longstreet, Jackson*, and *McLaws*, and, with the main body of the cavalry, will cover the route of the army, bringing up all stragglers that may have been left behind.

IX. The commands of *Generals Jackson, McLaws*, and *Walker*, after accomplishing the objects for which they have been detached, will join the main body of the army at Boonsborough or Hagerstown. . . .

By command of *General R. E. Lee:* [*O.R.*, XIX, Part 2, pp. 603–4.] *R. H. Chilton*, Assistant Adjutant General.

THE BATTLE OF SOUTH MOUNTAIN
14 September, 1862

Report of Maj. Gen. Daniel H. Hill, CSA,
Commanding Division.

On the 13th, I was ordered by *General Lee* to dispose of my troops so as to prevent the escape of the Yankees from Harper's Ferry, then besieged, and also to guard the pass in the Blue Ridge near Boonsborough. *Major-General Stuart* reported to me that two brigades only of the Yankees were pursuing us, and that one brigade would be sufficient to hold the pass. I, however, sent the brigades of *Garland* and *Colquitt,* and ordered my other three brigades up to the neighborhood of Boonsborough.

An examination of the pass, very early on the morning of the 14th, satisfied me that it could only be held by a large force, and was wholly indefensible by a small one. I accordingly ordered up *[G. B.] Anderson's* brigade. A regiment of *Ripley's* brigade was sent to hold another pass, some 3 miles distant, on our left. I felt reluctant to order up *Ripley* and *Rodes* from the important positions they were holding until something definite was known of the strength and design of the Yankees. [*O.R.,* XIX, Part 1, pp. 1019–20.]

From his lookout station near the Mountain House, now a fashionable restaurant, perched at the crest of South Mountain where the National Road [Alternate 40] crosses through Turner's Gap, Hill could see McClellan's "vast army" spread out before him, blue marching columns extending back as far as the eye could see. "It was a grand and glorious spectacle," he later recalled, "and it was impossible to look at it without admiration. I had never seen so tremendous an army before . . ." [General Daniel H. Hill, "The Battle of South Mountain, or Boonsboro'," Robert Underwood Johnson and Clarence Clough Buel, editors, *Battles and Leaders of the Civil War* (4 vols, New York: The Century Company, 1914) II, p. 564.]

TOUR BEGINS – MIDDLETOWN, MARYLAND

Starting from the intersection of ALTERNATE 40 [Main Street] and MARYLAND STATE 17 [Church Street] in Middletown, Maryland, drive WEST on ALTERNATE 40 for *3 miles* to the intersection of ALT 40 and BOLIVAR ROAD. Turn left onto Bolivar Road. Drive about 200 feet and you will see a fuel storage tank on your right. Pull over and stop.

As you look to your right up Alt 40 you will see Turner's Gap. The hilltop just to the right of the Gap was a major objective of Hooker's I Corps, which in the afternoon was deployed along the base of the mountain to the right of Alt 40. The IX Army Corps commanded by Maj. Gen. Jesse L. Reno was deployed to the left of Alt 40, along the base of South Mountain.

The Confederate position was along the ridge line and on the forward slopes of South Mountain running about four miles from the FROSTOWN ROAD, which crosses South Mountain about a mile northeast of Alt 40, to about half a mile south of RENO MONUMENT ROAD, which runs through FOX'S GAP a mile to the south. The National Road (Alt. 40) cuts through the middle of the Confederate lines.

On your left, about 400 yards from Bolivar Road, is a tree line. McClellan's headquarters was located near the right end of this tree line.

Report of Brig. Gen. Alfred Pleasonton, USA, Commanding Cavalry Division.

Satisfied that the enemy would defend his position at Turner's Gap with a large force, I sent back to General Burnside for some infantry, and in the intermediate time I caused a force of dismounted cavalry to move up the mountain on the right of the turnpike, to examine the position on that side. This produced some skirmishing with the enemy, and induced him to mass a considerable force on that side during the night. I learned also that there were two roads, one on the right [Frostown Road] and the other to the left [Reno Monument Road] of the gap, both of which entered the turnpike beyond the gap, and would assist us materially in turning the enemy's position on both flanks. General Burnside . . . on the morning of the 14th . . . kindly sent me a brigade of infantry, under Colonel Scammon, and some heavy batteries. Scammon's brigade I directed to move up the mountain on the left-hand road, gain the crest, and then move to the right to the turnpike in the enemy's rear. At the same time I placed Gibson's battery and the heavy batteries in position to the left, covering the road on that side, and obtaining a direct fire on the enemy's position in the gap.

Shortly after this, General Cox arrived with a second brigade of infantry, and upon my explaining the position to him, he moved to the support of Scammon, who was successful in his movement to gain the crest of the mountain. During the cannonading that was then going on, the enemy's batteries were several times driven from the gap, but the contest assuming on each side large proportions, and Major General Reno having arrived on the field, I pointed out to him the positions of the troops as I had placed them, giving him at the same time those of the enemy. He immediately assumed the direction of the operations, passed to the front on the mountain height, and was eminently successful in driving the enemy. . . . [*O.R.*, XIX, Part 1, pp. 209–10.]

Continue on BOLIVAR ROAD for 0.4 mile. To the right you will see, about 400 yards distance, a knoll with a stonewall running parallel to Bolivar Road ending at a rock outcropping. In this area Benjamin's Union battery of 20 pdr Parrott Artillery rifles was positioned. These were large caliber guns for that time and gave the Union the capability of supporting the forces that were attacking both Fox's and Turner's Gaps. As Lieut. Samuel N. Benjamin reported:

We engaged three batteries in the course of the day, one on a knoll to the right of the turnpike, about 2,600 yards from us, the others on the right and left of the pike on the hills. The first two commanded our position, the third we commanded. The first we silenced twice, after which it did not open again. The second and third we fired at to draw the fire from our infantry. We also shelled the wood in several places, and shelled a column far up the pass, apparently with some effect. . . . We had no casualties, no projectiles of any kind coming near us. *O.R.* XIX, Part 1, pp. 435 – 36.

Drive for another 0.3 mile to the intersection with RENO MONUMENT ROAD. Turn right and proceed 0.3 mile to the intersection of RENO MONUMENT ROAD and FOX'S GAP ROAD. Pull over to the right and stop.

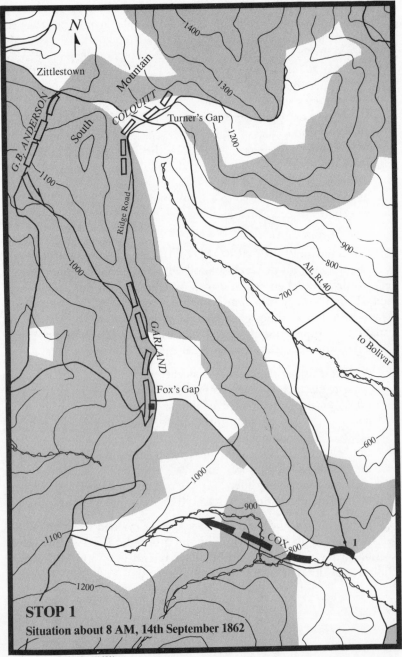

STOP 1

Situation about 8 AM, 14th September 1862

Approximate Scale 1″ = 1666′

STOP 1

Reno Monument Road in front of you continues up the mountain to Fox's Gap. On your left, about 50 feet up Reno Monument Road, you will see a house with a separate garage. What appears to be a driveway going into the property is in fact an old farm road, which today ends at a farm about a quarter of a mile from the entrance.

At the time of the battle this old farm road ran up a small gully to the ridgeline south of Fox's Gap. [The road is no longer passable by vehicle but can be comfortably hiked.] On the ridgeline above the gully you can see the upper portion of a tall power line tower, which is located close to where the road comes out at the top. This was the road that Brig. Gen. Jacob D. Cox's Kanawha Division followed to turn the flank of *Brig. Gen. Samuel Garland's* Confederate Brigade, which was deployed at the extreme right of *Hill's* line.

Later Brig. Gen. Orlando B. Willcox moved his division up the Sharpsburg or Reno Monument Road to join Cox, then skirmishing in the woods several hundred yards south of the gap, and about 1 o'clock the division of Brig. Gen. Samuel D. Sturgis followed in support of Willcox. A short distance down the road to your right were the trains of Reno's Corps.

Report of Maj. Gen. Ambrose E. Burnside, USA, Commanding Right Wing, Army of the Potomac

General Pleasanton had reconnoitered the ground fully, and after posting Benjamin's and Gibson's batteries on the high ground immediately in front of the gap, indicated to Cox's division the road that should be taken in order to turn the enemy's right. This division and Willcox's division became engaged immediately. Soon after, I arrived on the ground with General Reno, and directed him to order up General Rodman's and General Sturgis' divisions to support Cox's division, which had passed up to the left of the main gap by the Sharpsburg road over the South Mountain. After these divisions had passed on to the front, General Reno moved on and took the immediate command of his corps. [*O.R.*, XIX, Part 1, p. 417.]

Report of Brig. Gen. Jacob D. Cox, USA, Commanding Kanawha Division, IX Corps

At 6 o'clock in the morning of September 14 the division marched from Middletown under an order . . . from Major-General Reno, directing me to support . . . the advance of General Pleasanton, who, with his brigade of cavalry and artillery, was moving up the Hagerstown turnpike toward the positions of the enemy in the pass of South Mountain. The First Brigade . . . Col. E. P. Scammon commanding . . . : was ordered to proceed by the Boonsborough road, moving to the left of the Hagerstown turnpike, and to feel of the enemy, ascertaining whether the crest of South Mountain on that side was held by any considerable force. . . .

It soon became evident the enemy held the crest in considerable force, and the whole division was ordered to advance to the assault of the position, word being received from Major-General Reno that the column would be supported by the whole corps. Two 20-pounder Parrott guns from Simmonds' battery and two sections [4 guns] from McMullin's battery were left in the rear, in positions on the turnpike where they were most efficiently served during the action in opposition to the enemy's guns . . . along the Hagerstown road. The First Brigade being in advance, the Twenty-third Ohio Regiment, Lieut. Col. Rutherford B. Hayes commanding, was deployed to our left and ordered to move through the woods to the left of the [Sharpsburg] road and up to the crest of the mountain, gaining, if possible, the enemy's right, so as to turn it and attack his flank. The Twelfth Ohio Regiment . . . occupied the center of the line, and the Thirtieth Ohio Regiment . . . was on the right. These movements were successfully made and the troops brought into position by Colonel Scammon before the arrival of the rest of the division. The Second Brigade marched in column of reserve, and within easy supporting distance. The whole line in advancing was well covered with skirmishers. . . . [*O.R.*, XIX, Part 1, pp.458–9.]

Writing years after the battle, Cox recreated the situation that he had encountered on the morning of the 14th.

The notion that Pleasonton was authorized to put the infantry in position for an unexpected battle is wholly a mistake. No battle was expected at Turner's Gap. *Lee's* order, of which a copy had fallen into McClellan's hands, directed the concentration of the forces under *Longstreet* and *D. H. Hill* at Boonsboro', where they were to be joined

by those under *Jackson* as soon as Harper's Ferry should be taken. . . .
Pleasonton had found a rear-guard at Turner's Gap, but the support
of a single brigade of infantry was assumed to be enough to enable his
cavalry to clear the way. Pleasonton asked for one brigade of infantry
to report to him for the purpose . . . and I detailed the brigade under
command of Colonel E. P. Scammon.

As Cox rode forward he met one of his brigade commanders who
had been captured in an insignificant skirmish near Frederick two days
earlier and was returning from beyond the mountain after being paroled.
The colonel felt honor-bound not to violate his parole by revealing precise
information of what he had seen on top of South Mountain, but he did
manage to gasp "My God! be careful" as he rode to the rear.

I galloped to Scammon and told him that I should follow him in
close support with Crook's brigade, and as I went back along the
column I spoke to each regimental commander, warning them to be
prepared for anything, big or little, — it might be a skirmish, it might
be a battle. Hurrying back to the camp, I ordered Crook to turn out
his brigade prepared to march at once. I then wrote a dispatch to
General Reno, saying I suspected we should find the enemy in force
on the mountain-top, and should go forward with both brigades
instead of sending one. Starting a courier with this, I rode forward to
find Pleasonton, who was . . . where the old Sharpsburg road leaves
the turnpike. I found that he was convinced that the enemy's position
in the gap was too strong to be carried by a direct attack, and that he
had determined to let his horsemen demonstrate on the main road,
supporting the batteries . . . while Scammon should march by the
Sharpsburg road and try to reach the flank of the force on the
summit. Telling him of my suspicion as to the enemy, I also informed
him that I had determined to support Scammon with Crook, and if it
became necessary to fight with the whole division I should do so. . . .
It was about half-past 7 o'clock when Crook's column filed off on the
old Sharpsburg road, Scammon having perhaps half an hour's start.
We had fully two miles to go before we should reach the place where
our attack was made, and, as it was a pretty steep road, the men
marched slowly with frequent rests. On our way up we were over-
taken by my courier who had returned from Reno with approval of
my action, and the assurance that the rest of the Ninth Corps would
come forward to my support. [Jacob D. Cox, "Forcing Fox's Gap and
Turner's Gap," *Battles and Leaders*, II, pp. 585–86.]

Reno Monument. Photo by Diane U. Kallmann. (DUK)

Proceed now to **STOP 2.** Continue west on Reno Monument Road. At 0.5 mile you will observe a lightly wooded area on your right: here Captain Asa M. Cook's battery, supporting Willcox's division, was later located.

At 0.8 mile you will pass the **RENO MONUMENT** on your left. Immediately beyond this monument is a small hard-surfaced road on your left. **TURN LEFT ONTO THIS ROAD.** The Wise house, a small log structure mentioned frequently in accounts of the battle, was located in the angle formed by this road and the Reno Monument or Sharpsburg road. Drive 0.5 mile, stopping briefly at the turnout on your right just short of the tall power line. If you look to the left you will see the stone wall behind which *Gen. Samuel Garland* deployed several regiments from his brigade to anchor the Confederate right flank. Continue to drive across the cleared area under the power line and stop in one of the turnouts beyond. Proceed on foot to the narrow dirt road on the left that intersects the road you have been following (about 200 yards beyond the powerline). Follow that road about 225 yards into the woods, take the left fork, and continue to a position under the powerline where you can look back across the field toward the stone wall defended by the Confederates. You are now in the position of the Union attackers.

STOP 2, POSITION A

As you look north across the fields you can view the terrain over which Scammon's brigade moved to assault *Garland's* line. Immediately in front of you was the 23rd Ohio, commanded by Rutherford B. Hayes, the man to be elected President of the United States fourteen years after the battle. Serving in the ranks of this regiment was Sgt. William McKinley, another future president. The commander of the 30th Ohio, Col. Hugh Ewing, was Gen. William T. Sherman's foster brother.

Report of Col. Eliakim P. Scammon, USA, Commanding First Brigade, Kanawha Division, IX Corps

The First Brigade . . . reached the immediate vicinity of the scene of action at about 9 o'clock. I ordered the Twenty-third Regiment, under Lieutenant-Colonel Hayes, to move through the woods on the left of the road, crossing the mountain so as to attack the enemy on the right and rear of the right flank. The regiment moved up promptly and effectively. Early in the encounter, Lieutenant-Colonel Hayes . . . who had gallantly and skillfully brought his men into action and charged the enemy in his front, was severely wounded and carried to the rear. He remained on the field a considerable time after receiving his wound, and left it only when compelled to retire.

On arriving at the foot of the slope in front of the enemy, I sent the Thirtieth Regiment, commanded by Col. Hugh Ewing, to attack the left of that position of the enemy which was immediately opposed to us, with orders, if practicable, to seize a battery in that part of the enemy's lines. In executing this order it was ascertained that the battery was beyond our reach, and that its infantry support far outnumbered the force opposed to it; but the Thirtieth Regiment attacked vigorously, and drove the enemy from their immediate front. They were assailed by a shower of grape from the battery, whose real position and strength were not previously known, but they seized and held the crest of the mountain until they nobly bore their part in the charge by our whole line.

In all this . . . there was no faltering. It was the thorough work of good soldiers. The Twelfth Regiment being in the center of the brigade, was moved directly to the front, and briskly engaged the enemy. Its first advance, deployed as skirmishers, told upon the enemy with marked effect. It was more like a charge than an advance of skirmishers. They soon gained the crest, and drove the enemy back to the cover of the thicket behind it.

Meantime a section of artillery [2 guns], under Lieutenant Crome, took position on top of the slope, and opened an effective fire upon the enemy. It was, of necessity, advanced so near the enemy's lines as to expose the men to a most effective fire from his infantry. Lieutenant Crome was mortally wounded while serving a piece whose gunners had already fallen. The two pieces of artillery were, in fact, silenced by the killing of the men who served them. . . .

Total of First Brigade taken into action, 1,455. [Killed 63, wounded 201, missing 8.]. The killed of the enemy far outnumbered our own, besides which the First Brigade sent to the rear a number of prisoners fully equal to its total loss. [*O.R.*, XIX, Part 1, pp. 461–62.]

Report of Capt. James R. McMullin, USA, First Ohio Battery

About 11 o'clock, in obedience to an order . . . I sent one section, under command of First Lieut. George L. Crome, to take position on the top of South Mountain, which Lieutenant Crome reached with difficulty, being compelled to move his pieces by manual force, and opened on the enemy, in position behind a stone wall, with canister at a distance of 40 yards. After expending four double rounds, Lieutenant Crome was struck in the breast with a musket-ball while engaged in loading one of his pieces, three of his cannoneers being wounded. The enemy was driven from his position, and the section remained on the field. [*O.R.*, XIX, Part 1, p. 464.]

General Cox recalled:

At about half a mile from the summit . . . the enemy had opened upon Scammon with case shot from the edge of the timber above the open fields, and the latter had judiciously turned off upon a country road leading still farther to the left and nearly parallel to the ridge above. Here I overtook him, his brigade being formed in line, under cover of the timber, facing open pasture fields, having a stone-wall along the upper side, with the forest again beyond this. Crook was brought up close in his rear. The ascent and the formation of the division had occupied more than an hour, and it was now about 9 o'clock. Bayonets were fixed, and at the word the lines charged forward with loud hurrahs. The enemy opened with musketry and shrapnel; our men fell fast, but they kept up their pace, and in a few moments they were on and over the wall, the center of *Garland's*

View directly north of Reno Monument Road just east of summit. (DUK)

North Carolina brigade breaking before them. They hung on a little longer at right and left, and for some time it was a fierce melee, hand to hand, but the Ohio boys were the victors. We found that there was a country road behind the wall on top of the ridge, and the cover of the forest had enabled the enemy's guns to get away toward our right. The 11th Ohio was sent from Crook's brigade beyond Scammon's left, where part of the enemy's force held a hill and summit higher than the ridge at the stone-wall. This seems to have been held by *Rosser's* cavalry with a battery. The 36th Ohio was, in similar manner, sent beyond Scammon's right. The whole line again sprung forward. The high knoll on the left was carried, the enemy's center was completely broken and driven down the mountain, while on the right our men pushed the routed Carolinians beyond the Sharpsburg road, through Wise's fields, and up the slope of the crest toward the Mountain House at Turner's Gap. The regiment on the enemy's extreme right had been cut off from the others and retreated south-westwardly down the mountain toward Rohrersville. . . . The cavalry also took refuge on a wooded hill west of the Mountain House. [Cox, "Forcing Fox's Gap," *Battles and Leaders* II, pp. 586–87.]

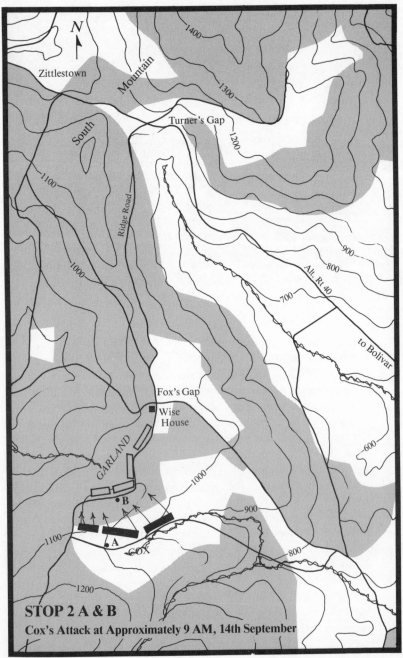

N

Zittlestown

South Mountain

1400

1300

Turner's Gap

1200

1100

Ridge Road

1000

900

800

Alt. Rt 40

700

to Bolivar

600

Fox's Gap

Wise House

GARLAND

1000

B

900

COX

A

1100

800

1200

STOP 2 A & B

Cox's Attack at Approximately 9 AM, 14th September

Approximate Scale 1″ = 1666′

STOP 2, POSITION B

Return to your car. Turn around and drive back to the first turnout back beyond the powerline. Dismount and move to a position along the wall where you can see out into the field.

Report of Col. D. K. McRae, CSA, 5th North Carolina Infantry, Commanding Garland's Brigade.

Gen. Garland and I had been but a few moments in this field when our attention was directed to persons moving at some distance upon this road. . . . He ordered me to advance a body of 50 skirmishers into the woods to our right oblique front to . . . explore. This was done, and they had not passed 50 steps from where we then stood when they encountered the enemy's skirmishers and the fight commenced.

This was about 9 a.m. I was then ordered to take out my regiment to their support, which I did. We found the growth very thick, so much so that it was impossible to advance in line of battle. The enemy's skirmishers had advanced almost to the very edge of the woods nearest us, and, as we appeared at the edge, a sharp skirmish fire ensued, with much more effect on our side than on that of the enemy. . . . At this moment I found that the raw troops on my right [12th North Carolina] who had never been under fire, had had no drill, and had but few officers, were breaking in some confusion, the rest of the line remaining firm. I immediately hastened back and rallied those retreating at our first position, and at *Gen. Garland's* suggestion recalled the regiment back to that point. I then stated to *General Garland* my belief that the enemy had massed a very large force in those woods, and were preparing to turn our right, and suggested that he might be dislodged or his position discovered by shelling the woods, when *Gen. Garland* informed me that *Capt. Bondurant's* battery, which had previously been put in position, had been so severely pressed by the enemy's sharpshooters that it had been necessary to withdraw it. He then passed to the left, and in a few moments intelligence was brought me that this useful and brave officer had received a mortal wound and was no more, and that the command of the brigade had devolved upon me.

I felt all the embarrassment which this situation was calculated to inspire. The brigade numbered scarce 1,000 men. I was satisfied that the enemy, largely superior in numbers and having the advantage of position, was immediately in our front and on the right, and was preparing a heavy movement against us. Previous to this time the Twenty-third North Carolina had been advanced into the field in front of the ridge road, under cover of some piles of stone which afforded shelter to his men, and from this point they had been, with great coolness, pouring a constant and destructive fire into the enemy as they attempted to pass from the woods into the ravines or to advance upon our position. . . . Most gallantly for an hour and a half did this regiment, from this advanced position, harass the enemy and retard his movements. The Twelfth North Carolina had been ordered forward to the support of the Fifth, but a large portion of this regiment, led by its captain commanding, had fled the field early in the fight, and he has not since reported for duty, that I am aware of. By this time the Thirteenth and Twentieth had been ordered up from the left, and both had engaged the enemy from their respective positions. . . .

I then hastened to the right, intending, if time allowed, to move the Fifth North Carolina to the left and fill with it the space vacant in the line, but I found that, under my previous order, this regiment had already been advanced into the field on the right of the Twenty-third, and it was dangerous to withdraw it. . . .

The position now stood thus: the Fifth, on the extreme right, was nearest to the intersecting road, which was threatened. It was advanced into the field, sheltered in some degree by a fence which ran perpendicularly to its line. Next, in the field, under cover of the piles of stone, was the Twenty-third. Back on the ridge road, to the left and rear of the Twenty-third, was the Twentieth. This regiment could not be advanced with the others because of the exposed position and because this would discover [sic] to the enemy at once the vacuum in our line. Between this and the Thirteenth was the open space of 250 to 300 yards, which I had been so anxious to fill. The enemy, having now filed through the succession of ravines and formed in three lines, approached under entire cover toward the brow of the plateau in our front, and, with a long-extended yell, burst upon our line, surrounding the Twentieth on both flanks, and passing to the rear of the Twenty-third. The distance was so short that no opportunity was given for more than a single fire, which was delivered full in the enemy's face, and with great effect, for his first line staggered and some of his forces retreated. A portion of the Twenty-third received his advance upon their bayonets, and men on both sides fell from bayonet wounds; but the enemy's strength was overpowering, and could not be resisted. The Twentieth and a portion of the Twenty-third, finding themselves surrounded, were compelled to retreat . . . under a severe fire, down the mountain side. With the aid of *Colonels Iverson* and *Christie,* I rallied the men as soon as possible, and, obtaining a courier from *Colonel Rosser,* of the cavalry, I communicated with *General Hill.* At *Colonel Rosser's* request, I occupied an adjacent height, with remnants of the Twentieth and Twenty-third, to support a battery which he proposed to put in position. . . .

When I took command of the brigade, I placed the Fifth under the command of *Capt. Thomas M. Garrett.* When the enemy charged upon the front and flank of the Twentieth and Twenty-third, this officer found his regiment, with the right of the Twenty-third, cut off, so that he was obliged to make his way out by moving off to the right and rear. This was done for a short space in some confusion, but *Capt. Garrett* ordered his flag to be placed upon the ridge road, and was endeavoring to make a rally there, when his color-bearer was shot down, and he was compelled to fall back farther down the hill. He did, however, rally the regiment, and, passing out to the turnpike, reported to *General Hill,* when this regiment was assigned to a position, which it occupied the remainder of the day.

Notwithstanding the disadvantage of position, the absence of artillery support, and the injurious effect produced by the death of its general, who had possessed in the warmest degree the confidence and affection of the troops, and the great superiority of the enemy's numbers (a prisoner taken early reported the force in our front at sixteen regiments, naming many of them), this brigade maintained its ground for more than three hours, and inflicted heavy loss on the enemy, destroying his cannoneers, compelling him to abandon his guns . . . and so intimidating him as to prevent pursuit, and the consequent passage of his force into the valley between us and Sharpsburg, which was evidently his first intention. [*O.R.,* XIX, Part 1, pp. 1041–43.]

Report of Lieut. Col. Thomas Ruffin, Jr., CSA, Thirteenth North Carolina

Early in the morning . . . we were ordered by *General Garland* to go, in company with the Twentieth North Carolina, commanded by *Colonel Iverson*, out by a road leading along the top of the mountain, and then to occupy a position on the left of the old Sharpsburg road, which we did at about sunrise, and remained there about two hours. We were then ordered to move farther to the right to the support of the Fifth North Carolina . . . which we proceeded to do, and, being met by *General Garland*, were directed to take position in an open field upon the brow of a high hill. The enemy, we found, were posted upon a high hill densely wooded, and immediately facing the hill occupied by ourselves. There was also a regiment under cover of a rail fence upon our left. Not being able to see the enemy in our front, our whole fire was directed upon those upon the left, and, as our men were cool and fired with precision and effect, they soon drove that portion of the enemy entirely off the field. All this, while those in our front were firing constantly into us, and it was then that *General Garland* fell. Not deeming it prudent to advance down the hill in the face of an enemy so strongly posted, and whose force, though we could not see them, we judged, by their fire, to be very strong, the regiment was withdrawn about 50 yards from the brow of the hill. There I received an order from *Colonel McRae*, in person . . . to move by the left flank until our left was brought in contact with the right of *General Anderson's* brigade, which we did, and took our new position upon the road on the right of *General Anderson*, and supposed that our own brigade was extended in one continuous line on our right.

The enemy advancing in our front, we became soon entirely engaged, and were evidently getting the advantage of him, but to our great surprise a heavy fire was opened upon us from the right, which we supposed to be occupied by our own brigade. Our adjutant was immediately dispatched to see what was the matter, and, returning, reported that the enemy had obtained the road on our right, and were coming down upon us from that direction. An order for a charge to the front was immediately given, and, the men obeying it with alacrity, we had the satisfaction to see the enemy give way. We pursued as far as it was thought to be prudent, and, falling back, changed front, so as to meet those on the right; charged them also and drove them back. While thus engaged, the enemy appeared upon our left, which position had been occupied by *General Anderson's* brigade, but which had been removed without our knowledge. Finding this to be so, our regiment about faced and charged, and, as it turned out to be but a party of the enemy's skirmishers, there was no difficulty in repulsing them. It was then determined to get into position somewhere from which we could communicate with our commanding officer, and with this view the regiment was removed to the Sharpsburg road, where we found *General Anderson's* brigade. Not being able to find *Colonel McRae,* and, indeed, hearing that he and his command had been cut off, we reported to *General Anderson,* and asked to be taken under his command, to which he assented, and we remained with him the rest of the day. By him we were formed in line of battle in the old Sharpsburg road, our regiment being on the right of his brigade. . . . [*O.R.*, XIX, Part 1, pp. 1045–46.]

Narrative of General Cox, USA, continued.

Although *Garland's* line had been broken in the first charge, the rallying and fighting had been stubborn for more than an hour. Our position was now diagonally across the mountain-top, the shape of the ridges making our formation a hollow curve with our right too much in the air, where it was exposed to a severe artillery fire, not only from the batteries near the Mountain House but from one on a high hill north of the turnpike. . . . We had several hundred prisoners in our hands, and learned from them that *D. H. Hill's* division, consisting of five brigades, was opposed to us, and that *Longstreet* was said to be in near support. Our own losses had not been trifling, and it seemed wise to contract our lines a little, so that we might have some reserve and hold the crest we had won till the rest of the Ninth Corps should arrive.

Our left and center were strongly posted, but the right was partly across Fox's Gap, at the edge of the woods beyond Wise's house, around which there had been a fierce struggle. The 30th and 36th were therefore brought back to the crest on the hither side of the gap, where we still commanded the Sharpsburg road, and making the 30th our right flank, the 36th and the 28th were put in second line. My right thus occupied the woods looking northward into Wise's fields. About noon the combat was reduced to one of artillery, and the enemy's guns had so completely the range of the sloping fields behind us that their canister shot long furrows in the sod, with a noise like the cutting of a melon rind. [Cox, "Forcing Fox's Gap," *Battles and Leaders,* II, p. 587.]

Wise house and field on South Mountain near Fox's Gap. Early postwar photograph. U.S. Army Military History Institute. (USAMHI)

Return to your car. Drive back out to Reno Monument Road. As you approach that road, note the ramshackle homestead on your left. That was the site of the Wise house. When you reach Reno Monument (the Old Sharpsburg) Road, turn right and then immediately turn right again into the unimproved parking space next to the west wall at the Reno Monument site. Dismount and walk to the monument.

The insignia on the monument depicting a fouled anchor and cannon later became the official badge of the Ninth Corps. The design was suggested in the Seal of the State of Rhode Island, which was General Burnside's home state, and was especially appropriate in view of the amphibious nature of the first operation of his corps in capturing Roanoke Island on February 8, 1862.

STOP 3, HILL'S SPOILING ATTACK

You are standing in the middle of what at the time was *Wise's Field*, which was then surrounded by a rail fence. The field filled with second-growth timber that you see on the other side of the Old Sharpsburg Road to the north was an open pasture at the time of the battle, bordered on the west and south by a stone wall. The main Confederate position on this part of the battlefield was near the edge of the woods to the left of the Wise pasture, behind the stone fence on the east side of Ridge Road and along the Old Sharpsburg Road as it descends to the west.

The first Confederate infantry in this immediate area belonged to *Garland's* brigade. About 10 a.m., by which time *General Garland* had been killed and his brigade routed, *G. B. Anderson's* brigade arrived to take up the fight. Repulsed by Cox's division, *Anderson* together with remnants of *Garland's* brigade then deployed along the Old Sharpsburg Road west of Fox's Gap, where he was joined on his left by *Ripley's* brigade and ultimately by four brigades from *Longstreet's* division. Meanwhile Willcox's division had arrived to extend the Union lines across the Old Sharpsburg Road about a quarter of a mile to your right, and in the late afternoon these troops swept across Wise's field and pasture, forcing the Confederates to retire down the west face of the mountain and back some distance along Ridge Road.

Narrative of Maj. Gen. D. H. Hill, CSA

General Cox, having beaten the force in his front, now showed a disposition to . . . advance to the Mountain House by the [Ridge] road running south from it on the summit of the mountain. There was nothing to oppose him. My other three brigades had not come up; *Colquitt's* could not be taken from the pike [at Turner's Gap] except in the last extremity. So two guns were run down from the Mountain House and opened a brisk fire on the advancing foe. A line of dismounted staff-officers, couriers, teamsters, and cooks was formed behind the guns to give the appearance of battery supports. I do not remember ever to have experienced a feeling of greater *loneliness*. It seemed as though we were deserted "by all the world and the rest of mankind." Some of the advancing Federals encountered *Colquitt's* skirmishers under *Captain Arnold*, and fell back to their former positions. . . .

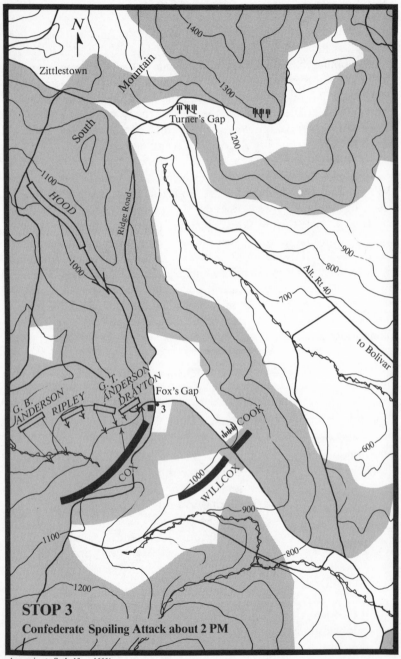

N

Zittlestown

South Mountain

1400

1300

Turner's Gap

1200

Ridge Road

1100

HOOD

1000

900

800

Alt. Rt. 40

700

to Bolivar

600

G. B. ANDERSON

RIPLEY

G. T. ANDERSON

DRAYTON

Fox's Gap

3

COOK

COX

WILLCOX

1000

900

800

1100

1200

STOP 3

Confederate Spoiling Attack about 2 PM

Approximate Scale 1″ = 1666′

It was more than half an hour after the utter rout and dispersion of *Garland's* brigade when *G. B. Anderson* arrived at the head of his small but fine body of men. He made an effort to recover the ground lost by *Garland*, but failed and met a serious repulse.

Ripley, of my division, reported to me for orders [and] . . . was directed to attach himself to *G. B. Anderson's* left. . . . About 3.30 p.m. the advance of *Longstreet's* command arrived and reported to me—one brigade under *Colonel G. T. Anderson* and one under *General Drayton*. They were attached to *Ripley's* left and a forward movement was ordered. In half an hour or more I received a note from *Ripley* saying that he was progressing finely; so he was—to the rear of the mountain on the west side. Before he returned the fighting was over, . . . Ripley did not draw trigger; why, I do not know. [Hill, "Battle of South Mountain," *Battles and Leaders*, II, pp. 566–69; *O.R.*, XIX, Part 1, p. 1021.]

Col. William L. De Rosset, CSA, 3rd North Carolina, Ripley's Brigade

The facts are these. . . . We reached a position at the foot of the mountain—on the west side—when *General Ripley* said to me that we were entirely cut off from the rest of the army, except *G. B. Anderson's* brigade, which was on our right, and that he assumed the command of the two brigades, directing me to take command of [his own] . . . three regiments and to advance slowly up the mountain with a strong line of skirmishers in front. Upon reaching the summit, after toiling through the dense undergrowth of laurel, *Major Thruston*, in command of the skirmish line, reported troops in his front, a few minutes later confirming his first impression that they were *G. B. Anderson's* brigade, presenting their flank and advancing toward his left. This was promptly reported . . . to *General Ripley*, who directed me to withdraw to my original position . . . [where] I was directed to hold my . . . position until further orders. After nightfall I moved forward, changing front to the left, a short distance, to the support of *General Drayton*, remaining there 'without drawing a trigger' until we took up the line of march for Sharpsburg, about 10 to 12 at night. . . . We accomplished nothing tangible. . . . [*Battles and Leaders*, II, p. 569 n.]

Report of Brig. Gen. Roswell S. Ripley, CSA, Commanding Brigade, Hill's Division

At about 9 o'clock I received orders to send forward my artillery, and, soon after, to move with the whole force to the main pass east of Boonsborough. Upon arriving, I was directed to follow the road leading to Braddock's [Fox's] Gap, and place myself in communication with *Brigadier-General [G. B.] Anderson*, who had preceded me in that direction. Upon coming up and communicating with that officer, it was arranged that he should extend along the Braddock [Old Sharpsburg] road and make room for the troops of my command, and that the attack should be made upon the enemy, then occupying the heights to the south. While taking position, *General Hill* arrived, and with him *Brigadier-General Drayton's* command. *General Hill* directed *General Anderson's* and my command to extend still farther on the road, making room for *General Drayton's* troops, and that the attack should be made as soon as all were in position.

General Anderson's and my own brigade got into position on the road, and *General Drayton's* command was rapidly forming when the action commenced by the enemy attacking him in force. This he sustained for some time, *General Anderson's* and my own brigade pushing forward through dense thickets and up very steep acclivities to outflank the enemy and come into *General Drayton's* support. The natural difficulties of the ground and the condition of the troops prevented these movements being made with the rapidity which was desirable, and the enemy forced his way to the Braddock road between *General Drayton's* force and my own, and sent a column of troops down the road as if to cut off the troops forming our right. In this object he was thwarted by two pieces of artillery belonging to *Colonel Rosser's* cavalry, which was speedily placed in position a short distance in our rear on the Braddock road. A few well-directed shot and shell drove the enemy up the hill, leaving the road in our possession.

Meantime *General Anderson* had extended far to the right and come up with the enemy, with whom he had a short engagement. My own brigade had pressed up to within a short distance of the crest of the heights, and held its position under a noisy but comparatively harmless fire, but *Anderson's* brigade having extended far to the right, it was for the time unsupported by any other troops. [*O.R.*, XIX, Part 1, pp. 1031–32.]

Ripley mentioned Confederate cavalry under *Col. T. L. Rosser.* This was the Fifth Virginia Cavalry of *Brigadier General Fitz Lee's* brigade, fighting dismounted and reinforced by the Stuart Horse Artillery, which had been sent by *Major General J. E. B. Stuart* to occupy Fox's Gap the previous evening. *Stuart*, whose skillful withdrawal from Frederick the previous day, had gained time for *D. H. Hill* to occupy the South Mountain gaps with infantry, quickly decided that "this was obviously no place for cavalry operations" and had spent the night of the 13th in Boonsboro before rejoining the main part of his command at Crampton's Gap, six miles to the south. "I had not, up to this time, seen *General D. H. Hill,*" he reported, "but about midnight he sent *General Ripley* to me to get information concerning roads and gaps in a locality where *General Hill* had been lying for two days with his command. All the information I had was cheerfully given, and the situation of the gaps explained by map. [*O.R.*, XIX, Part 1, p. 817.]

This is all that *Stuart* reported about the part played by cavalry in the battle of South Mountain and there is no published official report written by *Rosser. McRae* reported that at *Rosser's* request he had occupied an adjacent height with two regiments to support a battery that *Rosser* wished to put into position (*Ibid.*, p. 1042), and in the afternoon, about 3 o'clock, *D. H. Hill* ordered the brigades of *Ripley, Drayton* and *G. T. Anderson,* then approaching the gap, "to follow a path until they came in contact with *Rosser,* when they should change their flank, march into line of battle, and sweep the woods before them." [*Ibid.*, p. 1020] According to *Hill,* even after *Drayton's* men "went streaming to the rear *Rosser, Anderson* and *Ripley* still held their ground, and the Yankees could not gain our rear." [*Ibid.*, p. 1021.]

Report of Col. George T. Anderson, CSA, Commanding Brigade, D. R. Jones' Division, Longstreet's Corps

My brigade, in conjunction with *General Drayton's*, was ordered forward to report to *Maj. Gen. D. H. Hill.* I found *General Hill* at the Mountain House, and he conducted us in person to the right of our line, and, after giving the necessary orders, left for other parts of the field. *Brigadier-General Ripley,* the next senior officer, was then left in command of the four brigades, viz, *Brig. Gen. G. B. Anderson's,* his own, my brigade, and *General Drayton's,* in line from right to left as enumerated.

Before *Drayton* had formed his line, *General Ripley* ordered the whole line to move by the right flank, and about this time the enemy opened a heavy fire on *Drayton*. I had, by moving to the right under *General Ripley's* order, become separated at least 300 yards from *General Drayton's* right, when *General Ripley* came by and ordered me to move by the left flank into the wood, which I did. My skirmishers (the right wing of the Georgia Regulars, *Captain Wayne* commanding), not having the command to change direction, had continued moving by the flank, and uncovered my front. Having moved some distance over the mountain side, I halted, and sent forward to find *Captain Wayne*, but could not for the reason above given, and, finding that the fire of the enemy was more to my left than front, I changed front forward on the left, and had the left wing of the Georgia Regulars, under direction of *Colonel Magill*, deployed as skirmishers; and as I was in the act of advancing to find the enemy, *Lieutenant Shellman* . . . reported the enemy as having turned *Drayton's* right flank, and being on our left and rear. A few of them were taken prisoners, and several of *Drayton's* men, who had been captured, released.

To prevent the enemy from cutting off my small brigade, being at the time alone (*General Ripley's* brigade, on my right, being several hundred yards away, as I found by sending *Captain Montgomery* . . . to report for orders, who reported him at least one-quarter of a mile from my right, after a long search), I ordered my brigade to move by the left flank and recross the road, in our original rear, and there reformed my line of battle, and was advancing to find the right of *Drayton's* brigade when *Captain Twiggs* . . . in charge of skirmishers, called my attention to the fact that the enemy were crossing the road in considerable force on my left flank. Seeing this myself, and to prevent my left from being turned, I moved by the left diagonally to the rear to intercept them, and at this time found *General Hood's* two brigades coming up to support that part of the line. He engaged the enemy [from Willcox's division] and drove him back.

Not knowing where to find *General Ripley* or *General Drayton*, I reported to *General Hood* for instructions, and was requested by him to hold my position to protect his left flank, and remained there until drawn off the field after night.

In consequence of being separated from *Drayton's* right by the order of *General Ripley*, and having to recross the road to avoid being surrounded, my men were not engaged in the fight, except the first line of skirmishers. . . . Falling back from this place, I was ordered to report to *Brigadier-General Hood*, commanding the rear guard, and remained with him until our arrival at Sharpsburg. [*O.R.*, XIX, Part 1, pp. 908–9.]

Report of Brig. Gen. Jacob D. Cox, USA, Commanding Kanawha Division

About noon . . . a lull occurred in the contest, which lasted some two hours, during which our supports from the remainder of the corps were arriving and taking position. General Willcox's division being the first to arrive, took position on the right, sending one regiment, however, to the extreme left, which was threatened to be turned by a column of the enemy which moved in that direction. General Sturgis' [division] arriving subsequently supported General Willcox's, and General Rodman's was divided; Colonel Fairchild's brigade being posted on the extreme left, and Colonel Harland's (under General Rodman's personal supervision) being placed on the right.

While these supports were arriving the enemy [*G. B. Anderson's* brigade] made several vigorous efforts to regain the crest, directing their efforts chiefly upon our right, which was exposed not only to the fire in front, but to the batteries on the opposite side of the gorge beyond our right, through which the Hagerstown turnpike runs.

About 4 o'clock p.m., most of the re-enforcements being in position, the order was received to advance the whole line and take or silence the enemy's batteries immediately in front. The order was immediately obeyed, and the advance was made with the utmost enthusiasm. The enemy made a desperate resistance, charging our advancing lines with fierceness, but they were everywhere routed and fled with precipitation. In this advance the chief loss fell upon the division of General Willcox, which was most exposed, being on the right . . . but it gallantly overcame all obstacles, and the success was complete along the whole line of the corps. The battery of the enemy was found to be across a gorge and beyond reach of our infantry, but its position was made untenable, and it was hastily removed and not again put in position near us.

General Sturgis' division was now moved forward to the front of General Willcox's position, occupying the new ground gained on the farther side of the slope. About dark a brisk attack was made by the enemy upon the extreme left, but was quickly repulsed by Colonel Fairchild's brigade, of Rodman's division, with little loss.

About 7 o'clock still another effort to regain the lost ground was made by the rebels in front of General Sturgis' division and part of the Kanawha Division. This attack was more persistent, and a very lively fire was kept up for about an hour, but they were again repulsed, and, under cover of the night, retreated in mass from our entire front.

Just before sunset Major-General Reno was killed while making a reconnaissance at the front. . . . [*O.R.*, XIX, Part 1, pp. 459–60.]

Cox now assumed command of the corps. The Ninth Corps reported 889 casualties, 356 of which were from Cox's division. [*Ibid.*, p. 187.]

Report of Brig. Gen. John B. Hood, CSA, Commanding Division

On the morning of September 14, we marched back to Boonsborough Gap, a distance of some 13 miles. This division, arriving between 3 and 4 p.m., found the troops of *General D. H. Hill* engaged with a large force of the enemy. By direction of the general commanding, I took up my position immediately on the left of the pike. Soon, orders came to change over to the right, as our troops on that side were giving way to superior numbers. On the march to the right, I met *General Drayton's* brigade coming out, saying that the enemy had succeeded in passing to their rear. I at once inclined more to the right over a very rugged country and succeeded in getting in a position to receive the enemy. I at once ordered the Texas Brigade, *Col. W. T. Wofford* commanding, and the Third Brigade, *Col. E. M. Law* commanding, to move forward with bayonets fixed, which they did with their usual gallantry, driving the enemy and regaining all of our lost ground, when night came on and further pursuit ceased. . . . Soon after night, orders were received to withdraw and for this division to constitute the rear guard of the army. The march was accordingly taken up in the direction of Sharpsburg. [*O.R.*, XIX, Part 1, p. 922.]

STOP 3, EXCURSION

Walk along Reno Monument Road to your left about 35 yards and turn right onto the old Ridge Road, opposite the road you just used to reach Stop 2. Follow that trail about 200 yards to a fork, take the right fork and continue about 60 yards further until you notice a prominent rock knoll a few yards off the trail to your left.

Rock ledges located just west of the crest of the ridge about ½ mile north of the Reno Monument. (DUK)

You will be walking along *Drayton's* line of battle before he gave way. *Law's* brigade of *Hood's* division later occupied this position until driven back by Willcox late in the evening. The fighting described above by *G. T. Anderson* took place down the wooded slopes to your left.

When you approach the northwest corner of the 'Wise pasture' on your right, look for a suitable site for the Confederate battery that is mentioned in many of the Union reports. This battery drove off a section of Cook's Union battery located near the Reno Monument, and subsequently played a significant part in opposing the advance of Willcox's division. Keep in mind that a good battery position not only provided a clear field of fire, but also had to have shelter nearby for the horses and ammunition chests.

When you reach the prominent rock ledges that would have been an obvious obstacle to troops working their way along this ridge, you have probably reached the place described by *General Hill* (see above, p. 29) where he threw dismounted staff officers, couriers, teamsters and cooks into the fight, and where it seemed that "all of the world and the rest of mankind" had deserted the Confederates. This position also represents the farthest advance by Union forces on this part of the battlefield that night.

As you return to your car, try to imagine what it must have been like to advance in line of battle in such terrain. It is little wonder that whole brigades got lost or turned around.

STOP 4, 17TH MICHIGAN

Back your car out into Reno Monument Road, heading back down the way you first approached this site. Drive slightly less than 0.1 mile and pull off to the left side of the road just short of the barn. Willcox's division was deployed in your front and on the higher ground to your right, the Confederates at the far end of the field to your left and rear, where a troublesome battery was located in the northwest corner of the old pasture. The charge of the 17th Michigan, mentioned in the following accounts, took place on your immediate left: the remnants of the stone wall to the right of the lane leading to the house is probably the wall that the regiment "leaped over" in its charge up the slope to meet the advancing Confederates.

Report of Brig. Gen. Orlando B. Willcox, USA, Commanding First Division, IX Corps

I was ordered by General Burnside to . . . march up by the Sharpsburg road, and take up a position near Cox. Found the latter to the left of the road some few hundred yards, skirmishing on the wooded slope with the enemy. The Sharpsburg road here crosses South Mountain near a hollow called Shriver's Gap. . . .

At General Cox's request I sent two regiments . . . to follow up his line, and was proceeding to take up a position on his right, when I was ordered by General Reno to take position overlooking the main pike to our right. I planted a section of Cook's battery near the turn of the road, and opened fire on enemy's battery across the main pike. After a few good shots, the enemy unmasked a battery on his left, over Shriver's Gap, from a small field [to your left] enveloped by woods. He threw canister and shell, and drove Cook's cannoneers and drivers down the road with their limbers. . . . The attack was so sudden, the whole division being under this . . . flank fire, that a temporary panic occurred until I caused the Seventy-ninth New York . . . and Seventeenth Michigan . . . on the extreme left, to draw across the road, facing the enemy, who were so close that we expected a charge to take Cook's battery. The Seventy-ninth and Seventeenth here deserve credit for their coolness and firmness in rallying and changing front under a heavy fire.

I now made a new disposition of the division, viz: The rear, Seventy-ninth up in front and left of Cook's pieces, and Seventeenth on right and little in rear; Seventy-ninth as skirmishers along whole line, supported by Forty-fifth Pennsylvania . . . connected Welsh's brigade with Cox's right, and stretched Christ's brigade from Welsh and across the road, holding the One Hundredth Pennsylvania . . . in reserve, and moved up my whole command under cover of the hillside.

Meantime the enemy's guns continued to play on us, killing and wounding at all points, but few in number. We lay silent and kept concealed. Our picket officers reported the enemy in heavy force of regiments in rear of their skirmishers.

I soon received orders from Generals Reno and McClellan to silence the enemy's battery at all hazards. Sent picket report to Reno, and was making disposition to charge, moving the Seventeenth Michigan so as to cross the hollow and flank the enemy's guns, when the enemy charged out of the woods on their side directly upon our front in a long, heavy line, extending beyond our left to Cox's right. I instantly gave the command "Forward," and we met them near the foot of the hill, the Forty-fifth Pennsylvania in front. The Seventeenth Michigan rushed down into the hollow [directly ahead of your car], faced to the left, leaped over a stone fence, and took them in flank. Some of the supporting regiments over the slope of the hill fired over the heads of those in front, and after a severe contest of some minutes the enemy was repulsed, followed by our troops to the opposite slope and woods, forming their own position. Their battery in front of us was withdrawn, but the guns across the main pike played upon us heavily with shot and shell. Cook reopened his fire. Reno and Sturgis came up. The firing, except from artillery, had about ceased. Sturgis' regiments relieved my division in the front as soon as our ammunition was exhausted. Sturgis opened with his artillery on the enemy's battery and troops across the main pike, and night came on. . . .

After dark the enemy opened fire on Sturgis with musketry, in which the gallant and beloved Reno was killed, and a temporary confusion occurred until Sturgis' troops were handsomely rallied, and my division took position close up in their support. Still later a heavy fire of musketry opened on us, the enemy (as was learned from a prisoner) being re-enforced by a brigade . . . [probably *Hood's* small division] and the troops were engaged until 10 o'clock, our soldiers firmly holding the ground they had won. Before 12 o'clock, the enemy was in full retreat, abandoning his wounded. . . .

The Seventeenth Michigan . . . performed a feat that may vie with any recorded in the annals of war, and set an example to the oldest troops. This regiment had not been organized a single month, and was composed of raw levies. [*O.R.*, XIX, Part 1, pp. 428–29.]

Report of Col. Benjamin C. Christ, USA, Commanding First Brigade, First Division, IX Corps

Before reaching the summit, I was ordered to form in line of battle on the right of the [Sharpsburg] road, but before this movement was completed the enemy opened a battery, which commanded this road. Cook's battery, which was just being placed in position at this time, received this fire directly in front, and from its great severity they were obliged to retire with their caissons, leaving two of their pieces in danger of being taken by the enemy. The Seventy-ninth New York . . . was immediately ordered to the front on the left of the road, and the Seventeenth Michigan . . . on the right of the road, to protect these pieces. The enemy held their position . . . and fired their shot and shell with terrible effect until about 2 o'clock, when he commenced the attack with his infantry. From the previous disposition of my command, it was impossible for me to give my attention to the whole. I therefore led forward the Seventeenth Michigan on the right of the road, while Colonel Welsh advanced on the left with the Forty-fifth Pennsylvania and Forty-sixth New York Volunteers. Supported by the Seventy-ninth New York, the Seventeenth Michigan moved steadily forward until they arrived within good range, and then opened a fire on the enemy with terrible effect, piling the road and field with his dead and wounded, and finally completely routing him, driving him in the utmost confusion across the field into the woods, and capturing a number of prisoners. [*O.R.*, XIX, Part 1, p. 436.] The Seventeenth Michigan lost 132 killed and wounded in this action. [*Ibid.*, p. 186.]

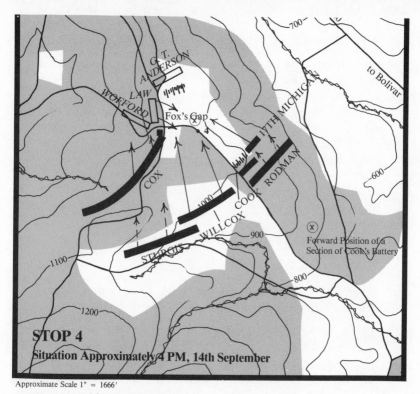

STOP 4

Situation Approximately 4 PM, 14th September

Approximate Scale 1" = 1666'

STOP 5, GIBBON'S ATTACK

Continue down the mountain to Stop 1 (Fox Gap Road—about 0.8 mile). Turn left and follow Fox Gap Road (an all-weather road, but not hard-surfaced) nearly a mile to the STOP sign at ALT 40. Pull off to the side a few yards short of the STOP sign.

Report of Maj. Gen. Joseph Hooker, USA, Commanding I Corps

In front of us was South Mountain, the crest of the spinal ridge . . . which was held by the enemy in considerable force. Its slopes are precipitous, rugged, and wooded, and difficult of ascent to an infantry force, even in the absence of a foe in front. The National turnpike crosses the summit of this range of mountains through a gentle depression, and near this point a spur projects from the body of the ridge, and running nearly parallel with it about a mile, where it is abruptly cut by a rivulet from the main ridge, and rises again and extends far to the northward. At and to the north of the pike this spur is separated from the main ridge by a narrow valley, with cultivated fields, extending well up the gentle slope of the hill on each side. Here the enemy had a strong infantry force posted, and a few pieces of artillery. Through the break in the spur at the base of the principal ridge were other cleared fields occupied by the enemy. . . .

From my observation, anticipating no important sequence from the attack to the south of the turnpike, it was resolved to move to the assault at once, [which was] commenced with throwing forward a heavy body of skirmishers along my whole line, and directions were given for Meade and Hatch to support them with their divisions. . . . An excellent brigade had been withdrawn from [Hatch's] division by the major-general commanding the right wing without my knowledge, and ordered to advance to the turnpike. . . . I . . . call your attention to their list of casualties; it speaks for itself. [O.R., XIX, Part 1, pp. 214–15.]

Reports of Brig. Gen. John Gibbon, USA, Commanding Fourth Brigade, First Division, I Corps

On the afternoon of that day my brigade was detached from the division and ordered to report for duty to Major-General Burnside. Late in the afternoon I was ordered to move up the Hagerstown turnpike with my brigade and one section of Gibbon's battery, to attack the position of the enemy in the gorge. The Seventh Wisconsin and the Nineteenth Indiana were placed respectively on the right and left of the turnpike, to advance by the head of the company, preceded by two companies of skirmishers from the Sixth and Second Wisconsin, and followed by these regiments, formed in double column at half distance, the section of the battery under Lieutenant Stewart, Fourth Artillery, keeping on the pike a little distance in rear of the first line. The skirmishers soon became engaged, and were supported by the leading regiments, while our guns moved forward on the turnpike until within range of the enemy's guns, which were firing on our column from the top of the gorge, when they opened with good effect. My men steadily advanced on the enemy, posted in the woods and behind stone walls, driving him before them until he was re-enforced by three additional regiments, making five in all opposed to us.

Seeing we were likely to be outflanked on our right, I directed Lieutenant-Colonel Bragg, of the Sixth Wisconsin, to enter the wood on his right, and deploy his regiment on the right of the Seventh. This was successfully accomplished, while the Nineteenth Indiana, supported by the Second Wisconsin, deployed, and, swinging around parallel to the turnpike, took the enemy in the flank. Thus the fight continued until long after dark, Stewart using his guns with good effect over the heads of our own men. My men, with their ammunition nearly exhausted, held all the ground they had taken, and were late in the night relieved, with the exception of the Sixth Wisconsin, which occupied the battlefield all night, by General Gorman's brigade. . . .

The loss in the brigade was 37 killed, 251 wounded, 30 missing; total, 318. [*O.R.*, XIX, Part 1, pp. 247–48.]

Report of Col. Solomon Meredith, USA, Nineteenth Indiana Infantry, Fourth Brigade, First Division, I Corps

On arriving near South Mountain, it was ascertained that the enemy was in force on the mountain and in the pass. I was ordered to form a line of battle about 3 o'clock p.m., which was done on the hill facing the mountain. Remained there until about 5 o'clock, when we were ordered to go forward. We went forward in line of battle on the left of the pike leading through the pass, supported by the Second Wisconsin, two companies of which . . . had been deployed as skirmishers. I also deployed Company B . . . as flankers to protect our left flank. We moved slowly and cautiously, but steadily, forward. The skirmishers were soon fired on, but pressed forward with caution.

On arriving near a house on our extreme left, surrounded on the southwest and north by timber, I discovered large numbers of the enemy in and around the house. They had been annoying us as well as the skirmishers by firing from the house and outhouses; also from the woods near the house. I ordered Lieutenant Stewart, who commanded a section of Battery B, Fourth Artillery, to come forward and open fire upon the house. He moved forward his section of two pieces and threw several splendid shots, the first of which took effect in the upper story, causing a general stampede of their forces from that point, enabling us to go forward more rapidly, and with less loss from their sharpshooters. Their skirmishers soon opened a sharp fire upon ours, which made it necessary for us to push forward. We then opened fire on the enemy at short range, who were concealed in part under cover. The fire became general on both sides. The Nineteenth gave a shout, and pressed forward . . . cheering all the time. . . .

After driving the enemy about three-quarters of a mile, I discovered a stone fence in front, which the enemy had fallen back to. At that point they were annoying us very much. I then ordered Captain Clark, Company G, to wheel . . . to the left, and move by the right flank until he could command the line of battle lying directly behind the stone fence. They then opened a flank fire upon the enemy, causing them to retreat precipitately, which gave us an opportunity of pouring upon them a raking fire as they retreated. Captain Clark here took 11 prisoners. . . . The firing then ceased in front of us. The Second Wisconsin came to our support promptly as soon as the firing became general, and stood by the Nineteenth until the enemy fled over the mountain.

After the firing ceased in front, we discovered the enemy, who was concealed behind a stone fence on the right of the pike, in front of the Seventh Wisconsin, annoying them by a deadly fire behind their breastworks. Colonel Fairchild, commanding Second Wisconsin, wheeled the left wing of his regiment, and opened an enfilading fire upon the enemy. After exhausting their ammunition, he withdrew them and ordered up his right wing to take their place, in which position they remained until they exhausted their ammunition, when they were withdrawn. I then took forward my regiment and occupied the same position, and continued an enfilading fire upon the enemy, who soon fell back from their strong position, the Wisconsin and Indiana boys giving three hearty cheers as the fate of the day was thus decided.

It was then after 9 o'clock in the night, and pursuit being considered dangerous, we lay down on our arms, holding the battle-field. Small detachments of my command were now engaged in bringing in wounded prisoners. We held the field until about 12 o'clock, when we were relieved by fresh troops. . . .

It was a glorious victory on the part of General Gibbon's brigade, driving the enemy from their strong position in the mountain gorge. [*O.R.*, XIX, Part 1, pp. 249–50.]

As you drive up to the summit, try to visualize the fighting over the terrain on both sides of the old turnpike. On the steep hills to the right the Sixth Wisconsin executed a similar flanking movement against Confederates sheltered among the rocks and trees, with comparable success.

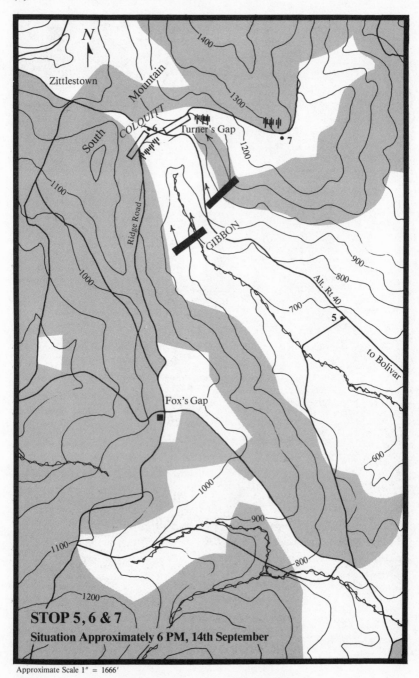

STOP 5, 6 & 7

Situation Approximately 6 PM, 14th September

Approximate Scale 1″ = 1666′

"Rations from the Stalk." (B&L)

STOP 6, MOUNTAIN HOUSE

Turn left and follow 40 Alternate slightly more than a mile to Old South Mountain Inn at the top of the pass. Turn around there and park. Note the high ground to the North (your left after you park). This became the key terrain used to overcome the Confederate defenders.

Hill relied upon Colquitt's brigade, which was deployed on both sides of the Hagerstown turnpike, to hold Turner's Gap. Lane's battery of artillery was in support.

Today's view from the Confederate artillery positions at Stop 7. (DUK)

Report of Col. A. H. Colquitt, CSA, Sixth Georgia Infantry, Commanding Brigade, Hill's Division, Jackson's Corps

On the night of September 12 I left the camp of the division with the brigade and *Captain Lane's* battery, with instructions to occupy the commanding points at Boonville [*sic*], 4 miles to the rear. The march and the unavoidable delay in selecting positions in the dark consumed most of the night.

Early the next morning *General Hill* arrived. While engaged in making a reconnaissance, he received information that *General Stuart*, commanding the cavalry in rear, stood in need of support, I was ordered to move at once with my brigade and the battery of artillery. Proceeding along the turnpike 2½ or 3 miles, I reached the summit of South Mountain, and discovered the enemy's cavalry advancing and ours gradually giving back. I reported my arrival to *General Stuart*, and consulted with him as to the best disposition of the forces. Two pieces of artillery were ordered to the front, to a position commanding the turnpike leading down the valley. The continued advance of the enemy rendered the execution of the order impracticable. They were thrown rapidly into position at the most available points, and the infantry disposed upon the right and left of the road. The enemy [Pleasonton's cavalry] made no further efforts to advance, and at dark withdrew from my immediate front.

To the right and left of the turnpike, a mile distant on either side, were practicable roads leading over the mountain, and connecting by a cross-road along the ridge with the turnpike. Upon each of these roads I threw out strong infantry pickets, the cavalry being withdrawn, and my main body was retired to the rear of the cross-road, leaving a line of skirmishers in front.

Early the next morning my pickets were called in, being relieved by other forces which had arrived during the night, and my brigade advanced to the position it occupied the day previous. Upon the right of the road, across the valley and upon the hillside, three regiments were placed, with instructions to connect with *General Garland's* line on the right. The force was insufficient to reach that distance, and there was a gap left of 300 or 400 yards between the two brigades. The remaining regiments of my brigade, to wit, the Twenty-third Georgia and Twenty-eighth Georgia, were put in position on the left of the turnpike, under cover of a stone fence and a channel worn by water down the mountainside.

The first attack of the enemy was made upon the extreme right of my line, as with the view to pass in the opening between *Garland's* and my command. This was met and repulsed by a small body of skirmishers and a few companies of the Sixth Georgia.

At 4 o'clock in the afternoon a large force [Gibbon's brigade] had been concentrated in my front and was moving up the valley along each side [of] the turnpike. I informed *General Hill* of the movement, and asked for supports. Being pressed at other points, he had none to give me. The enemy advanced slowly, but steadily, preceded by skirmishers. Upon the right of the road, 400 yards in advance of my line, was a thick growth of woods, with fields opening in front and around them. In these I had concealed four companies of skirmishers, under the command of *Captain Arnold.* As the enemy advanced, these skirmishers poured upon the flank a sudden and unexpected fire, which caused the troops on this part of his line to give back in confusion. They were subsequently rallied and thrown to the right, strengthening the attack to be made upon my left.

Two regiments here were to meet at least five, perhaps ten, times their numbers. Nobly did they do it. Confident in their superior

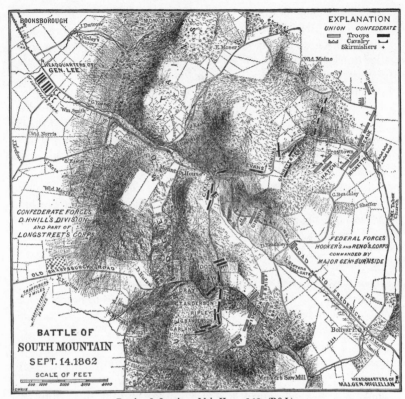

Battles & Leaders, Vol. II, p. 568. (B&L)

numbers, the enemy's forces advanced to a short distance of our lines, when, raising a shout, they came to a charge. As they came full into view upon the rising ground, 40 paces distant, they were met by a terrific volley of musketry from the stone fence and hillside. This gave a sudden check to their advance. They rallied under cover of the uneven ground, and the fight opened in earnest. They made still another effort to advance, but were kept back by the steady fire of our men. The fight continued with fury until after dark. Not an inch of ground was yielded. The ammunition of many of the men was exhausted, but they stood with bayonets fixed.

I am proud of the officers and men of my command for their noble conduct on this day. Especial credit is due to *Colonel Barclay,* of the Twenty-third Georgia, and *Major [Tully] Graybill,* Twenty-eighth Georgia, who, with their regiments, met and defeated the fiercest assaults of the enemy. [*O.R.,* XIX, Part 1, pp. 1052–53.]

STOP 7, ARTILLERY POSITION

Drive forward down the east slope of South Mountain on 40 A the same way you approached the summit. At slightly less than 0.1 mile, turn left onto Dahlgren Road. This is an all-weather road, but it is inferior to Fox Gap Road. You may encounter some erosion at the shoulders and some sharp bumps from water washing across the road, so drive carefully and avoid the extreme edges of the road immediately after rains. After driving 0.4 mile on Dahlgren Road, pull off to the right next to a field where a long curving driveway intersects Dahlgren Road from the right near the crest of the hill. As you look across the valley to the mountain on your right, you should be able to see a microwave tower at the crest. Below that you will see a long slash through the trees where a powerline runs—the same powerline you passed under at Stop 2. Below the powerline is a dark patch of pine trees filling the ground that was Wise's Field on the day of the battle. Reno's Monument (Stop 3) is just short of the right side of that patch of pines.

Report of Maj. Gen. Daniel H. Hill, CSA, Commanding Division, Jackson's Corps (detached)

There was . . . a solitary peak on the left, which, if gained by the Yankees, would give them control of the ridge commanding the turnpike. The possession of this peak was, therefore, everything to the Yankees, but they seemed slow to perceive it. I had a large number of guns from *Cutts'* artillery placed upon the hill on the left of the turnpike, to sweep the approaches to this peak. From the position selected, there was a full view of the country for miles around, but the mountain was so steep that ascending columns were but little exposed to artillery fire. The artillerists of *[A. S.] Cutts'* battalion behaved gallantly, but their firing was the worst I ever witnessed. *Rodes* and *Ripley* came up soon after *Anderson*. *Rodes* was sent to the left, to seize the peak . . . and Ripley was sent to the right to support *Anderson*. . . .

This artillery position is not indicated in the map found in *Battles and Leaders*. The map in the *Official Records*, however, shows Confederate artillery on the same contour line where you are now located about 200 yards to your right, just east of the wall bordering Dalhgren Road. This map also places a "Georgia Bat." immediately behind you, on the far side of the road and slightly to your left. Since the Confederate order of battle includes no Georgia infantry *battalions* identified as such, lists four of *Cutts'* five batteries as Georgia batteries and indicates that the only other Georgia batteries in *Lee's* army were with *McLaws'* division to the south, near Harper's Ferry, this is probably where *Lieutenant Colonel A. S. Cutts'* guns were employed. From here Confederate guns could easily fire into Union positions in Wise's field.

Rodes initially deployed his brigade in this vicinity, about where *Garnett's* brigade is located on the map, near the woodline at the east end of the field to your left front. After remaining here about 45 minutes, "part of the time under artillery fire and throwing out scouts and skirmishers to the left and front," he was ordered to occupy another bare hill about three-quarters of a mile still farther to the left, across a deep gorge separating the hills. *Hill* continues:

It was now past noon, and the Yankees had been checked for more than five hours; but it was evident that they were in large force on both sides of the road, and the Signal Corps reported heavy masses at the foot of the mountain. In answer to a dispatch from *General Longstreet*, I urged him to hurry forward troops to my assistance. *General Drayton* and *Col. G. T. Anderson* came up, I think, about 3 o'clock, with 1,900 men, and I felt anxious to beat the force on my right before the Yankees made their grand attack, which I feared would be on our left. . . . Affairs were now very serious on our left. [*O.R.*, XIX, Part 1, pp. 1020–21.]

The advance of Hatch's division in three lines, 2 brigade in each, was . . . grand and imposing . . . Hatch's general and field officers were on horseback, his colors were all flying, and the alignment of his men seemed to be perfectly preserved. From the top of the mountain the sight was grand and subline. . . . Doubtless The Hebrew poet whose idea of the awe-inspiring is expressed by the phrase, "Terrible as an army with banners," had his view of the enemy from the top of a mountain. [*Battles and Leaders*, II, pp. 573–74.]

For a better view of the terrain over which *Longstreet's* brigades contested the advance of Hatch's Union division, resume your tour. Continue on Dahlgren Road for a little more than 0.1 mile, over the crest of the hill. Pull out into the exit of the farm lane on the right.

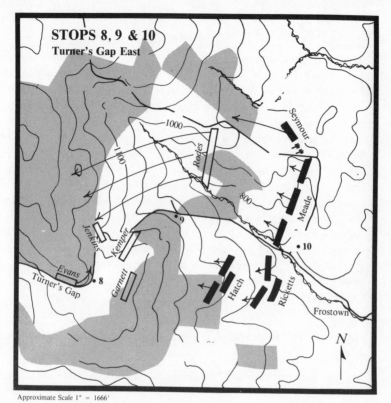

Approximate Scale 1" = 1666'

STOP 8, THE FIGHT FOR THE CREST

The ground between this spot and the curve ahead was where Hatch's Union division endeavored to reach the top of the mountain. Across the fields to your right, at the edge of the woods, is where the Confederate brigades of *Garnett* and *Kemper* did most of their fighting. *Rodes'* brigade of Hill's division had previously deployed in this vicinity, but after remaining here for about 45 minutes, "part of the time under artillery fire and throwing out scouts and skirmishers to the left and front," *Rodes* was ordered to occupy another bare hill about three-quarters of a mile ahead of you, across the deep gorge separating the hills.

Report of Lieut. Gen. James Longstreet, CSA, Commanding Army Corps

I reached Boonsborough about 3 o'clock in the afternoon, and, upon ascending the mountain, found *General Hill* heavily engaged. My troops were hurried to his assistance as rapidly as their exhausted condition would admit of. The brigades of *Brigadier-Generals Evans*, *Pickett* (under *Garnett*), *Kemper*, and *Jenkins* (under *Colonel Walker*) were extended along the mountain to our left; *Brigadier-General Hood,* with his own, and *Whiting's* brigade (under *Colonel Law*), *Drayton's* and *D. R. Jones'* (under *Col. G. T. Anderson*), were extended to the right. *Major-General Hill* had already placed such batteries in position as he could find ground for, except one position on the extreme left. It was my intention to have placed a battery in this position, but I was so much occupied in front that I could find no time to do so before nightfall. We succeeded in repulsing the repeated and powerful attacks of the enemy and in holding our position until night put an end to the battle. It was short, but very fierce. . . . Had the command reached the mountain pass in time to have gotten into position before the attack was made, I believe that the direct assaults of the enemy could have been repulsed with comparative ease. Hurried into action, however, we arrived at our position more exhausted than the enemy. [*O.R.*, XIX, Part 1, p. 839.]

Report of Maj. Gen. David R. Jones, CSA, Commanding Division, Longstreet's Corps

On the 14th I marched on the Frederick road in the direction of that city, hearing heavy firing, leaving *Toombs'* brigade in command of Hagerstown, and Eleventh Georgia Regiment, of *Anderson's* brigade, in charge of wagon-train. Halting beyond Boonsborough, *Drayton's* and *Anderson's* brigades were temporarily detached from my command and ordered to report to *General D. H. Hill.* With my three other brigades present I was ordered by *General Longstreet* to march to a pass about a mile to the right of the main road [Fox's Gap], through which the enemy was said to be flanking our army. Reaching the pass and finding the report incorrect, I was directed to bring my brigades as rapidly as possible back to the main road and to the mountain top, and, under orders from *General Longstreet,* placed *Kemper* and *Garnett,* supported by *Jenkins'* brigade, in position on the ridge to the left of the road and above it.

While taking position my troops were exposed to severe shelling, and shortly afterward to a heavy infantry attack in overwhelming numbers. Despite the odds they held their ground till dark, when, the brigades on my left giving way, they were withdrawn in comparatively good order to the foot of the mountain. The enemy did not pursue . . . and our troops were marched to Sharpsburg, which we reached on the morning of the 15th. [*O.R.*, XIX, Part 1, pp. 885–86.]

Report of Brig. Gen. Richard B. Garnett, CSA, Commanding Pickett's Brigade, Jones' Division, Longstreet's Corps

This command . . . reached Boonsborough . . . in the afternoon, after a hot, dusty, and fatiguing march of some 18 miles. A short distance beyond the village, *Kemper's*, *Pickett's*, and *Jenkins'* brigades (the latter commanded by *Colonel Walker*) . . . were moved in a southerly direction on a road running perpendicular to the pike. Having proceeded over a mile, these troops were directed on another route parallel to the turnpike, leading toward . . . [Fox's] gap in the South Mountain, farther south than . . . the Hagerstown and Frederick road. . . . After marching nearly half a mile, *Kemper* filed to the left, and again moved in the direction of the pike. At this time I received an order, by *Major Mayo [Moses?]*, of *General Jones'* staff, to bring my troops to an about-face, and to return the way I came until I reached a path, which I must take. He was unable to give me any information respecting the path in question, but said he would go forward and try to obtain some. I did not, however, see him again.

I followed *Jenkins'* brigade, which was now in front some distance; but hearing musketry open on the mountain, I took what I supposed to be a near cut in the direction where I presumed I was wanted. This took me over rough and plowed ground up the mountain side. I at length found an old and broken road, along which *General Kemper* must have moved. Here I met *Capt. Hugh Rose*, of *General Jones'* staff, who had orders for me to return to the turnpike. When I got back to this road my troops were almost exhausted. I consequently lost the services of a number of men by straggling.

After a short rest, I proceeded up the mountain, and, having gained the summit on the main road, I was sent, by a narrow lane bearing to the left, [Dahlgren Road] to a higher position. A portion of this route was commanded by several pieces of the enemy's artillery, which opened upon my column (marching by the flank) as soon as it came in sight, which they were enabled to do with considerable accuracy, as they had previously been practicing on other troops which had preceded mine. Several casualties occurred from this cause while I was approaching and forming my line of battle, which I did by filing my command to the right through an open field. My right rested in thick woods, which descended quite abruptly in front, and my left in a field of standing corn.

As soon as my troops were formed, I sent forward a line of skirmishers to ascertain the position of the enemy. When these dispositions had been completed (which was only a short time before sunset), I received an order from *General Jones* to detach my left regiment to *Kemper's* right (he being on my left), and to withdraw the rest of the brigade to a wooded ridge a little to the left and rear [immediately behind Dahlgren Road]. The first part of this order had scarcely been executed when the Federal skirmishers made their appearance, immediately followed by their main body, so that the action at once became general. . . .

It is due to the brigade to say that it went into the battle . . . under many serious disadvantages. It had marched (a portion of the time rapidly) between 22 and 23 miles before it went into action, much oppressed by heat and dust; reached its position a short time before sunset under a disheartening fire of artillery, and was attacked by a much superior force as soon as it was formed in line of battle. [*O.R.*, XIX, Part 1, pp. 894–95.]

Report of Major George C. Cabell, CSA, Eighteenth Virginia Infantry, Pickett's Brigade (Garnett), Jones' Division

About 5 p.m. on . . . September 14, the Eighteenth Virginia Regiment, about 120 strong, under my command, after a rapid and fatiguing march from Hagerstown, was directed to a position a little north of the gap in South Mountain. . . . We were not fairly in position before the enemy's skirmishers were seen not far off and, to their rear, their line of battle approaching. Fire was soon opened along the entire front of the . . . regiment, when the skirmishers retired, and soon the main body of the enemy fell back a short distance, sheltered themselves behind trees, rocks, etc., and opened a heavy fire upon us, which was replied to with spirit and vigor for some time.

After some three-quarters of an hour, word was brought that the regiments on our left had fallen back, and that the left of the Eighteenth was wavering. I at once repaired to the left of the regiment and aided in restoring comparatively good order, but soon after the order came along the lines to fall back, which was done, halting in a ravine about 100 yards to the rear of the position we had just left. Here the regiment was reformed. *General Garnett* did not approve of this last position, so he ordered the regiment to the edge of the wood and across a fence some 200 yards distant. In going to this position, the ground being uneven, rocky, and covered with bushes and briars, the regiment became a good deal scattered. As many of the regiment as could be were collected, and, together with *Captains Claiborne* and *Oliver*, I marched them forward and took position on the left of *Jenkins'* brigade, which had just come up, and again engaged the enemy, the men fighting bravely. In some . . . thirty minutes information was brought that *General Garnett's* brigade was ordered to retire. The men were then withdrawn, and, together with *General Garnett*, who was upon our left, retired from the field.

It is but just to say that the regiment was very much exhausted when it went into the fight, having marched in quick time from Hagerstown and around the mountain some 4 or 5 miles, and therefore fought under disadvantages. It nevertheless did good and effective fighting, and, had it been supported on the left, would have maintained its ground. . . . There were only seven officers besides myself with the regiment, and three of the companies were commanded by second sergeants. [*O.R.*, XIX, Part 1, pp. 899–900.]

Report of Capt. B. Brown, CSA, Nineteenth Virginia Infantry, Pickett's Brigade (Garnett), Jones' Division

The sun was nearly setting behind the western hills when the regiment . . . numbering 150 men . . . was formed in a line of battle on the top of a hill, with an open space in front, where the enemy lay concealed behind a stone fence, at the distance of 15 paces. A murderous fire was at once opened upon the regiment by the concealed foe, which was manfully replied to by the Nineteenth for more than an hour, when the ranks were thinned to such an extent as to prove a withdrawal absolutely necessary. One-third of the men were rendered unable to fight, and a precipitous retreat from the hill was ordered. [*O.R.*, XIX, Part 1, p. 901.]

Report of Col. Montgomery D. Corse, CSA, Seventeenth Virginia Infantry, Kemper's Brigade, Jones' Division

My regiment was placed in line of battle about 4 p.m. in a field to the right of the road [Frostown] leading to the summit of the mountain and to the left of Crampton's [Turner's] Gap. In the act of taking that position the regiment was subjected to a very fierce shelling from a battery of the enemy about 600 or 800 yards on our right, which enfiladed our line. Fortunately, however, we suffered very little loss from that, having but 2 men slightly wounded.

I moved the regiment forward about 100 yards, by your orders, toward a woods in our front, and ordered *Lieutenant Lehew*, with his company, to deploy forward as skirmishers into the woods and to engage the enemy, which were supposed to be there. Very soon I heard shots from our skirmishers. Your aide . . . at this time delivered me an order to move my regiment by the left flank and to connect my line with the Eleventh, occupying a corn-field, which order was obeyed, when *Colonel Stuart's* regiment (Fifty-sixth Virginia), of *Pickett's* brigade [commanded by *Garnett*] joined my right. Immediately the brigade on our right *[Garnett]* became hotly engaged. We reserved our fire, no enemy appearing in our front. After the fire had continued about fifteen minutes, *Colonel Stuart* reported to me that the troops on his right had fallen back. I observed that they had abandoned the left of the Eleventh. I communicated my intention to *Colonel Stuart* and *Major Clement*, of the Eleventh, to fall back about 10 or 15 steps behind a fence, which was simultaneously done by the three regiments in good order. We held this position until long after dark, under a severe fire of musketry obliquely on our right flank and in front, until nearly every cartridge was exhausted.

Shortly after the enemy had ceased firing (about 7.30 p.m.), I received your order to withdraw my regiment, which was done in good order, and halted to rest on the Boonsborough and Fredericktown road, with the other regiments of your brigade. [*O.R.*, XIX, Part 1, p. 904.]

Report of Brig. Gen. Abner Doubleday, USA, Commanding Hatch's Division, Hooker's Corps

To avoid the fire of [Confederate] batteries, the division . . . diverged from the main road and struck off into a by-road to the right, which led to a stone church at the foot of the mountain, where we found General Hooker and his staff. The division at this time consisted of Doubleday's, Patrick's, and Phelps' (late Hatch's) brigades, General Gibbon having been detached with his brigade on special service.

The general order of battle was for two regiments of Patrick's brigade to precede the main body, deployed as skirmishers, and supported by Patrick's two remaining regiments; these to be followed by Phelp's brigade, 200 paces in the rear, and this in turn by Doubleday's brigade, with the same interval. . . .

By General Hatch's order, Phelps' brigade advanced in column of divisions at half distance, preserving the intervals of deployment. My brigade advanced in the same order. On reaching a road part way up the mountain, and parallel to its summit, each brigade deployed in turn and advanced in line of battle. Colonel Phelp's brigade, owing to an accidental opening, preceded for a while our line of skirmishers, but soon halted, and advanced in line some 30 paces in their rear. General Patrick rode to the front with his skirmishers, drew the fire of the enemy, and developed their position. They lay behind a fence on the summit, running north and south, fronted by a woods and backed by a corn-field, full of rocky ledges. Colonel Phelps now ordered his men to advance, and General Hatch rode through the lines, pressing them forward. They went in with a cheer, poured in a deadly fire, and drove the enemy from his position behind the fence, after a short and desperate conflict, and took post some yards beyond.

Here General Hatch was wounded and turned over the command to me, and . . . the command of my brigade . . . devolved upon Lieutenant-Colonel Hofmann. . . . Phelps' brigade being few in number, and having suffered severely, I relieved them just at dusk with my brigade, reduced by former engagements to about 1,000 men, who took position beyond the fence . . . the enemy being in heavy force some 30 or 40 paces in our front. They pressed heavily upon us, attempting to charge at the least cessation of our fire. At last I ordered the troops to cease firing, lie down behind the fence, and allowed the enemy to charge to within about 15 paces, apparently under the impression that we had given way. Then, at the word, my men sprang to their feet and poured in a deadly volley, from which the enemy fled in disorder, leaving their dead within 30 feet of our line.

I learned from a wounded prisoner that we were engaged with 4,000 to 5,000, under the immediate command of *General Pickett [Garnett]*, with heavy masses in their vicinity. He stated also that *Longstreet* in vain tried to rally the men, calling them his pets, and using every effort to induce them to renew the attack. The firing on both sides still continued, my men aiming at the flashes of the enemy's muskets, as it was too dark to see objects distinctly, until our cartridges were reduced to two or three rounds.

General Ricketts now came from the right and voluntarily relieved my men at the fence, who fell back some 10 paces and lay down on their arms. A few volleys from Ricketts ended the contest in about thirty minutes, and the enemy withdrew from the field — not, however, until an attempt to flank us on our left, which was gallantly met by a partial change of front of the Seventy-sixth New York Volunteers . . . and the Seventh Indiana. . . . In this attempt the enemy lost heavily, and were compelled to retreat in disorder.

While the main attack was going on at the fence . . . Colonel Rogers, with . . . the Twentieth New York State Militia and Twenty-first New York Volunteers, of Patrick's brigade, rendered most essential service by advancing his right and holding a fence bounding the northeast side of the same corn-field, anticipating the enemy, who made a furious rush to seize this fence, but were driven back. Colonel Rogers was thus enabled to take the enemy in flank, and also to pick off their cannoneers and silence a battery which was at the right and behind their main body.

Our men remained in position all night, sleeping on their arms and ready for any attack; but with the dawn it was discovered that the enemy had fled. . . . [O.R., XIX, Part 1, pp. 221–22.]

Continue downhill another 0.45 mile. Stop short of the driveway entering the road from the left. Note the deep narrow valley to your left and the ridgeline beyond.

STOP 9, RODES' RESISTANCE

Between this point and the high ground on the ridge opposite, *Rodes'* brigade fought desperately to hold the left of *Hill's* line. His left regiment, the Sixth Alabama commanded by *Colonel John B. Gordon*, was deployed on the hill near the house that you can see on the far side of the gorge.

Report of Brig. Gen. R. E. Rodes, CSA, Commanding Brigade, D. H. Hill's Division

The whole brigade was moved to that hill, crossing, in doing so, a deep gorge which separated the hills. This movement left a wide interval between the right of my brigade, which in its last position rested in the gorge, and the balance of the division, which being reported to *General Hill*, together with the fact that no troops supported the battery *[Cutts]* on the first . . . ridge, by his order I sent back . . . the Twelfth Alabama to support the battery.

By this time the enemy's line of battle was pretty well developed and in full view. It became evident that he intended to attack with a line covering both ridges and the gorge . . . and extending some half a mile to my left. I had, immediately after my arrival on the extreme left, discovered that the hill there was accessible to artillery, and that a good road [Frostown Road], passing by the left of said hill from the enemy's line, continued immediately in my rear and entered the main road about half a mile west of the gap. Under these circumstances, I sent for artillery, and determined upon the only plan by which the enemy could be prevented from immediately obtaining possession of said road, and thus marching entirely in our rear without difficulty, and that was, to extend my line as far as I could to the left, to let the right rest in the gorge, . . . and to send . . . for re-enforcements to continue the line from my right to the gap on the main road, an interval of three-quarters of a mile at least. Having thrown out skirmishers along the whole front and to the left, they very soon became engaged with the enemy's skirmishers.

This was about 3 p.m., and it was perfectly evident then that my force of about 1,200 muskets was opposed to one which outflanked mine on either side by at least half a mile. I thought the enemy's force opposed to my brigade was at least a division. In a short time the firing became steady along the whole line, the enemy advancing very slowly. The danger of his possessing the top of the left hill, and thus being in my rear, became so imminent that I had to cause my left regiment (the Sixth Alabama) under *Colonel Gordon* to move along the brow of the hill, under fire, still farther to the left. He did so in good style, and, having a fair opportunity to do so with advantage, charged and drove the enemy back a short distance.

By this time the enemy, though met gallantly by all four of the regiments with me, had penetrated between them, and had begun to swing their extreme right around toward my rear, making for the head of the gorge, up the bottom and sides of which the whole of my force, except the Sixth Alabama, had to retreat, if at all. I renewed again, and yet again, my application for re-enforcements, but none came. Some artillery, under *Captain Carter,* who was moving up without orders, and some of *Colonel Cutts',* under a gallant lieutenant whose name I do not now recollect, was reported . . . to be on its way to my relief; but at this time the enemy had obtained possession of the summit of the left hill . . . and had command of the road in rear of the main mountain. The artillery could only have been used by being hauled up on the high peak, which arose upon the summit of the ridge just at the head of the gorge. . . . This they had not time to do, and hence I ordered it back.

Just before this, I heard that some Confederate troops [*Kemper's* brigade] had joined my right very nearly. Finding that the enemy were forcing my right back, and that the only chance to continue the fight was to change my front so as to face to the left, I ordered all the regiments to fall back up the gorge and sides of the mountain, fighting, the whole concentrating around the high peak. . . . This enabled me to face the enemy's right again, and to make another stout stand with *Gordon's* excellent regiment (which he had kept constantly in hand, and had handled in a manner I have never heard or seen equaled during this war), and with the remainder of the Fifth, Third, and Twelfth Alabama Regiments. I found the Twelfth had been relieved by other troops and closed in toward my right, but had passed in rear of the original line so far that, upon re-establishing the line on the main peak . . . the Third Alabama came upon its right. The Twenty-sixth Alabama, which had been placed on my right, was by this time completely demoralized; its colonel [*Col. E. A. O'Neal*] was wounded, and the men mingled in utter confusion with some South Carolina stragglers [probably from *Jenkins'* brigade] on the summit of the hill, who stated that their brigade had been compelled to give way and had retired. Notwithstanding this, if true, left my rear entirely exposed again (I had no time or means to examine the worth

The gorge on the east side of South Mountain. (DUK)

of their statements), I determined, in accordance with the orders I received about this time, in reply to my last request for re-enforcements, to fight on on the new front.

My loss up to this time had been heavy in all the regiments except the Twelfth Alabama. The Fifth Alabama, which had occupied the left center, got separated into two parts in endeavoring to follow up the flank movement of *Gordon's* regiment. Both parts became engaged again before they could rejoin, and the right battalion was finally cut off entirely. The left and smaller battalion, under *Major Hobson's* gallant management, though flanked, wheeled against the flanking party, and, by desperate fighting, silenced the enemy so far as to enable his little command to make its way to the peak. . . . In the first attack of the enemy up the bottom of the gorge, they pushed on so vigorously as to catch *Captain Ready* and a portion of his party of skirmishers, and to separate the Third from the Fifth Alabama Regiment. The Third made a most gallant resistance at this point, and had my line been a continuous one it could never have been forced.

Having re-established my line, though still with wide intervals . . . on the high peak (this was done under constant fire and in full view of the enemy, now in full possession of the extreme left hill and of the gorge), the fight at close quarters was resumed, and again accompanied by the enemy throwing their . . . right around toward my rear. In this position the Sixth Alabama and the Twelfth suffered pretty severely. The latter, together with the remainder of the Third . . . was forced to retire, and in so doing lost heavily. . . . *Gordon's* regiment retired slowly, now being under an enfilading as well as, direct fire and in danger of being surrounded, but was still, fortunately for the whole command, held together by its able commander.

After this, I could meet the enemy with no organized force except *Gordon's* regiment. One more desperate stand was made by it from an advantageous position. The enemy by this time were nearly on top of the highest peak, and were pushing on, when *Gordon's* regiment, unexpectedly to them, opened fire on their front and checked them. This last stand was so disastrous to the enemy that it attracted the attention of the stragglers . . . many of whom *Colonel Battle* and I had been endeavoring to organize, and who were just then on the flank of that portion of the enemy engaged with *Gordon*. . . . For a few minutes they kept up a brisk enfilading fire upon the enemy, but, finding his fire turning from *Gordon* upon them, and that another body of Federal troops were advancing upon them, they speedily fell back.

It was now so dark that it was difficult to distinguish objects at short musket range, and both parties ceased firing. Directing *Colonel Gordon* to move his regiment to his right and to the rear, so as to cover the gap, I endeavored to gather up stragglers from the other regiments. . . . The remnants . . . were assembled at the gap, and were speedily placed alongside of *Gordon's* regiment, which by this time had arrived in the road ascending the mountain . . . forming a line on the edge of the woods . . . about 200 yards from the main road. The enemy did not advance beyond the top of the mountain. . . .

This position we held until about 11 o'clock at night, when we were ordered to take the Sharpsburg road and to stop at Keedysville, which we did. We had rested about an hour, when I was ordered to proceed to Sharpsburg . . . to drive out a Federal cavalry force reported to be there. . . .[see below, p. 99]

In this engagement my loss was killed 61, wounded 157, missing 204: Total 422. . . . We did not drive the enemy back or whip him, but with 1,200 men we held his whole division at bay without assistance during four and a half hours' steady fighting, losing in that time not over half a mile of ground. [*O.R.*, XIX, Part 1, pp. 1034–36.]

Today's view of Meade's position prior to launching his attack. Note the stone wall referred to in the text. (DUK)

Continue downhill 0.5 mile to the next intersection. At the foot of the hill and the eastern side of the woods in the 'gorge,' you will see the remnants of a stone wall running at right angles to the road. This was where Meade's division deployed before launching its attack. Shortly beyond and to the right of this road you will see a lane leading back to your right. This was in fact a continuation of the same road that you followed on your way to STOP 5, and was the road where the divisions of Hatch and then Ricketts deployed before advancing up the mountain.

At the intersection, turn left on FROSTOWN ROAD and drive nearly 0.1 mile. Pull off to your right in the cattle crossing (farmer's field access).

Modern view of a mid-point on the east slope of South Mountain near path of Meade's attack. (DUK)

STOP 10, MEADE'S ATTACK

General D. H. Hill considered Meade "one of our most dreaded foes; he was always in deadly earnest, and he eschewed all trifling." [*Battles and Leaders*, II, p. 574]. As you look to your left you see the terrain over which Meade's troops attacked.

Report of Brig. Gen. George G. Meade, USA, Commanding Third Division, I Corps

I was directed to move the division on a road leading off to the right of the turnpike and toward the enemy's left. After advancing over a mile on this road, the division, which was the advance of the corps, was turned across the field to the left, and moved in an advantageous position to support Cooper's battery, which it was proposed to establish on an adjoining eminence.

The enemy, perceiving these dispositions, opened on the column from a battery on the mountain side, but without inflicting any injury. Captain Cooper's battery of 3-inch ordnance guns was immediately put in position on the ridge . . . and at the same time, by direction of the general commanding the corps, the regiment of First Rifles of the division was sent forward to feel for the enemy. Being well satisfied, from various indications, that the enemy occupied the mountain in force with his infantry, the general commanding the corps directed me to advance my division to the right, so as, if possible, to outflank them, and then to move forward to attack him.

A slight description of the features of the ground is necessary to properly describe the movements of the division. The turnpike from Fredericktown to Hagerstown in crossing the mountains takes a general direction of northwest and southeast. The mountain ridge occupied by the enemy was perpendicular in its general direction to the road. Parallel to the mountain was another ridge, separated from it at the turnpike by a deep valley, but connected at the upper end by a very small depression. Over this second ridge there was a road, along which I advanced Seymour's brigade of the division, directing him to push forward and feel the enemy.

Soon after advancing, General Seymour reported that he could take the crest of the first ridge, along which ran the road, and could then advance across the ravine to the second ridge, which I immediately ordered him to do. At the same time I deployed Gallagher's (Third) brigade parallel to the mountain, and also Magilton's (Second) brigade on the same line, but down in the valley, and, when the line of battle was completely formed, directed a general advance of the whole.

Seymour soon gained the crest of the first ridge, and then moved in the same direction as the other two brigades. Gallagher and Magilton advanced steadily to the foot of the mountain, where they found the enemy's infantry. In a short time the action became general throughout the whole line. Steadily the line advanced up the mountain side, where the enemy was posted behind trees and rocks, from whence he was slowly, but gradually, dislodged, Seymour first gaining the crest of the hill, and driving the enemy to the left along the ridge, where he was met with the fire of the other two brigades.

Soon after the action commenced, having reason to believe the enemy was extending his left flank to outflank us, I sent to the general commanding the corps for re-enforcements, which were promptly furnished by sending General Duryea's brigade of Ricketts' division. Owing, however, to the distance to be travelled to reach the scene of action, Duryea did not arrive on the ground till just at the close of the engagement. His men were promptly formed in line of battle, and advanced on the left of Seymour, but only one regiment had an opportunity to open fire before the enemy retired and darkness intervened. . . .

I am greatly indebted to Brigadier-General Seymour for the skill with which he handled his brigade on the extreme right flank, securing by his maneuvers the great object of our movements, viz, the outflanking the enemy. To Colonel McNeil, of the first Pennsylvania Rifles, who with his regiment has always been in the advance, I am indebted for ascertaining the exact position of the enemy. . . .

The command rested on their arms during the night. The ammunition train was brought up and the men's cartridge boxes were filled, and every preparation made to renew the contest at daylight the next morning should the enemy be in force. Unfortunately, the morning opened with a heavy mist, which prevented any view being obtained, so that it was not till 7 a.m. that it was ascertained the enemy had retired entirely from the mountain.

I . . . accompany this report with a consolidated return of the killed and wounded and missing, amounting . . . to 399 [392] in all, or about 10 per cent. of the force taken into action. [O.R., XIX, Part 1, pp. 267–68.]

Report of Brig. Gen. Truman Seymour, USA, Commanding First Brigade, Meade's Division

This brigade was placed on the extreme right, and after being massed at the base of the slope, was advanced through open woods and over cultivated ground, on the right of a road leading up a ravine and intersecting the turnpike in rear of the mountain. The Bucktails were thrown forward as skirmishers, supported by the Second [Pennsylvania Reserves] and two companies of the First; the remainder of the brigade followed closely.

On a prominent hill on his extreme left, and on our right of the road . . . the rebels had posted a regiment, the Sixth Alabama. A brisk fire was opened upon our skirmishers by this regiment, and by a battery on the mountain to our left. The exposure was great, and numbers fell under the accurate fire of the shell from these guns, but the enemy was rapidly driven, the hill won, and many prisoners taken.

Looking to the left, an extended field of corn led directly to the main position on the mountain itself. The First, Second, and Fifth [Pennsylvania Reserves] changed direction, and, supported by the Sixth in column of companies, continued the attack. A few volleys were fired, bayonets were leveled, three hearty cheers given, and the whole line moved quickly up the hillside with an impetus that drove the enemy from cover and gave us the crest in time to anticipate a fresh brigade which was advancing to support their line, but which then turned in retreat. Later other brigades came up on our left, and night coming on, the pursuit, from the rough nature of the ground, had to be abandoned. [*O.R.*, XIX, Part 1, p. 272.]

Drive straight ahead and follow the road around to the left. As you approach the first house on your left, after about 0.6 mile, you cross the position of *Gordon's* 6th Alabama. From here, as you look across the valley to your left front, you get a good idea of the difficult terrain over which the troops of Meade and *Rodes* fought. Imagine, if you will, groups of Confederates falling back toward the summit, while the Union commanders endeavored to keep their brigades aligned on this rough terrain.

At 1.6 miles the Frostown Road intersects **MICHAEL ROAD. TURN LEFT.** Go 0.2 mile and turn left again at the STOP sign. After driving another 0.3 mile you may want to take an excursion into Washington Monument State Park for the picnic and rest room facilities as well as the view from the monument site—used by Union signallers after South Mountain was cleared of Confederates.

WASHINGTON MONUMENT EXCURSION

Turn right into the Park and follow the signs directing you to the parking area. Traffic is ONE WAY through the Park, so you will emerge at the same entrance when you have finished your excursion in the Park.

Leave the intersection at the entrance to Washington Monument Park: you want to go south on ZITTLESTOWN ROAD (straight ahead if you did not visit the Park, a right turn if you did). Drive one mile to the STOP sign. TURN RIGHT on U.S. 40 Alternate. Drive 1.1 mile to the Junction with Maryland ROUTE 67 (HARPER'S FERRY). TURN LEFT onto Route 67.

Drive 7.1 miles. TURN LEFT onto GAPLAND ROAD. Drive 1 mile. When you reach the intersection at the TOWNSEND MONUMENT to war correspondents, you can either pull off to the right on Gapland Road or take the hard right turn up into the parking lot if you wish to explore this area in more detail. Picnic and restroom facilities are available.

If you choose the latter course, ignore the sign for Civil War trenches that you will see in the parking lot. These are of doubtful provenance. Simply walk back to the Townsend Monument for the view that can also be seen from the roadside.

STOP II, Townsend Monument Overview

This elaborate structure was built by George Alfred Townsend in 1896 as a memorial to his fellow war correspondents, principally those who had accompanied Union armies during the Civil War. Townsend himself had covered the Peninsular campaign and the initial stages of the Second Bull Run campaign. He was not present during the fighting on South Mountain, for after the battle of Cedar Mountain he embarked upon an extended lecture tour in England followed by a trip to the Continent. Townsend returned to the war in time to accompany Sheridan and the Fifth Corps during the Appomattox campaign. One year later he published *Campaigns of a Non-Combatant* which he himself described as "desultory chapters of [a] desultory life."

It is sad to have written so much at twenty-five, and yet to have only drifting convictions. I may have succeeded in depicting the lives of certain young men who reported the war. All of us, who were young, loved the business, and were glad to quit it. Geo. Alfred Townsend, *Campaigns of a Non-Combatant, and his Romaunt Abroad during the War* (New York: Blelock and Company, 1866), pp. 367–68.

FROM SOUTH MOUNTAIN
TO ANTIETAM

Report of Maj. Gen. D. H. Hill, CSA, Commanding Division

We retreated that night to Sharpsburg, having accomplished all that was required—the delay of the Yankee army until Harper's Ferry could not be relieved.

Should the truth ever be known, the battle of South Mountain, as far as my division was concerned, will be regarded as one of the most remarkable and creditable of the war. The division had marched all the way from Richmond, and the straggling had been enormous in consequence of heavy marches, deficient commissariat, want of shoes, and inefficient officers. Owing to these combined causes, the division numbered less than 5,000 men the morning of September 14, and had five roads to guard, extending over a space of as many miles. This small force successfully resisted, without support, for eight hours, the whole Yankee army, and, when its supports were beaten, still held the roads, so that our retreat was effected without the loss of a gun, a wagon, or an ambulance. *Rodes'* brigade had immortalized itself; *Colquitt's* had fought well, and the two regiments most closely pressed (Twenty-third and Twenty-eighth Georgia) had repulsed the foe. *Garland's* brigade had behaved nobly, until demoralized by the fall of its gallant leader, and being outflanked by the Yankees. *Anderson's* brigade had shown its wonted gallantry. *Ripley's* brigade, for some cause, had not been engaged, and was used with *Hood's* two brigades to cover the retreat.

Had *Longstreet's* division been with mine at daylight in the morning, the Yankees would have been disastrously repulsed; but they had gained important positions before the arrival of re-enforcements. These additional troops came up, after a long, hurried, and exhausting march, to defend localities of which they were ignorant, and to fight a foe flushed with partial success, and already holding key points to further advance. Had our forces never been separated, the battle of Sharpsburg never would have been fought, and the Yankees would not have even the shadow of consolation for the loss of Harper's Ferry.

We reached Sharpsburg about daylight on the morning of the 15th. The Yankees made their appearance that day, and some skirmishing and cannonading occurred.[*O.R.*, XIX, Part 1, pp. 1021–22.]

Report of General Robert E. Lee, CSA, Commanding Army of Northern Virginia

The [Union] effort to force the passage of the mountains had failed, but it was manifest that without re-enforcements we could not hazard a renewal of the engagement, as the enemy could easily turn either flank. Information was also received that another large body of Federal troops had during the afternoon forced their way through Crampton's Gap, only 5 miles in rear of *McLaws* [on Maryland Heights, overlooking Harper's Ferry]. Under these circumstances, it was determined to retire to Sharpsburg, where we would be upon the flank and rear of the enemy should he move against *McLaws*, and where we could more readily unite with the rest of the army. This movement was efficiently and skillfully covered by the cavalry brigade of *General Fitzhugh Lee*, and was accomplished without interruption by the enemy, who did not appear on the west side of the pass at Boonsborough until about 8 a.m. on the following morning. The resistance that had been offered to the enemy at Boonsborough secured sufficient time to enable *General Jackson* to complete the reduction of Harper's Ferry. . . .

The commands of *Longstreet* and *D. H. Hill*, on their arrival at Sharpsburg, were placed in position along the range of hills between the town and the Antietam, nearly parallel to the course of that stream, *Longstreet* on the right of the road and *Hill* on the left. The advance of the enemy was delayed by the brave opposition he encountered from *Fitzhugh Lee's* cavalry, and he did not appear on the opposite side of the Antietam until about 2 p.m. During the afternoon the batteries on each side were slightly engaged. [*O.R.*, XIX, Part 1, pp. 147–48.]

Army forge at McClellan's Sharpsburg headquarters. (USAMHI)

Report of Maj. Gen. George B. McClellan, USA,
Commanding Army of the Potomac

In the engagement at Turner's Pass our loss was 328 killed and
1,463 wounded and missing; that of the enemy is estimated to be, in
all, about 3,000. . . .

On the morning of the 15th I was informed by Union civilians
living on the other side of the mountains that the enemy were
retreating in the greatest haste and in disordered masses to the river.
There was such a concurrence of testimony on this point that there
seemed no doubt to the fact. The hasty retreat . . . from the mountain, and the withdrawal of the remaining troops from between
Boonsborough and Hagerstown to a position where they could resist
attack and cover the Shepherdstown ford and receive the re-enforcements expected from Harper's Ferry, were for a time interpreted as
evidences of the enemy's disorganization and demoralization.

As soon as it was definitely known that the enemy had abandoned the mountains, the cavalry and the corps of Sumner, Hooker, and Mansfield were ordered to pursue them, via the turnpike and Boonsborough, as promptly as possible. The corps of Burnside and Porter (the latter having but one weak division present) were ordered to move by the old Sharpsburg road, and Franklin to advance [from Crampton's Gap] into Pleasant Valley, occupy Rohrersville, and to endeavor to relieve Harper's Ferry. Burnside and Porter, upon reaching the road from Boonsborough to Rohrersville, were to re-enforce Franklin or to move on Sharpsburg, according to circumstances. . . . The cavalry advance overtook a body of the enemy's cavalry in Boonsborough, which it dispersed after a brief skirmish, killing and wounding many, taking some 250 prisoners and 2 guns.

Richardson's division, of Sumner's corps, passing Boonsborough to Centreville or Keedysville, found a few miles beyond the town the enemy's forces displayed in line of battle, strong both in respect to numbers and position, and awaiting attack. Upon receiving reports of the disposition of the enemy, I directed all the corps, except that of Franklin, upon Sharpsburg, leaving Franklin to observe and check the enemy in his front and avail himself of any chance that might offer. I had hoped to come up with the enemy during the 15th in sufficient force to beat them again and drive them into the river. My instructions were that if the enemy were on the march they were to be at once attacked; if they were found in force and in position, the corps were to be placed in position for attack, but no attack was to be made until I reached the front. [*O.R.*, XIX, Part 1, pp. 28–29.]

CRAMPTON'S GAP

Report of General Robert E. Lee, CSA, Commanding Army of Northern Virginia

General McLaws, with his own and *R. H. Anderson's* division, was ordered to seize Maryland Heights, on the north side of the Potomac, opposite Harper's Ferry. . . . *General McLaws.* . . . entered Pleasant Valley on the 11th. On the 12th he directed *General Kershaw,* with his own and *Barksdale's* brigade, to ascend [at Solomon's Gap, about one mile west of Rohrersville] the ridge whose southern extremity is known as Maryland Heights, and attack the enemy who occupied that position with infantry and artillery, protected by intrenchments. He disposed the rest of his command to hold the roads leading from Harper's Ferry eastward through Weverton and northward from Sandy Hook, guarding the pass in his rear, through which he had entered Pleasant Valley, with the brigades of *Semmes* and *Mahone.* . . .

In the mean time events transpired in another quarter which threatened to interfere with the reduction of the place. [Harper's Ferry] A copy of the order directing the movement of the army from Fredericktown had fallen into the hands of General McClellan, and disclosed . . . the disposition of our forces. He immediately began to push forward rapidly. . . .

Early on the 14th a large body of the enemy attempted to force its way to the rear of the position held by *[D. H.] Hill.* . . . Information was also received that another large body of Federal troops had during the afternoon forced their way through Crampton's Gap, only 5 miles in rear of *McLaws.* [*O.R.,* XIX, Part 1, pp. 145–47.]

Report of Maj. Gen. Lafayette McLaws, CSA, Commanding Division, Longstreet's Corps

On the 14th . . . hearing of an advance of the enemy toward the gap [Brownsville Gap, now only a jeep trail about a mile and a half south of Crampton's Gap] over which the command had passed into Pleasant Valley, I had, about 12 o'clock, ordered *General [Howell] Cobb* to return with his brigade to the camp near the point where the road came into the valley, and directed *General Semmes* to withdraw the brigade from Solomon's gap, leaving a mere guard, and to tell *General Cobb*, on his arrival in the vicinity, to take command of Crampton's Gap. This gap was over 5 miles from the positions of my main force. I was on Maryland Heights, directing and observing the fire of our guns, when I heard cannonading in the direction of Crampton's Gap, but I felt no particular concern about it, as there were three brigades of infantry in the vicinity, besides the cavalry of *Colonel Munford*, and *General Stuart*, who was with me on the heights and had just come in from above, told me he did not believe there was more than a brigade of the enemy. I, however, sent my adjutant general to *General Cobb* . . . with directions to hold the gap if he lost his last man in doing it, and shortly afterward went down the mountain and started toward the gap. [*O.R.*, XIX, Part 1, p. 854.]

Report of Brig. Gen. Howell Cobb, CSA, Commanding Brigade, McLaws' Division, Longstreet's Corps

On the 13th . . . I was ordered by you to take and hold possession of Sandy Hook . . . which was done, without serious opposition. On the 14th my command was ordered by you to return to our former camp, at Brownsville. This order was received about 1 o'clock p.m., and the brigade was immediately marched to that point, reaching there about 4 p.m. I had been in camp about an hour when I received a message from *Colonel Munford*, at Crampton's Gap, distant about 2 miles, recommending the removal of my command to that point, as the enemy were pressing the small force at the gap. I immediately ordered my two strongest regiments to march to their support. Before, however, the head of the column had filed into the road I received a message from *Colonel Parham*, who was in command of · *Mahone's* brigade at the gap, to the effect that the enemy was pressing him hard with overwhelming numbers, and appealing for all the support I could bring to him. I immediately ordered the remaining two regiments to march, and accompanied the command in person. As I was marching the last of the column, I received a message from you . . . that I must hold the gap if it cost the life of every man in my command. Thus impressed with the importance of the position, I went forward with the utmost dispatch. When I reached the top of the mountain, I found that the enemy had been repulsed and driven back in the center and had been pursued down the other side of the mountain by *Mahone's* brigade. [O.R., XIX, Part 1, p. 870].

STOP 12, SLOCUM'S ATTACK

Continue to the right on Gapland Road. Go downhill about 0.7 mile and turn left on Mountain Church Road. Drive about 0.8 mile until the view opens out on the right. Pull off to the right side of the road beyond the two farm lanes that enter from the right.

Report of Maj. Gen. William B. Franklin, USA, Commanding VI Corps

The corps advanced on the morning of the 14th from a point 3 miles east of Jefferson. . . . to the vicinity of the village of Burkittsville. Upon ascertaining that the pass over the mountains at this point, which I was directed to secure and hold, was occupied by the enemy in force, I caused immediate preparations to be made for an attack. The enemy was strongly posted on both sides of the road, which made a steep ascent through a narrow defile, wooded on both sides, and offering great advantages of cover and position. Their advance was posted near the base of the mountain, in the rear of a stone wall, stretching to the right of the road at a point where the ascent was gradual, and for the most part over open fields. Eight guns had been stationed on the road, and at points on the sides and summit of the mountain to the left of the pass.

It was evident that the position could be carried only by an infantry attack. Accordingly, I directed Major-General Slocum to advance his division through the village of Burkittsville, and commence the attack upon the right. Wolcott's First Maryland Battery was stationed on the left and to the rear of the village, and maintained a steady fire on the positions of the enemy until they were assailed and carried by our troops. Smith's division was placed in reserve on the east side of the village, and held in readiness to co-operate with General Slocum, or support his attack, as occasion might require. Captain Ayres' battery, of this division, was posted on a commanding ground to the left of the reserves, and kept up an uninterrupted fire on the principal battery of the enemy until the latter was driven from his position.

The advance of General Slocum was made with admirable steadiness through a well-directed fire from the batteries on the mountain, the brigade of Colonel Bartlett taking the lead, followed at proper intervals by the brigades of General Newton and Colonel Torbert. Upon fully determining the enemy's position, the skirmishers were withdrawn, and Colonel Bartlett became engaged along his entire line. He maintained his ground steadily under a severe fire for some time at a manifest disadvantage, until re-enforced by two regiments of General Newton's brigade on his right, and the brigade of Colonel Torbert and the two remaining regiments of Newton's on his left. The line of battle thus formed, an immediate charge was ordered, and most gallantly executed. The men swept forward with a cheer, over the stone wall, dislodging the enemy, and pursuing him up the mountain side to the crest of the hill and down the opposite slope. This single charge, sustained as it was over a great distance and on a rough ascent of unusual steepness, was decisive. The enemy was driven in the utmost confusion from a position of strength, and allowed no opportunity for even an attempt to rally until the pass was cleared and in the possession of our troops.

When the division under General Slocum first became actively engaged, I directed General Brooks' brigade, of Smith's division, to advance upon the left of the road, and dislodge the enemy from the woods upon Slocum's flank. The movement was promptly and steadily made, under a severe artillery fire. General Brooks occupied the woods after a slight resistance, and then advanced, simultaneously with General Slocum, rapidly and in good order, to the crest of the mountain. The victory was complete, and its achievement followed so rapidly upon the first attack that the enemy's reserves, although pushed forward at the double-quick, arrived but in time to participate in the flight, and add confusion to the rout. Four hundred prisoners from seventeen different organizations, 700 stand of arms, 1 piece of artillery, and 3 stand of colors were captured, while numberless articles of equipment, knapsacks, haversacks, blankets, etc., were abandoned by the enemy in their flight. [*O.R.*, XIX, Part 1, pp. 374–75.]

Report of Col. Joseph J. Bartlett, USA, Commanding Second Brigade, Slocum's Division, VI Corps

My command, after a march of nearly 10 miles, arrived opposite . . . Crampton's Pass about 12 o'clock p.m., with the Ninety-sixth Pennsylvania Volunteers . . . deployed as skirmishers. The enemy's pickets retired from the town and opened an artillery fire from two batteries upon my line of skirmishers. I was ordered by Major-General Slocum to halt until he could mass his troops and arrange the plan of the assault, as the appearance of the mountain pass convinced all that artillery was of no avail against it, and that nothing but a combined and vigorous charge of infantry would carry the mountain.

It being decided that the attack should be made on the right and flank of the road leading over the mountains, I was ordered to lead the column, under cover from artillery fire and as secretly as possible, to a large field near its base, where the column of attack was to be formed, each brigade in two lines, at 200 paces in rear. About 4 o'clock p.m. I ordered forward the Twenty-seventh New York Volunteers . . . to deploy as skirmishers, and, upon their placing the interval ordered between the column of attack and their line, I advanced at quick time the Fifth Maine Volunteers . . . and Sixteenth New York Volunteers. . . .

My line of skirmishers found the enemy at the base of the mountain, safely lodged behind a strong stone wall. Their entire line, being now developed, exhibited a large force. My first line advanced rapidly and steadily to the front under a severe fire of artillery from the heights above and musketry from behind the wall and the trees on the slope above it. Halting behind a rail-fence about 300 yards from the enemy, the skirmishers were withdrawn and the battle commenced.

By some unexplained and unaccountable mistake, more than 1,000 yards intervened between the head of the column of General Newton's brigade and my own line, and nothing but the most undaunted courage and steadiness on the part of the two regiments forming my line maintained the fight until the arrival of the rest of the attacking column. . . . On their arrival the Thirty-Second New York Volunteers . . . and the Eighteenth New York Volunteers . . . were sent to report to me by order of General Newton. . . . The Fifth Maine and Seventh New York Volunteers having expended their ammunition, I relieved them, and formed them 20 paces in rear.

The New Jersey brigade, Colonel Torbert commanding, now arrived on the left of the line, and commenced firing by its first line, and the Ninety-sixth Pennsylvania Volunteers having joined my command, and been positioned by me on the extreme right, it became apparent to all that nothing but a united charge would dislodge the enemy and win the battle. A moment's consultation with Colonel Torbert decided us to make the charge immediately at a double-quick, and the order was passed along the line to "Cease Firing," the command given to "Charge," and our whole line advanced with cheers, rushing over the intervening space to the stone wall and routing the enemy. The charge was maintained to the top of the mountain, up an almost perpendicular steep, over rocks and ledges, through the underbrush and timber, until the crest overlooking the valley beyond was gained. The victory was decisive and complete, the routed enemy leaving arms, ammunition, knapsacks, haversacks, and blankets in heaps by the roadside.

The great natural strength of the enemy's position, supported by his well-served batteries, made it absolutely necessary that the first attempt should be successful or great confusion and slaughter must ensue. The success was fully and clearly established by the masterly arrangement of the column of attack by Major-General Slocum. . . . All orders were carried out in detail. No more and no less was done than to execute the plan during the fiercely contested assault which was so clearly expressed in the bivouac. [*O.R.*, XIX, Part 1, pp. 388–89.]

Report of Brig. Gen. Paul J. Semmes, CSA, Commanding Brigade, McLaws' Division, Longstreet's Corps

By order of *Major-General McLaws*, a picket, consisting of a company, was posted in Burkittsville Gap, which, by my orders, was afterward increased to three regiments and five pieces of artillery, thus employing all the regiments of my brigade, except the Tenth Georgia, which had been previously sent to picket the Rohrersville road and other avenues leading down Pleasant Valley in the direction of Harper's Ferry. On the 13th . . . *Colonel Parham*, commanding *Mahone's* brigade, reported with his command to me by order of *Major General McLaws*, with directions to post one of his regiments in Solomon's Gap.

Having soon become more familiar with the roads and passes, on the morning of the 14th . . . I ordered *Colonel Parham*, with his three remaining regiments and battery, to Crampton's Gap for the purpose of guarding that pass; and directed him, if he should need support, to call upon *Major Holt*, commanding the Tenth Georgia Volunteers, for his regiment, then posted on the Rohrersville road.

On the morning of the 14th . . . *Brigadier-General Cobb*, with his command, was ordered up the valley to his old camp near mine. . . . *General McLaws* informed me that *General Cobb* would take command of Crampton's Gap, and directed that the troops under my command should be withdrawn therefrom. When *General Cobb* returned to his old camp, I called on him, and communicated *General*

McLaws' orders, and soon after set out to visit the picket guard in Burkittsville Gap. While on the mountain, the enemy engaged *Colonel Parham's* troops with artillery and infantry at the base of the mountain. I immediately dispatched this information to *General Cobb*, with the request that he would hurry forward his troops to Crampton's Gap, to the support of *Colonel Parham*, and in a few minutes I followed hurriedly on horseback, for the purpose of offering *General Cobb* whatever assistance it might be in my power to render him. . . . Soon after commencing the ascent of the mountain at Crampton's Gap, I encountered fugitives from the battle-field, and endeavored to turn them back. Proceeding farther up the mountain, the troops were met pouring down the road and through the wood, in great disorder, where I found *General Cobb* and his staff, at the imminent risk to their lives, using every effort to check and rally them. I immediately joined my efforts . . . to *General Cobb's*, and co-operated with him for a considerable time in the vain effort to rally the men. Finding it impossible to rally them so near the enemy, it was determined to post artillery about half a mile farther to the rear and bring up two of my regiments from Burkittsville [Brownsville?] Gap . . . and make a stand there to arrest the farther advance of the enemy during that night. Line of battle was finally formed here. The enemy made no farther advance.

Colonel Parham, commanding *Mahone's* brigade, and *Colonel Munford*, of the cavalry, as I was informed, jointly made the dispositions for the battle, which was conducted under their orders, and the troops under their command had been thrown into disorder and were retiring from the field before *General Cobb's* command came up. [*O.R.*, XIX, Part 1, pp. 872–73.]

From the crest of South Mountain at Brownsville Gap, fully a mile to the south, Confederate artillery also participated in the defense of Crampton's Gap.

Report of Col. E. B. Montague, CSA, Thirty-second Virginia Infantry, Semmes' Brigade, McLaws' Division, Longstreet's Corps

On the evening of the 13th I was ordered by *Brigadier-General Semmes* to proceed with the Fifteenth Virginia Regiment and my own, and two pieces of *Manly's* battery, to the top of South Mountain [Brownsville Gap] to watch for and report any advance of the enemy in that direction.

On the morning of the 14th I received a message from *Major-General [Jeb] Stuart* to the effect that the enemy were advancing in great force, and that I must defend the pass at all hazards, calling for re-enforcements if necessary, should the enemy select it as his point of attack, which, however, he thought doubtful.

At 9 or 10 o'clock the enemy's advance came in sight from the direction of Jefferson, seemingly in great force. At about 11 o'clock they masked the most of their force under a hill and wood about 3 miles, and advanced two brigades by the left flank into a field opposite our position. Meantime I had sent to *General Semmes* for re-enforcements, and he promptly ordered up the Fifty-third Georgia Regiment and three pieces of artillery (rifled). . . . I stationed a picket of about 200 men at the foot of the mountain, near Burkittsville, and a line of skirmishers along my whole front. . . . Shortly afterward the enemy threw out a large advance of skirmishers, who steadily advanced toward the base of the mountain, supported by a brigade of infantry, the other brigade remaining at a halt. I ordered *Captain Manly* to open upon them with his 3-inch rifled gun, which he did so effectally as to check the advance of the skirmishers and cause the advancing brigade to fall back on its reserve, beyond our range.

At about 3 or 4 o'clock, after withdrawing his skirmishers, he moved by the right flank, leaving Burkittsville on his left, formed three strong parallel lines of battle, and started the whole in advance, still leaving an immense force in reserve, and moved with great celerity and perfect order against Crampton's Gap. I was in a position to see every move that was made, and saw at once that, by moving my artillery to the left a few hundred yards, I could bring the advancing host within easy range. This was done, and *Macon's, Manly's,* and *Magruder's* guns were played upon the enemy with great effect, time and again their ranks being broken by their deliberate and well-directed fire, the enemy's guns not being able to reach us on account of our elevated position. *Captain Macon,* the senior artillery officer, managed his guns most handsomely. . . . I was more of a spectator than participant in the action. My infantry force was not engaged, though they were ready and anxious to take part in the conflict.

Our guns continued to play on the enemy until dark, long after our forces at Crampton's Gap had been driven from their position. At least three hundred guns [rounds?] were fired during the evening. At least eight brigades of the enemy were engaged in this fight, and many more were coming up when night closed the scene. I withdrew

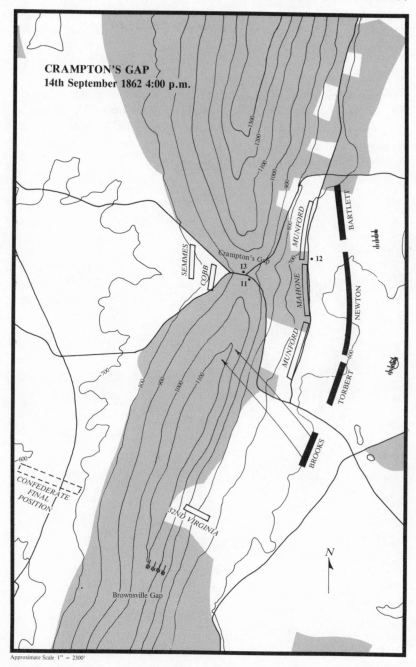

CRAMPTON'S GAP
14th September 1862 4:00 p.m.

Crampton's Gap

SEMMES

COBB

MUNFORD

MAHONE

MUNFORD

BARTLETT

NEWTON

TORBERT

• 12

13

11

BROOKS

32ND VIRGINIA

CONFEDERATE
FINAL
POSITION

Brownsville Gap

N

Approximate Scale 1" = 2300'

after dark, by order, and joined the balance of our force on the road just above Brownsville. [*O.R.*, XIX, Part 1, pp. 881–82.]

STOP 13

Drive straight ahead about 0.3 mile and turn left on Arnoldtown Road. Drive 0.7 mile to the Stop sign near the Townsend Monument. When you have passed the STOP sign, pull over to the right to read the reports and messages that explain the next phase of the operation. You should consult the map on pp. 83, 94–95.

FROM CRAMPTON'S GAP TO HARPERS FERRY

Report of Maj. Gen. Lafayette McLaws, CSA, Commanding Division, Longstreet's Corps

Fortunately, night came on and allowed a new arrangement of the troops to be made to meet the changed aspect of affairs. The brigades of *Generals Kershaw* and *Barksdale*, excepting one regiment of the latter and two pieces of artillery, were withdrawn from the [Maryland] heights, leaving the regiment and two rifle pieces on the main height overlooking the town, and formed line of battle across the valley about 1-1/2 miles below Crampton's Gap, with the remnants of the brigades of *Generals Cobb, Semmes,* and *Mahone,* and those of *Wilcox, Kershaw,* and *Barksdale,* which were placed specially under the command of *General [R. H.] Anderson. Generals Wright* and *Pryor* were kept in position guarding the Weverton Pass, and *Generals Armistead* and *Featherston* that from Harper's Ferry. That place was not yet taken, and I had but to wait and watch the movements of the enemy.

It was necessary to guard three positions: First, to present a front against the enemy advancing down the valley; second, to prevent them from escaping from Harper's Ferry and acting in conjunction with their troops in front; third, to prevent an entrance at Weverton Pass. The force of the enemy engaged and in reserve at Crampton's Gap was estimated to be from 15,000 to 25,000 and upward.

The loss in those brigades engaged was, in killed, wounded, and missing, very large, and the remnant collected to make front across the valley was very small. I had dispatched . . . my aide-de-camp, with a courier and guide, to report to *General Lee* the condition of affairs, but, on getting beyond our forces, he rode suddenly on a strong picket of the enemy, was halted, and fired on by them as he turned and dashed back. . . . *General Stuart* had, however, started couriers before that, and sent others from time to time during the night, and I, therefore, was satisfied that *General Lee* would be informed before morning.

On the 15th the enemy did not advance, nor did they offer any opposition to the troops taking position across the valley. The line to oppose them from that direction was, therefore, formed, and the artillery posted to the best advantage, our artillery on Maryland Heights firing on the enemy below so soon as light permitted.

About 10 a.m. it was telegraphed to me from Maryland Heights that the enemy at Harper's Ferry had hoisted a white flag and had ceased firing. I at once ordered the troops which were defending the pass from Harper's Ferry to advance their skirmishers along the road to the bridge, or until they were fired on, and directed all the trains to be sent toward the Ferry, still keeping the line of battle opposed to that of the enemy above. They, in the meantime, were planting batteries on the Blue Ridge to operate against the artillery on the left of the valley looking north, which had been advantageously placed in position by my chief of artillery . . . along the line formed across the valley. . . . The enemy showing no disposition to advance, I left the command to *General Anderson*, with directions to push the train across the river as fast as possible and follow with the infantry when the trains were well over. I then rode over and received orders to proceed to Sharpsburg with all possible dispatch. [*O.R.*, XIX, Part 1, p. 855.]

Report of Maj. Gen. George B. McClellan, USA, Commanding the Army of the Potomac

As soon as it was definitely known that the enemy had abandoned the mountains . . . Franklin [was ordered] to advance into Pleasant Valley, occupy Rohrersville, and to endeavor to relieve Harper's Ferry. . . . Franklin moved toward Brownsville and found there a force, largely superior in numbers to his own, drawn up in a strong position to receive him. Here the total cessation of firing in the direction of Harper's Ferry indicated but too clearly the shameful and premature surrender of that post. . . . [*O.R.* XIX, Part 1, p. 29.]

On the night of the 14th the following dispatch was sent to General Franklin.

Bolivar, September 15, 1 A.M.

The commanding general directs that you occupy with your command the road from Rohrersville to Harper's Ferry, placing a sufficient force at Rohrersville to hold that position in case it should be attacked by the enemy from Boonsborough. Endeavor to open communication with Colonel Miles [commanding] at Harper's Ferry, attacking and destroying such of the enemy as you may find in Pleasant Valley. Should you succeed in opening communication with Colonel Miles, direct him to join you with his whole command, with all the guns and public property that he can carry with him. . . . You will then proceed to Boonsborough, which place the commanding general intends to attack to-morrow, and join the main body of the army at that place; should you find, however, that the enemy have retreated from Boonsborough toward Sharpsburg, you will endeavor to fall upon him and cut off his retreat.

On the 15th the following were received from General Franklin:

In Pleasant Valley, 3 miles from Rohrersville,

September 15–8.50 A.M.

My command started at daylight this morning, and I am waiting to have it closed up here. General Couch arrived about 10 o'clock last night. I have ordered one of his brigades and one battery to Rohrersville or to the strongest point in its vicinity. The enemy is drawn up in line of battle about 2 miles to our front, one brigade in sight. As soon as I am sure that Rohrersville is occupied, I shall move forward to attack. . . . This may be two hours from now. If Harper's Ferry has fallen — and the cessation of firing makes me fear that it has — it is my opinion that I should be strongly re-enforced.

September 15–11 A.M.

I have received your dispatch. . . . The enemy is in large force in my front, in two lines of battle stretching across the valley, and a large column of artillery and infantry on the right of the valley looking toward Harper's Ferry. They outnumber me two to one. It will, of course, not answer to pursue the enemy under these circumstances. . . . I shall wait here until I learn what is the prospect of re-enforcement. I have not the force to justify an attack on the force I see in front. I have had a very close view of it, and its position is very strong. [O.R., XIX, Part 1, pp. 46–47.]

Maj. Gen. W. B. Franklin, USA, to McClellan,
September 15–3 P.M.

I made a demonstration on my left this morning at the gap, on the left of Burkittsville, with two regiments of infantry and a section of horse artillery. The enemy has begun to retreat, although I hardly consider that due to the demonstration. Smith is in pursuit, with a brigade and a battery, and will do good service.

Under your last orders I do not feel justified in putting my whole command in motion toward the front, but shall act according to the dictates of my judgment, as circumstances may occur. . . . I shall, however, try to carry out the spirit of your orders as nearly as possible.

September 15–4 P.M.

In consequence of the last orders received from you, I shall await further orders here. . . . I have not moved toward Sharpsburg. There is a pass opposite, west of Brownsville, through which part of the enemy retreated today.

Maj. Gen. McClellan, USA, to Franklin
Near Keedysville, September 15, 1982–9 P.M.

Your dispatches . . . have been received. Sumner's, Hooker's, and Banks' [XII Corps] move immediately. Mansfield's and Burnside's corps are here.

The regulars are also here, and the remainder of Porter's corps is at Middletown. The enemy was found in position in considerable force this afternoon, just beyond this place. The troops have not been able to come up sufficiently today to enable us to attack the enemy, but a reconnaissance will be made at daylight, and if he is found to be in position, he will be attacked. The general wishes you to send out tonight a squadron of cavalry to picket the Frederick pike. [*O.R.*, XIX, Part 2, pp. 296–97.]

Report of Maj. Gen. W. B. Franklin, USA,
Commanding VI Corps

For . . . two days I had been encamped in rear of Rohrersville, in Pleasant Valley. During the night of the 16th I received orders to move toward Keedysville in the morning with two divisions, and to dispatch General Couch's division to occupy Maryland Heights. I started at 5.30 a.m. General Smith's division led the column, and its head arrived at the field of battle about 10 o'clock. [*O.R.*, XIX, Part 1, p. 376.]

STOP 14, McLAW'S POSITION

Turn right onto Gapland Road. Retrace your route on the 1-mile drive down the west slope of South Mountain to Maryland Route 67. Turn left on Maryland 67. After driving about 0.5 miles on Maryland 67 you will pass the Christian Holiness Church. The Confederate Final Position shown on the Crampton's Gap map (p. 83) was on the Knoll about 0.1 mile south of that church and stretched across the valley as indicated on the map. Drive 2.5 miles to the Yarrowstown Road and pull off onto the shoulder near that intersection.

Three days before the battle of Crampton's Gap, Major General Lafayette McLaws moved with two divisions into Pleasant Valley. From here you can see the central features of the terrain that he describes in the report dealing with his operations leading to the capture of Harpers Ferry. You are in Pleasant Valley. The ridge to your right is Elk Ridge, that on your left is the Blue Ridge.

Report of Maj. Gen. Lafayette McLaws, CSA, Commanding Division, Longstreet's Corps

On the 10th . . . in compliance with Special Orders No. 191 . . . I proceeded with my own and *General Anderson's* division, via Burkittsville, to Pleasant Valley, to take possession of Maryland Heights, and endeavor to capture the enemy at Harper's Ferry and vicinity. I reached the valley on the 11th.

Pleasant Valley runs north and south, and is bounded on the east by the Blue Ridge, on the west by Elk Ridge, the southern portion of which . . . [is] specially designated as Maryland Heights, the distance across in an air-line between the summits of the two ridges being about 2-1/2 or 3 miles. The valley itself is rolling and irregular, having one main road along or near the foot of the Blue Ridge, and there is another along the base of Elk Ridge, but it is very much out of repair and not much used. The Potomac River runs along the south ends of both ridges, Harper's Ferry town being on the opposite side of the river but entirely commanded by Maryland Heights, from which a plunging fire, from musketry even, can be made into the place. The Baltimore and Ohio Railroad, the turnpike to Frederick, Md., through Middletown, and the canal to Washington City pass along the south end of Blue Ridge, there being just enough space for them between the mountains and the river. They also pass under the south end of Maryland Heights, where a crowded space for them has been made by blasting the rocks for a very considerable distance. The railroad bridge crosses the river just under the precipice of Maryland Heights, and about 50 yards above it the Yankees had a pontoon bridge for wagons, etc. The railroad bridge was defended by cannon placed on the farther end; the narrow causeway along the river under Elk Ridge, by cannon placed under the precipice and on the road. The river there is near 400 yards wide. On the west slope of Elk Ridge the enemy had three heavy guns, placed so as to command the approaches along the road and the town on the opposite side, and, I believe, the road coming from the west, and they also swept Bolivar Heights, which defended the approaches to the town from the side between the Shenandoah and the Potomac, west and south. So long as Maryland Heights was occupied by the enemy, Harper's Ferry could never be occupied by us. If we gained possession of the heights, the town was no longer tenable to them.

Pleasant Valley was approached from the east—first, by the railroad, turnpike, and canal, at the south end of the Blue Ridge; second, by a road over the ridge passing Burkittsville, a small town about a mile or less from the foot of the Blue Ridge, over Brownsville Gap, and by another through a gap to the North of the last-named road, known as Crampton's Gap. The two last were about 1 mile apart. The second road was distant from the one along the south end of the ridge 4 miles. Thus Crampton's Gap was 5 miles from the first road along the Potomac.

Passing from the valley going west were two roads—one along the south end of Maryland Heights . . . and another through Solomon's Gap, a slight depression in Elk Ridge, about 5 miles north of the first. At the south end of Blue Ridge, and just at the commencement of the pass, coming from the east, is the small town of Weverton. About half-way between that place and Harper's Ferry, along the turnpike, is another small place called Sandy Hook. The road from Sandy Hook ran about the middle of the valley, and joined the main road along the foot of the Blue Ridge 2 miles from the Potomac. Understanding that there was a road running from the top of Solomon's Gap along the ridge to the heights commanding Harper's

Ferry, I directed *General Kershaw*, with his brigade and that of *General Barksdale*, to proceed along that road and carry the heights, using infantry alone, as the character of the country forbade the use of any other arm.

On the 12th he proceeded to carry out the order. I then directed a brigade of *General Anderson's* division *(General Wright's)* to ascend the Blue Ridge with two pieces of artillery, and, proceeding down it to the point overlooking Weverton, to command the approaches to the pass there, along the turnpike, railroad, and canal. *General Semmes* was left opposite the [Brownsville] gap the troops had passed over into the valley . . . with his own and *General Mahone's* brigade, commanded by *Colonel Parham*, with orders to send a brigade to the top of Solomon's Gap, to protect the rear of *General Kershaw* and also to take precautions to guard the passes over the Blue Ridge. *General Cobb's* brigade was directed to cross the valley, and, marching along its base, to keep in communication with *General Kershaw* above and up to his advance, so as to give support, if possible, if it was needed, and to serve as a rallying force should any disaster render such necessary. I then moved down the valley toward the river with the rest of the command, the inhabitants generally impressing it upon me that Maryland Heights was lined with cannon for a mile and a half. The main force was kept with the advance of *General Kershaw*, of which I was constantly informed by signal parties stationed on the heights moving with *General Kershaw*. *General Kershaw* soon encountered the skirmishers of the enemy, and drove them before him until darkness put an end to the conflict. *General Wright* gained his position [on the Blue Ridge] without opposition, and at sundown *General Anderson* pushed forward a brigade *(General Pryor's)*, as I directed, and took possession of Weverton, and disposed the troops to effectually defend the pass. The brigades of *Generals Armistead* and *Cobb* were moved up, forming a line across the valley from the right, commanding the road from Sandy Hook.

On the 13th, *General Kershaw* — after a very sharp and spirited engagement through the dense woods and over a very broken surface, there being no road from the point he had ceased operations the night previous, and across two abatis, the last quite a formidable work, the east and west sides being precipices of 30 or 40 feet, and across the ridge were breastworks of heavy logs and large rocks — succeeded in carrying the main ridge, where the enemy had a telegraph station, and by 4.30 p.m. we had possession of the entire heights, the enemy going down a road which they had constructed on the side opposite the Ferry, invisible to our troops from the valley, and were fired on by our skirmishers as they crossed the pontoon bridge to Harper's Ferry town. The report concerning cannon along the heights proved to be false, as the enemy used but one battery on the heights, and that was placed on the road toward Harper's Ferry, and was withdrawn so soon as the main ridge was carried. The battery of heavy guns placed on the west slope of the mountains, which during the day fired frequently on the storming party and dropped shells into Pleasant Valley, was spiked and abandoned at the same time.

The troops in the valley were then advanced, and *General Cobb's* brigade occupied Sandy Hook with but little resistance, the enemy having abandoned the place with their main force of 1,500 the night previous, leaving several hundred new muskets and other stores. The road, then, from Harpers Ferry, which presented egress from the place, coming east, was now completely commanded. . . .

On the 14th, the morning was employed in cutting a road to the top of Maryland Heights practicable for artillery. . . . and by 2 p.m. *Captain Read* and *Captain Carlton* . . . had two pieces from each of their batteries in position overlooking Bolivar Heights and the town. [*O.R.*, XIX, Part 1, pp. 852–84.]

Continue on Maryland 67 for 2.5 miles to the junction with U.S. 340 (Harpers Ferry). Take WEST 340, cross the Potomac and drive along the base of Loudoun Heights. You may want to pull off into the parking area on the right side of the highway beneath Loudoun Heights for the view. Continue on US 340 across the Shenandoah.

Photo Opposite: The railroad bridge at Harpers Ferry at the confluence of the Potomac and Shenandoah Rivers. A vital rail link and site of the Federal Arsenal and Armory. (USAMHI)

EXCURSION INTO HARPERS FERRY

Immediately after you cross the Shenandoah you will see brown
National Park Service signs directing you to the Harpers Ferry National Historical Park. If you are interested in visiting the Park, take
the first exit after you leave the bridge, following the Park Service
signs down into Harpers Ferry. After driving about 0.5 mile you will
come to a parking area on your right. Park there and walk to the
Visitors' Center for information on the sights and activities available
in the Park. When you have finished, return to your car, retrace your
route to US 340 and turn right onto US 340 WEST.

Continue on US 340 to the exit beyond the National Park exit and
turn right onto Union Street. Drive 0.3 mile to a STOP sign and turn
left onto Washington Street. Follow Washington Street for nearly a
mile. Opposite the cemetery, turn right onto the road marked "Bolivar Heights." Drive about 0.25 mile to the turnout on the left, park
and dismount.

As you look back toward the town, Maryland Heights are on
your left and Loudoun Heights are on your right. The trench lines
constructed by the Union defenders can be seen by walking down the
asphalt path that follows the fence back from the left side of the
parking area.

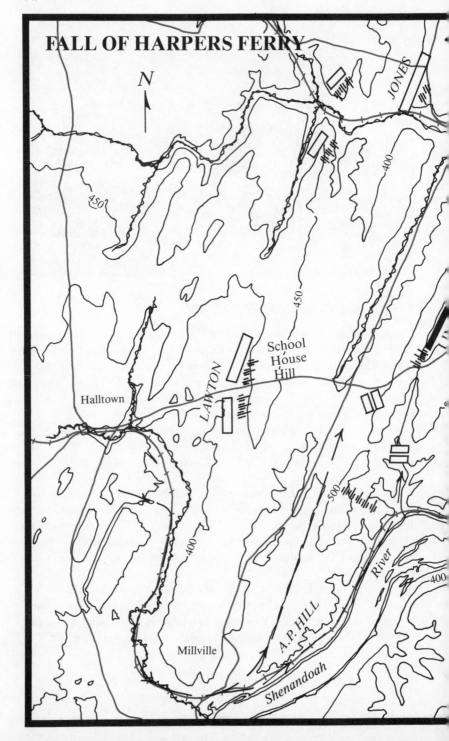

FALL OF HARPERS FERRY

N

JONES

School
House
Hill

LAWTON

Halltown

450

400

500

A.P. HILL

Millville

Shenandoah

River

400

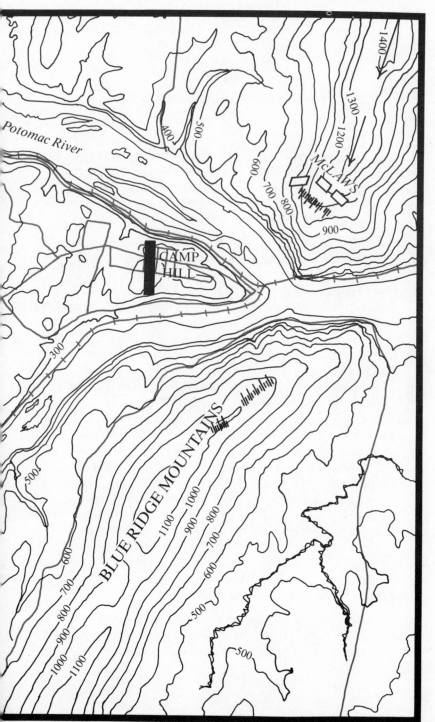

BOLIVAR HEIGHTS
The Defense of Harpers Ferry

You are now standing behind what one of the Union commanders described as "a slight earthwork" erected to protect Union batteries that commanded the approaches from the west. According to Brig. Gen. Julius White, the senior Union officer present—but *not* in command—during the siege:

> The defenses of Harper's Ferry, if worthy of the name, comprised a small work on the crest of Maryland Heights [and] . . . another well down the western slope, where a battery of heavy naval guns was established. . . . On Bolivar Heights a line of rifle-pits extended from near the Potomac southward to the Charlestown road, where a small work for the protection of artillery was situated.
>
> In the rear of this line eastward, and in the upper part of the town, was an earth-work known as Camp Hill. Loudoun Heights (east of the Shenandoah) were not occupied by our troops.
>
> The troops constituting the garrison were originally disposed by Colonel Miles as follows: on Maryland Heights, about 2,000; on Bolivar Heights, from the Potomac to the Charlestown road, thence at a right angle to the Shenandoah, a distance in all of at least a mile and a half, 7,000 men; in the work at Camp Hill, about 800; while the remainder, about 1,000, guarded the bridges and other points on the rivers.
>
> The distance from Maryland Heights to the nearest point on Bolivar Heights by way of the pontoon bridge was two and a quarter miles; to the intersection of the Charlestown road, three miles. Thus the principal points to be defended were not within supporting distance of each other in case of assault, nor was either of them properly fortified. [Brig. Gen. Julius White, "The Surrender of Harper's Ferry," *Battles and Leaders*, II, p. 612.]

To make matters worse, the works on Bolivar Heights were not well laid out or constructed. There was no place where troops could man the rifle pits "without their being slaughtered" by Confederate artillery fire,

and according to the testimony of one of the brigade commanders responsible for defending this line, enemy guns

> commanded every foot . . . around the batteries on the left and along
> the lines, enfilading that part of the ground, and producing a terrible
> cross-fire. . . . There was not a place where you could lay the palm of
> your hand and say it was safe. . . . The regiments between the
> Charlestown [pike] and the Shenandoah . . . rested with their flanks
> toward the batteries under Loudoun Heights, and, at the same time,
> they would have been in position to have been shelled from behind,
> from Loudoun Heights, and . . . they would have received the fire
> from the batteries on the ridge in front; and the regiments on Bolivar
> Heights, to the right of Rigby's batteries, were under range of three
> batteries on their flank . . . and also the shells from Loudoun Heights.
> [*O.R.*, XIX, Part 1, p. 743.]

Although Colonel D. Miles, who commanded the garrison at Harpers Ferry, had intended this to be the line to defend against any attack
from the west, he ignored suggestions to strengthen the works and to cut
down a belt of forest half a mile in front which could conceal enemy
movements.

Miles also neglected to take the necessary precautions to hold Maryland Heights, as the *Report* of the Military Commission appointed eight
days after the fall of Harpers Ferry to investigate events leading to the
surrender tartly concluded:

> On the 5th of September, Col. Thomas H. Ford, of the Thirty-
> second Ohio, took command of the forces on Maryland Heights.
> Forces were placed at Solomon's Gap and Sandy Hook. Those at
> Sandy Hook . . . retired, by order of Colonel Miles, to the eastern
> slope of Maryland Heights two or three days previous to their evac-
> uation by Colonel Ford.
>
> On the 11th . . . the force at Solomon's Gap was driven in by the
> enemy. Colonel Ford called upon Colonel Miles for re-enforcements,
> and on . . . the 12th . . . the Thirty-ninth and One hundred and
> twenty-sixth New York Regiments were sent him, and on the morn-
> ing of the 13th he was further re-enforced by the One hundred and
> fifteenth New York and a portion of a Maryland regiment. . . .
>
> Colonel Ford made requisition for axes and spades to enable him
> to construct defenses on the heights, but obtained none, and on the
> 12th, with twelve axes belonging to some Maryland regiment, being
> all he could obtain, a slight breastwork of trees was constructed near

the crest of the heights, and in front of which for a short distance a slashing of timber was made.

The forces under Colonel Ford were stationed at various points on Maryland Heights, the principal force being on the crest . . . near the breastwork and lookout. Skirmishing commenced on . . . the 12th, on the crest of the hill.

Early in the morning of the 13th the enemy made an attack on the crest of the hill, and, after a short engagement, the troops retired in some confusion to the breastwork, where they were rallied. About 9 o'clock a second attack was made, which the troops behind the breastwork resisted for a short time, and until Colonel Sherrill, of the One hundred and twenty-sixth New York, was wounded and carried off the field, when the entire . . . regiment . . . with the exception of two companies . . . broke and fled in utter confusion. Both men and most of the officers fled together, no effort being made to rally the regiment except by Colonel Ford . . . and some officers of other regiments, directed by Colonel Miles, who was then on the heights.

Soon after, the remaining forces at the breastwork fell back under a supposed order from Major Hewitt who himself says that he . . . merely sent instructions to the captains of his own regiment that, if they were compelled to retire, to do so in good order. Orders were given by Colonel Ford for the troops to return to their position, and they advanced some distance up the heights, but did not regain the breastwork.

That morning Colonel Miles was on the Maryland Heights for some hours, consulting with Colonel Ford. He left between 11 and 12 o'clock without directly ordering Colonel Ford to evacuate the heights, but instructing him, in case he was compelled to do so, to spike his guns and throw the heavy siege guns down the mountain. About 2 o'clock, perhaps a little later, by order of Colonel Ford, the heights were abandoned. . . .

The Commission blamed two officers for the "disgraceful surrender" of Harper's Ferry. Colonel Thomas H. Ford was accused of abandoning Maryland Heights prematurely. "Our forces were not driven from the field, as full time was given to spike the guns and throw the heavier ones down the precipice, and retreat in good order to Harper's Ferry." Nor did the loss in killed and wounded suggest anything approaching "a desperate conflict." Because Ford conducted the defense of Maryland Heights "without ability, abandoned his position without sufficient cause, and has shown throughout . . . a lack of military capacity," he was promptly dismissed from the service.

As for Colonel D. S. Miles, struck by a shell and mortally wounded while surrender negotiations were in process, the Commission approached its task with what it called "extreme reluctance."

> An officer who cannot appear before any earthly tribunal to answer or explain charges gravely affecting his character, who has met his death at the hands of the enemy, even upon the spot he disgracefully surrendered, is entitled to the tenderest care and most careful investigation. These this Commission has accorded Colonel Miles, and, in giving an opinion, only repeats what runs through our nine hundred pages of evidence, strangely unanimous upon the fact that Colonel Miles' incapacity, amounting to almost imbecility, led to the shameful surrender of this important post.

Major General H. W. Halleck, General in chief of the Union armies, testified that in his opinion, McClellan "could, and should, have relieved and protected Harper's Ferry," and in this judgment the Commission fully concurred.

> Had the garrison been slower to surrender or the Army of the Potomac swifter to march, the enemy would have been forced to raise the siege or have been taken in detail, with the Potomac dividing his forces. [*O.R.*, XIX, Part 1, pp. 795–800.]

Almost the only bright spot in the *Report* of the Commission was the brief mention of the cavalry at Harper's Ferry. On the night of the 14th, Colonel B. F. Davis and Lieutenant Colonel Hasbrouck Davis convinced their superiors that cavalry could be of little use in the defense of Harper's Ferry and received orders to attempt to break out with their regiments and reach McClellan before the surrender. Under the general command of the senior cavalry officer, Colonel Arno Voss, some 1,500 horsemen crossed the pontoon bridge, turned left onto the Sharpsburg road, and, in the dark, made their way through Confederate lines. They rode all of the way to Greencastle, Pennsylvania, capturing en route some 60 wagons loaded with ammunition and other supplies and 675 men belonging to *Longstreet's* trains. It was probably this cavalry force that was responsible for *Rodes'* worn division being sent to Sharpsburg after falling back from South Mountain. (See above, p. 64.) [*O.R.*, XIX, Part 1, p. 538; Part 2, p. 305; *Battles and Leaders*, II, p. 613.]

THE INVESTMENT OF HARPERS FERRY

Report of Brig. Gen. J. B. Kershaw, CSA, Commanding Brigade, McLaws' Division, Longstreet's Corps

On the morning of the 12th . . . I was directed, with *Barksdale's* Mississippi brigade and my own, to move from Brownsville and occupy the Maryland Heights, taking the road by Solomon's Gap to the summit of Elk Ridge, and thence, along the ridge, to the point which overlooks and commands Harper's Ferry. At an early hour the command was in motion and reached the gap without opposition. At this point, however, the pickets of the enemy were discovered, and it became necessary to approach the position carefully, with skirmishers thrown well to the right and left. This being done, the enemy withdrew . . . after a few scattering shots. Reaching the summit of the mountain, skirmishers were thrown well down the mountain to my right, while the column filed to the left along the ridge. *Captain Cuthbert*, Second South Carolina Regiment, commanding the skirmishers on the right, soon encountered a volley from about three companies of cavalry, but upon the fire being returned the enemy left with some loss. About a mile farther on, *Major Bradley*, Mississippi regiment, commanding skirmishers, reported an abatis across the line of march, from which he was fired upon by a picket. Directing him to press forward and ascertain the force in front, he soon overcame the obstacle without further resistance. Leaving then the path, which at that point passed down the mountain to the right, we filed along the crags on the ridge. The natural obstacles were so great that we only reached a position about a mile from the point of the mountain at 6 o'clock. Here an abatis was discovered, extending across the mountain, flanked on either side by a ledge of precipitous rocks. A sharp skirmish ensued, which satisfied me that the enemy occupied the position in force. I therefore directed *Major Bradley* to retire his skirmishers, and deployed my brigade in two lines, extending across the entire practicable ground on the summit of the mountain, the Eighth [South Carolina] . . . on the right, and the Seventh . . . on the left, constituting the first line; the Third Regiment . . . in the rear of the Eighth, and the Second . . . in rear of the Seventh, constituting the second line; *General Barksdale's* brigade immediately in rear. These dispositions being made, the approach of night prevented further operations. . . .

[On] the morning of the 13th . . . I moved forward my first line to the attack. Early in the advance, the Eighth Regiment encountered a ledge of rock which cut them off from further participation in the attack; but *Colonel Aiken* [7th South Carolina] moved briskly forward, under a heavy fire of musketry, surmounted the difficult abatis, and drove the enemy from his position in about twenty minutes. The enemy is stated by prisoners to have been 1,200 strong at this point. They retired about 400 yards, to a much stronger position, a similar abatis, behind which was a breastwork of logs, extending across the mountain, flanked, as before, by precipitous ledges of rock.

I had, at the commencement of the attack, directed *General Barksdale* to form his brigade down the face of the mountain to my left, in prolongation of the two lines on the summit, it having appeared the night before that the enemy's skirmishers occupied a part of that face of the mountain. I now directed *General Barksdale* to advance his command, and attack the enemy in flank and rear, while I pressed him in front. . . . Reaching the abatis, a most obstinate resistance was encountered, and a fierce fire kept up, at about 100 yards distance, for some time. Our loss was heavy, and I found it necessary to send in [the] . . . Third Regiment to support the attack. They, too, were stoutly resisted. *General Barksdale* then sent me word that he had, with great labor, overcome the difficulties of the route and had reached the desired position, but that he could not bring his men to the crest of the mountain without encountering our fire, as he was in rear of the enemy. I sent to direct our fire to cease, hoping that we might capture the whole force if *General Barksdale* could get up. Before this order was extended, the right company of *Colonel Fiser's* regiment, *Barksdale's* brigade, fired into a body of the enemy's sharpshooters lodged in the rocks above them, and their whole line broke into a perfect rout, escaping down the mountain sides to their rear.

This took place at 10.30 o'clock a.m. *General Barksdale* was directed to occupy the point of the mountain, which he did without encountering anything more than a picket of the enemy, which he soon disposed of. In their retreat the enemy abandoned and spiked three heavy guns, which were in position on the lower slope of the mountain toward Harper's Ferry, and left considerable commissary stores, ammunition, and a number of tents near the same place. The guns were left by me, as it was impossible to remove them without further time. . . .

In this engagement our loss was heavy; but three of my regiments were engaged, the ground not admitting of the employment of a larger number. The Seventh and Eighth Regiments exhausted their ammunition, and the Third Regiment had but a few rounds left when the place was carried. Prisoners were taken from three different regiments of the enemy, one of which was represented to number 1,000 men. . . . The conduct of the whole command, contending as they were against the most formidable natural obstacles, without water, which could not be obtained nearer than the foot of the mountain, and encountering an enemy most strongly posted and superior in numbers to all that could be brought into position against him, is worthy of the highest commendation. [*O.R.*, XIX, Part 1, pp. 863–64.]

As *McLaws'* guns in position on Maryland Heights bombarded Bolivar Heights, "driving the enemy from their works on the right" and throwing shells into the town, *General Walker's* guns opened fire from Loudoun Heights.

Report of Brig. Gen. John G. Walker, CSA, Commanding Division, Longstreet's Corps

On September 9 I was instructed by *General Lee* to proceed from Monocacy Junction, near Frederick, Md., to the mouth of the Monocacy, and destroy the aqueduct of the Chesapeake and Ohio Canal. We arrived at the aqueduct about 11 p.m., and found it occupied by the enemy's pickets, whose fire, as they fled, severely wounded *Captain Duffy*, of the Twenty-fourth North Carolina. . . . Working parties were at once detailed, and set to work to drill holes for blowing up the arches, but, after several hours of labor, it was apparent that, owing to the insufficiency of our tools and the extraordinary solidity and massiveness of the masonry, the work we had undertaken was one of days instead of hours.

The movement of our main army from Frederick toward Hagerstown, which I had been officially informed would take place on the 10th, would leave my small division in the immediate presence of a very strong force of the enemy, and, while it would be engaged in destroying the aqueduct, in a most exposed and dangerous position. I therefore determined to rejoin *General Lee* by way of Jefferson and Middletown, as previously instructed. . . . Before marching, however, I received instructions to cross the Potomac at Cheek's Ford and proceed toward Harper's Ferry, and cooperate with *Major-Generals Jackson* and *McLaws* in the capture of the Federal forces at that point.

Early on the morning of the 10th the aqueduct over the Monocacy was occupied by a large force of the enemy, with their artillery commanding the aqueduct and its approaches, as well as Cheek's Ford. I then determined to cross at Point of Rocks, which I effected during the night of the 10th and by daylight on the 11th, but with much difficulty, owing to the destruction of the bridge over the canal and the steepness of the banks of the Potomac. My men being much worn down by two days' and nights' marching, almost without sleep or rest, we remained in camp during the 11th, and proceeded the next day toward Harper's Ferry, encamping at Hillsborough.

On the morning of the 13th we reached the foot of the Blue Ridge, opposite the Loudoun Heights, which I was instructed to occupy. From such reconnaissance as could be made from below, it seemed certain that Loudoun Heights were unoccupied by the enemy. To ascertain if such was the case, I detached *Col. John R. Cooke*, with . . . the Twenty-Seventh North Carolina, and the Thirtieth Virginia Volunteers, who took possession of the heights without opposition and held them during the night.

In the mean time the enemy was being attacked on the Maryland Heights by the forces under *Major-General McLaws*, and in the afternoon it became apparent that our forces had possession of the summit, which commands Harper's Ferry as well as Loudoun Heights.

That night and the next, the entire division, except that portion of it occupying Loudoun Heights, was placed in a strong position to prevent the escape of the enemy down the right bank of the Potomac.

At daylight on the 14th, I sent *Captain French*, with three Parrott guns and two rifle pieces of *Branch's* battery . . . to Loudoun Heights, where I immediately proceeded and placed them in position. I informed *Major-General Jackson* of this, by signal, and awaited his instructions. In the mean time we had attracted the notice of the enemy, who opened their batteries upon us, and it became necessary either to reply or withdraw our pieces. About 1 p.m. I therefore gave orders to open fire upon the enemy's batteries and the troops upon Bolivar Heights. . . . Our guns were served admirably and with great rapidity, and in two hours we had silenced an eight-gun battery near the Barbour House, except one gun, which was so close under the mountain that we could not see it. What other effect our fire had we could not tell, but it evidently produced great consternation and commotion among the enemy's troops, especially the cavalry.

During the engagement, one of the enemy's caissons was blown up by a well-directed shot from *French's* battery. On our side we lost *Lieutenant Robertson*, of *French's* battery, killed; *Major Wiatt*, Forty-eighth North Carolina . . . and two privates, of *French's* battery, wounded. Our guns and horses sustained no injury.

Owing to a heavy mist, which concealed Harper's Ferry from view, we did not open our fire until after 8 o'clock in the morning of the 15th, the enemy replying very feebly at first, and, finally, about 9 o'clock, ceased firing altogether. [*O.R.*, XIX, Part 1, pp. 912–14.]

Report of Lieut. Gen. T. J. Jackson, CSA, Commanding Army Corps, Army of Northern Virginia

In obedience to instructions . . . and for the purpose of capturing the Federal forces and stores then at Martinsburg and Harper's Ferry, my command left the vicinity of Frederick City on the 10th, and, passing rapidly through Middletown, Boonsborough, and Williamsport, recrossed the Potomac into Virginia, at Light's Ford, on the 11th. *General [A.P.] Hill* moved with his division on the turnpike direct from Williamsport to Martinsburg. The divisions of *Jackson* and *Ewell* proceeded toward the North Mountain Depot, on the Baltimore and Ohio Railroad, about 7 miles northwest of Martinsburg. They bivouacked that night in the vicinity of the depot. In order to prevent the Federal forces then at Martinsburg from escaping westward unobserved, *Major Myers*, commanding the cavalry, sent part of his troops as far south as the Berkeley and Hampshire turnpike. *Brigadier-General White*, who was in command of the Federal forces at Martinsburg, becoming advised of our approach, evacuated the place on the night of the 11th and retreated to Harper's Ferry.

On the morning of the 12th our cavalry entered the town, as, in the course of the day, did the main body of my command. At this point, abandoned quartermaster's, commissary, and ordnance stores fell into our hands.

Proceeding thence toward Harper's Ferry, about 11 o'clock on the following morning (13th), the head of our column came in view of the enemy drawn up in force upon Bolivar Heights. *General Hill*, who was in the advance, went into camp near Halltown, about 2 miles from the enemy's position. The two other divisions encamped near by.

The commanding general having directed *Major-General McLaws* to move, with his own and *General R. H. Anderson's* divisions, to take possession of the Maryland Heights, overlooking Harper's Ferry, and *Brig. Gen. J. G. Walker*, pursuing a different route, to cross the Potomac and move up that river on the Virginia side and occupy the Loudoun Heights, both for the purpose of co-operating with me, it became necessary, before making the attack, to ascertain whether they were in position. Failing to learn the fact by signals, a courier was dispatched to each of those points for the required information. During the night the courier to the Loudoun Heights returned with a message from *General Walker* that he was in position. In the mean time *General McLaws* had attacked the Federal force posted to defend the Maryland Heights; had routed it and taken possession of that commanding position.

The Potomac River flowed between the positions respectively occupied by *General McLaws* and myself, and the Shenandoah separated me from *General Walker*, and it became advisable, as the speediest mode of communication, to resort to signals. Before the necessary orders were thus transmitted the day was far advanced. The enemy had, by fortifications, strengthened the naturally strong position which he occupied along Bolivar Heights, extending from near the Shenandoah to the Potomac. *McLaws* and *Walker*, being thus separated from the enemy by intervening rivers, could afford no assistance beyond the fire of their artillery and guarding certain avenues of escape to the enemy, and, from the reports received from them by signals, in consequence of the distance and range of their guns, not much could be expected from their artillery so long as the enemy retained his advanced position on Bolivar Heights.

In the afternoon *General Hill* was ordered to move along the left bank of the Shenandoah, turn the enemy's left, and enter Harper's Ferry. *General Lawton*, commanding *Ewell's* division, was directed to move along the turnpike for the purpose of supporting *General Hill*, and of otherwise operating against the enemy to his left. *General J. R. Jones*, commanding *Jackson's* division, was directed, with one of his brigades and a battery of artillery, to make a demonstration against the enemy's right, while the remaining part of his command, as a reserve, moved along the turnpike. *Major Massie*, . . . commanding the cavalry, was directed to keep upon our left flank, for the purpose of preventing the enemy from escaping. *Brigadier-General Walker* guarded against an escape across the Shenandoah River. Fearing lest the enemy should attempt to escape across the Potomac, by means of signals I called the attention of *Major-General McLaws*, commanding on Maryland Heights, to the propriety of guarding against such an attempt.

The demonstration on the left against the enemy's right was made by *Winder's* brigade, *Colonel Grigsby* commanding. It was ordered to secure a commanding hill to the left of the heights near the Potomac. Promptly dispersing some cavalry, this eminence, from which the batteries of *Poague* and *Carpenter* subsequently did such admirable execution, was secured without difficulty.

In execution of the orders given *Major-General Hill*, he moved obliquely to the right until he struck the Shenandoah River. Observing an eminence crowning the extreme left of the enemy's line occupied by infantry, but without artillery, and protected only by an abatis of fallen timber, *Pender, Archer,* and *Brockenbrough* were directed to gain the crest of that hill, while *Branch* and *Gregg* were directed to march along the river and during the night to take advantage of the ravines cutting the precipitous banks of the river and establish themselves on the plain to the left and rear of the enemy's works. *Thomas* followed as a reserve. The execution of the first movement was intrusted to *Brigadier-General Pender*, who accomplished it with slight resistance, and during the night *Lieutenant-Colonel Walker*, chief of artillery of *Hill's* division, brought up the batteries of *Captains Pegram, McIntosh, Davidson, Braxton,* and *Crenshaw*, and established them upon the position thus gained. *Branch* and *Gregg* also gained the positions indicated for them, and day-break found them in rear of the enemy's line of defense.

As directed, *Brigadier-General Lawton*, commanding *Ewell's* division, moved on the turnpike in three columns, one on the road and another on each side of it, until he reached Halltown, when he formed line of battle and advanced to the woods on School-House Hill [a modern school stands today on the same hill]. The division laid on their arms during the night, *Lawton* and *Trimble* being in line on the right of the road and *Hays* on the left, with *Early* immediately in his rear.

During the night, *Colonel Crutchfield*, my chief of artillery, crossed ten guns of *Ewell's* division over the Shenandoah and established them on its right bank, so as to enfilade the enemy's position on Bolivar Heights and take his nearest and most formidable fortifications in reverse. The other batteries of *Ewell's* division were placed in position on School-House Hill, on each side of the road.

At dawn, September 15, *General Lawton* advanced his division to the front of the woods. *Lawton's* brigade . . . moved by flank to the bottom between School-House Hill and Bolivar Heights, to support the advance of . . . *Hill.* *Lieutenant-Colonel Walker* opened a rapid enfilade fire from all his batteries at about 1,000 yards range. The batteries on School-House Hill attacked the enemy's lines in front. In a short time the guns . . . under the direction of *Colonel Crutchfield*, opened from the rear. The batteries of *Poague* and *Carpenter* opened fire on the enemy's right. The artillery upon the Loudoun Heights, of *Brigadier-General Walker's* command . . . which had silenced the enemy's artillery near the superintendent's house on the preceding afternoon, again opened upon Harper's Ferry, and also some guns of *Major-General McLaws* from the Maryland Heights.

In an hour the enemy's fire seemed to be silenced, and the batteries of *General Hill* were ordered to cease their fire, which was the signal for storming the works. *General Pender* had commenced his advance, when, the enemy again opening, *Pegram* and *Crenshaw* moved forward their batteries and poured a rapid fire into the enemy. The white flag was now displayed, and shortly afterward *Brigadier-General White* (the commanding officer, *Col. D. S. Miles* having been mortally wounded), with a garrison of about 11,000 men, surrendered as prisoners of war. Under this capitulation we took possession of 73 pieces of artillery, some 13,000 small-arms, and other stores. Liberal terms were granted to *General White* and the officers under his command in the surrender, which, I regret to say, do not seem, from subsequent events, to have been properly appreciated by their Government. Leaving *General Hill* to receive the surrender of the Federal troops and take the requisite steps for securing the captured stores, I moved, in obedience to orders from the commanding general, to rejoin him in Maryland with the remaining divisions of my command. By a severe night's march we reached the vicinity of Sharpsburg on the morning of the 16th. [*O.R.*, XIX, Part 1, pp. 953–55.]

Boteler's Ford from the right bank of the Potomac. (HWN)

HARPERS FERRY
TO ANTIETAM

TO SHARPSBURG VIA BOTELER'S FORD

Since the next phase of this battlefield tour is in the vicinity of Sharpsburg, and the Confederate soldiers who took these positions were on their way there after this battle, you should now follow their principal route to the Antietam Battlefield.

Drive back down to Washington Street the same way you came in. TURN RIGHT onto WASHINGTON Street and drive about 0.1 mile, following the signs to US 340. TURN RIGHT onto US340, and drive about 0.8 mile to BAKERTON ROAD. TURN RIGHT. Drive about 1.5 miles on Bakerton Road, through the railroad underpass, and TURN LEFT.

Drive about 5.0 miles, winding through the countryside near the Potomac, to the Bethesda Church intersection (Moler Crossroads). TURN LEFT and then immediately TURN RIGHT. Drive about 1.6 miles to TROUGH ROAD (the unmarked gravel road at the crest of the hill). Turn right and follow Trough Road about 1.6 miles down to the Potomac at Boteler's Ford (known also as Packhorse or Shepherdstown ford). Turn left and pull off into one of the available spaces if you want to consider the ford or read the historical markers.

Here on September 20 was fought a little-known but significant action that marked the end of the Maryland campaign.

General R. E. Lee to His Excellency Jefferson Davis, September 20, 1862

Since my last letter to you of the 18th, finding the enemy indisposed to make an attack on that day, and our position being a bad one to hold with the river in rear, I determined to cross the army to the Virginia side. This was done at night successfully, nothing being left behind, unless it may have been some disabled guns or broken-down wagons, and the morning of the 19th found us satisfactorily over on the south bank of the Potomac, near Shepherdstown, when the army was immediately put in motion toward Williamsport. Before crossing the river, in order to threaten the enemy on his right and rear and make him apprehensive for his communications, I sent the cavalry forward to Williamsport, which they successfully occupied. At night the infantry sharpshooters, left, in conjunction with *General Pendleton's* artillery, to hold the ford below Shepherdstown, gave back, and the enemy's cavalry took possession of that town, and, from *General Pendleton's* report after midnight, I fear much of his reserve artillery has been captured. I am now obliged to return to Shepherdstown, with the intention of driving the enemy back if not in position with his whole army; but if in full force, I think an attack would be inadvisable, and I shall make other dispositions.

Lee to Davis, September 21, 1862

General Jackson's corps was turned back toward Shepherdstown, to rectify occurrences in that quarter. Only one or two brigades of the enemy's infantry with cavalry had crossed the river, none of whom had entered Shepherdstown. They displayed a large force of artillery on the opposite bank. *General A. P. Hill's* division pushed forward, and soon drove them across the river, when this army resumed its march. Only four pieces of artillery fell into the hands of the enemy, which they had carried across the river before they were attacked by *A. P. Hill.* [*O.R.*, XIX, Part 1, p. 142.]

Report of Maj. Gen. Fitz-John Porter, USA, Commanding V Corps

At an early hour on the 19th it was discovered that the enemy had nearly evacuated Sharpsburg, and the Fifth with other corps was directed to take up a position in line beyond the town, but afterward ordered to pursue the enemy and give aid to the cavalry brigade, then in advance. I found that the enemy, pressed by Pleasonton, had crossed the river, and was holding the right bank, defending the fords, with artillery well posted. I determined to clear the fords, and, if possible, secure some of the enemy's artillery. With this view I caused the banks of the river and canal to be well lined with skirmishers and sharpshooters, supported by portions of their respective divisions (Morell's and Sykes') while the artillery and that of the reserve was posted to control the opposite bank. While these were driving from their guns the cannoneers and horses, and silencing the fire of the infantry, an attacking party from Griffin's and Barnes' brigades, composed of the Fourth Michigan and parts of the One hundred and eighteenth Pennsylvania and the Eighteenth and Twenty-second Massachusetts Regiments, volunteers for the occasion, was formed under the immediate direction of General Griffin, and moved across the river in face of a warm fire from the enemy's infantry. Through some misunderstanding, an order for Sykes to move over a similar party did not reach him. His skirmishers, under the immediate direction of Colonel [Gouverneur K.] Warren, were busy keeping down the fire of the enemy's infantry, and with the artillery effectually prevented the enemy's cannoneers from manning their guns.

Darkness concealed the movements of the enemy and enabled them to remove a portion of their artillery before our attacking party scaled the heights. The result of the day's action was the capture of 5 pieces, 2 caissons, 2 caisson bodies, 2 forges, and some 400 stand of arms; also 1 battle-flag. Our loss was small in numbers. . . . The party was recalled during the night, and the whole command bivouacked within reach of the fords.

Cavalry having been directed to cross the river at daybreak and the commander to co-operate with me in an advance, I directed Generals Morell and Sykes to cross about 7 a.m. on the 20th their divisions, preceding their main columns by advanced guards thrown well forward on the roads to Shepherdstown and Charlestown. About 8 a.m. I was informed by General Sykes that the skirmishers of his advanced guard (cavalry not having then crossed) had met the enemy advancing in large force on the Charlestown road. I directed the recall at once of this force, and proceeded immediately to the ford, over which I found rapidly returning such of the cavalry as had crossed. Seeing the small force of infantry on the opposite bank (two brigades of Sykes' and a part of one of Morell's), and the impossibility of getting over and forming sufficient force in time to meet the attack, I ordered all to withdraw and take shelter within the canal, which afforded admirable protection and means of using effectually our own fire. At the same time the hills immediately on the banks of the river were well lined with skirmishers, and the artillery, well posted, commenced playing on the advancing foe. Under cover of our guns the whole command recrossed with little injury except to the One hundred and eighteenth Pennsylvania Volunteers, a small portion of which became confused early in the action. Their arms (spurious Enfield Rifles) were so defective (these defective arms had been reported to the General in Chief, but all efforts to replace them had failed) that little injury could be inflicted by them upon the enemy. Many of this regiment, new in service, volunteered the previous evening, and formed part of the attacking party which gallantly crossed the river to secure the enemy's artillery. . . .

The attacking column was from a part of *Jackson's* corps, the main portion of which lay concealed in the adjacent woods. . . . A return of ordnance captured accompanies this report; also a list of casualties [363, including 131 captured or missing]. [*O.R.*, XIX, Part 1, pp. 204, 339–40.]

Report of Maj. Gen. Ambrose P. Hill, CSA, Commanding Division, Jackson's Corps

On the morning of the 20th, at 6.30 o'clock, I was directed by *General Jackson* to take my division and drive across the river some brigades of the enemy who had crossed during the night, driven off *General Pendleton's* artillery, capturing four pieces, and were making preparations to hold their position. Arriving opposite Boteler's Ford, and about half a mile therefrom, I formed my line of battle in two lines, the first the brigades of *Pender, Gregg,* and *Thomas,* under command of *General Gregg,* and the second, *Lane (Branch's brigade), Archer,* and *Brockenbrough,* under the command of *General Archer.* The enemy had lined the opposite hills with some seventy pieces of artillery, and the infantry who had crossed lined the crest of the high banks on the Virginia shore.

My lines advanced simultaneously, and soon encountered the enemy. This advance was made in the face of the most tremendous fire of artillery I ever saw, and too much praise cannot be awarded my regiments for their steady, unwavering step. It was as if each man felt that the fate of the army was centered in himself. The infantry opposition in front of *Gregg's* center and right was but trifling, and soon brushed away. The enemy, however, massed in front of *Pender,* and, extending, endeavored to turn his left. General *Pender* became hotly engaged, and informing *Archer* of his danger, . . . *Archer* moved by the left flank, and forming on *Pender's* left, a simultaneous, daring charge was made, and the enemy driven pell-mell into the river. Then commenced the most terrible slaughter that this war has yet witnessed. The broad surface of the Potomac was blue with the floating bodies of our foe. But few escaped to tell the tale. By their own account they lost 3,000 men, killed and drowned, from one brigade alone. Some 200 prisoners were taken. My own loss was 30 killed and 231 wounded; total, 261.

This was a wholesome lesson to the enemy, and taught them to know that it may be dangerous sometimes to press a retreating army. In this battle I did not use a piece of artillery. [*O.R.*, XIX, Part 1, p. 982.]

Now follow the road along the river into Shepherdstown (about 1.6 miles). When you come to the intersection with West Virginia 480, TURN RIGHT. This will carry you across the bridge into Maryland, where the Highway number changes to Maryland 34. Drive on in to Sharpsburg.

As you cross the bridge, notice the handsome mansion on the hill to your left, overlooking the Potomac. This is "Ferry Hill Place," the boyhood home of *Henry Kyd Douglas,* who at the time of the battle of Antietam served as Assistant Inspector General on *Stonewall Jackson's* staff. In his memoirs, written soon after the war and re-worked near the turn of the century, *Douglas* commented that "my early acquaintance with the Antietam, Blackford's Ford, and the fields around Sharpsburg was of much service to me at the time of the battles there." On the day before the battle of Antietam, *Jackson* directed *Douglas* to ascertain the position of all the artillery which would be engaged, to refamiliarize himself with all the roads leading to and from their positions to Sharpsburg and the rear, so as to direct in what manner to get ammunition, to take off disabled guns or caissons and bring up new ones, and to get any reports that needed attention; and for this purpose to visit them as frequently as possible. [Henry Kyd Douglas, *I Rode with Stonewall* (Chapel Hill: The University of North Carolina Press, 1940), pp. 1, 169.]

Today Ferry Hill is owned by the Government and serves as the Administration center for the Chesapeake and Ohio Canal National Historical Park.

About 2.1 miles east of the bridge you will notice that old trees begin to overarch the highway. Here the road veers away from the railroad, which was not in existence at the time of the war, and the trees reportedly were planted by the citizens of Sharpsburg so that veterans returning to the battlefield many years after the war could walk in the shade from the station—a white building, now a private dwelling—a mile into town.

Just on the western edge of town, in a grove of trees on your left, is a small blue and white sign, "Headquarters site of General R. E.

Sharpsburg after the battle. St. Paul's Lutheran Church shows evidence of damage from artillery fire. (USAMHI)

Lee." This is Stop 1 of the Antietam tour. You may not want to dismount, but you should pause to consider the location. Alternatively, you may wish to begin your Antietam tour by proceeding directly to the VISITOR'S CENTER. In this case continue on Maryland 34 for 0.8 mile, turn left, and at a distance of somewhat less than one mile you will see the Visitor's Center on your right. If you decide first to stop at the Visitor's Center, then begin the Antietam Tour with directions leading to Stop 1 from the Visitor's Center.

STOP 1, LEE'S HEADQUARTERS

You should begin the Antietam phase of this tour at the Visitor's Center located slightly less than one mile north of Sharpsburg on Maryland Route 65. The route to the Visitor's Center is clearly marked whether you approach the site from north or south. By checking in at the Visitor's Center before you begin your tour, you can take advantage of their facilities, check their programs and special events, and get current advice on road conditions.

TO STOP ONE

Return to Maryland 65, turn left and go south into Sharpsburg (slightly less than one mile). Turn right at the Stop sign (East Main Street) onto Maryland 34. Continue straight through Sharpsburg 0.8 mile to the Lee Headquarters site, located in a grove of trees on your right and marked by a small blue and white sign, "Headquarters site of General R. E. Lee." Park on the shoulder. You may not want to dismount, but you should pause to consider the location.

Report of General R. E. Lee, CSA, Commanding the Army of Northern Virginia

The effort to force the passage of the mountains had failed, but it was manifest that without re-enforcements we could not hazard a renewal of the engagement, as the enemy could easily turn either flank. Information was also received that another large body of Federal troops had during the afternoon [of the 14th] forced their way through Crampton's Gap, only 5 miles in rear of *McLaws*. Under these circumstances, it was determined to retire to Sharpsburg, where we would be upon the flank and rear of the enemy should he move against *McLaws*, and where we could more readily unite with the rest of the army. This movement was efficiently and skillfully covered by the cavalry brigade of *General Fitzhugh Lee*, and was accomplished without interruption by the enemy, who did not appear on the west side of the pass at Boonsborough until about 8 a.m. on the following morning. The resistance that had been offered to the enemy at Boonsborough [South Mountain] secured sufficient time to enable *General Jackson* to complete the reduction of Harper's Ferry. . . .

Leaving *General A. P. Hill* to receive the surrender of the Federal troops and secure the captured property, *General Jackson*, with his other two divisions, set out at once for Sharpsburg, ordering *Generals McLaws* and *Walker* to follow without delay. Official information of the fall of Harper's Ferry and the approach of *General Jackson* was received soon after the commands of *Longstreet* and *D. H. Hill* reached Sharpsburg, on the morning of the 15th, and reanimated the courage of the troops. *General Jackson* arrived early on the 16th and *General Walker* came up in the afternoon. The presence of the enemy at Crampton's Gap embarrassed the movements of *General McLaws*. . . . until the capitulation [of Harper's Ferry] . . . when, finding the enemy indisposed to attack, he gradually withdrew his command toward the Potomac. Deeming the roads to Sharpsburg on the north side of the river impracticable, he resolved to cross at Harper's Ferry and march by way of Shepherdstown. Owing to the condition of his troops and other circumstances, his progress was slow, and he did not reach the battlefield . . . until some time after the engagement of the 17th began.

The commands of *Longstreet* and *D. H. Hill*, on their arrival at Sharpsburg, were placed in position along the range of hills between the town and the Antietam, nearly parallel to the course of that stream, *Longstreet* on the right of the road to Boonsborough and Hill on the left. The advance of the enemy was delayed by the brave opposition . . . from *Fitzhugh Lee's* cavalry, and he did not appear on the opposite side of the Antietam until about 2 p.m. During the afternoon the batteries on each side were slightly engaged.

On the 16th the artillery fire became warmer, and continued throughout the day. The enemy crossed the Antietam beyond the reach of our batteries and menaced our left. In anticipation of this movement, *Hood's* two brigades had been transferred from the right and posted between *D. H. Hill* and the Hagerstown road *General*

Jackson was now directed to take position on *Hood's* left, and formed his line with his right resting upon the Hagerstown road and his left extending toward the Potomac, protected by *General Stuart* with the cavalry and horse artillery. *General Walker*, with his two brigades, was stationed on *Longstreet's* right. As evening approached, the enemy opened more vigorously with his artillery, and bore down heavily with his infantry upon *Hood*, but the attack was gallantly repulsed. At 10 p.m. *Hood's* troops were relieved by the brigades of *Lawton* and *Trimble*, of *Ewell's* division, commanded by *General Lawton*. *Jackson's* own division, under *General J. R. Jones*, was on *Lawton's* left, supported by the remaining brigades of *Ewell*.

At early dawn on the 17th the enemy's artillery opened vigorously from both sides of the Antietam, the heaviest fire being directed against our left. [*O.R.*, XIX, Part 1, pp. 147–49.]

Lee's command post was in the grove of trees to the north [right], about where the large stone marker is located. Here he could keep in touch with events elsewhere on the battlefield. From the high ground behind his tent he could get a good view of the terrain near the West Woods and the open ground east of the Hagerstown pike. It was also but a short ride to the commanding heights east of Sharpsburg, the present location of the National Cemetery, where he could observe the movements of both armies over much of the battlefield. From this command post *Lee* was able to direct troops as they arrived from Harper's Ferry to the sector where they were most desperately needed.

This location is quite in keeping with *Lee's* philosophy of command as he later described it to Captain Justus Scheibert, the official Prussian military observer, during the Chancellorsville and Gettysburg campaigns.

I do my duty insofar as my powers and capabilities will permit, until the moment when battle begins: I then leave the matter to God and the . . . subordinate officers. . . . My supervision during the battle does more harm than good. It would be unfortunate if . . . I could not rely upon my division and brigade commanders. I think and work with all my powers to bring my troops to the right place at the right time; then I have done my duty. ["General Robert E. Lee, Ober-Commandeur der ehemaligen Sudstaatlechen Armee im Nord Amerika," *Jahrbucher fur die Deutsche Armee und Marine*, XVI (September 1875), pp. 208–9; *La Guerre Civile*, pp. 66–67.]

The Pry House, site of McClellan's headquarters during the Battle of Antietam. Battles & Leaders. (B&L)

If you have come from Shepherdstown, continue in the same direction. If you have come from the Visitor's Center, then you must turn around. To avoid turning in a dangerous spot or in a private driveway, continue 0.5 mile to an old service station on the right where you can safely reverse your route.

The tour continues straight through Sharpsburg on Maryland 34. As you pass over the hill directly east of the town you will see the National Cemetery on your right. The high ground on both sides of the road was an important Confederate artillery position throughout the battle and *Lee* spent much of his time in this sector, where he could oversee the battle. You will next travel over a portion of the battlefield and cross the Antietam.

After you have driven 3.7 miles from the turnaround (3.2 miles from the *Lee* Headquarters site) you will come to a small blue and white sign on the right hand side of the road ("PRY HOUSE: Headquarters of G. B. McClellan") pointing LEFT toward a narrow driveway piercing a high bank. Turn left onto that drive and follow it 0.2 mile to the Pry House. Park in front of the house and walk along the track to the northwest of the house, where the National Park Service has cleared an overlook.

STOP 2, McCLELLAN'S HEADQUARTERS

As you look west across the Antietam you can clearly see the Visitor's Center highlighted against the distant mountain. Shifting your gaze further north, to the right of the white barn at the same range, you will discern the line of monuments that mark the location of the North Woods at the time of the battle. Farther to the south, and on a nearer ridge, you will see the square stone tower that marks the east end of the sunken road (Bloody Lane). This was constructed by the War Department in the 1890's to enable soldiers visiting the field to have a bird's eye view of the terrain.

The ridge you are standing on is cut by several ravines running down to the Antietam. At the time of the battle the heights south of the Pry House were lined with McClellan's "artillery of position"—mostly 20 pounder Parrott guns of the Reserve Artillery. These guns overlooked the Confederate positions and "their field of fire was extensive." On the morning of the 17th several of these batteries enfiladed *Jackson's* lines, deployed a short distance north of the white barn and at right angles to the ridgeline where you now stand, producing what *Jackson* described as "a severe and damaging fire."

The prominent tree-covered hill to your left rear (Elk Mountain) was the main Union signal and observation station. Signallers near the Pry House sent and received signals by semaphore, both through Elk Mountain to the rear and through forward stations to subordinate generals commanding at the front. By this means McClellan learned that Hooker had been wounded and that Sedgwick was in trouble in the West Woods.

General McClellan and his headquarters staff observed the battle from the lawns of the Pry House behind you. Through a telescope mounted on stakes he enjoyed a panoramic view of the fighting in the vicinity of the stone observation tower. He could see Richardson's division break through the Confederate position at the Bloody Lane. He could not, however, follow the movements of the First and the Twelfth Corps once they disappeared into the East Woods, which masked the fight for the Cornfield, nor did he witness the attempts to seize Burnside's bridge to the south because the view from the Pry House was blocked by trees and high ground.

In contrast to *Lee*, who was frequently close at hand in moments of crisis, McClellan was personally out of touch with the ebb and flow of battle. He did not ride to the front to consult any of his generals until after two o'clock, when fighting on the northern half of the battlefield had virtually ceased. After his return to the Pry House he observed the final assault and repulse of Burnside's troops against Confederates holding the dominant ridge south of Sharpsburg and what is now the National Cemetery, but the only way he could have influenced this phase of the battle was by sending in the Fifth Corps, which he had been holding in reserve. This he declined to do.

Report of Major General George B. McClellan, USA, Commanding the Army of the Potomac.

On arriving at the front [Keedysville] in the afternoon I found but two divisions—Richardson's and Sykes'—in position. The rest were halted in the road. . . . After a rapid examination of the position, I found that it was too late to attack that day, and at once directed locations to be selected for our batteries of position, and indicated the bivouacs for the different corps, massing them . . . on both sides of the Sharpsburg pike. . . .

On the 16th the enemy had slightly changed their line, and were posted upon the heights in rear of Antietam Creek, their left and center being upon and in front of the road from Sharpsburg to Hagerstown, and protected by woods and irregularities of the ground. . . . The ground between their immediate front and the Antietam is undulating. Hills intervene, whose crests are commanded by the crests of others in their rear. On all favorable points their artillery was posted. It became evident from the force of the enemy and the strength of their position that desperate fighting alone could drive them from the field, and all felt that a great and terrible battle was at hand. . . .

The design was to make the main attack upon the enemy's left—at least to create a diversion in favor of the main attack, with the hope of something more by assailing the enemy's right—and, as soon as one or both of the flank movements were fully successful, to attack their center with any reserve I might then have on hand.

The morning of the 16th . . . was spent in obtaining information as to the ground, rectifying the position of the troops, and perfecting the arrangements for the attack. On the afternoon . . . Hooker's corps . . . was sent across the Antietam Creek, by a ford and bridge . . . with orders to attack, and, if possible, turn the enemy's left. Mansfield, with his corps, was sent in the evening to support Hooker. [*O.R.*, XIX, Part 1, pp. 29–30.]

Report of Maj. Gen. Joseph Hooker, USA, Commanding
I Corps, Army of the Potomac

As soon as I saw my command under way, I rode to the headquarters of the commanding general for any further orders he might
have to give me, when I was informed that I was at liberty to call for
re-enforcements if I should need them, and that on their arrival they
would be placed under my command, and I returned and joined my
troops on their march. Our direction was nearly perpendicular to the
river we had crossed, my object being to gain the high ground or
divide between the Potomac and Antietam Rivers, and then incline to
the left, following the elevation toward the left of the rebel army. Two
regiments of Meade's division were thrown forward as skirmishers,
followed by a squadron of Owen's cavalry, and all supported by
Meade's division.

We had not proceeded over a half a mile before the commanding
general with his staff joined me, apparently to see how we were
progressing. Among other topics of conversation, I said to the general
that he had ordered my small corps, now numbering between 12,000
and 13,000 (as I had just lost nearly 1,000 men in the battle of South
Mountain), across the river to attack the whole rebel army, and that if
re-enforcements were not forwarded promptly, or if another attack
was not made on the enemy's right, the rebels would eat me up.
Pretty soon after this interview, my skirmishers became engaged with
the enemy's advanced post, and the firing was continued incessantly
until dark, we advancing slowly, and the enemy retiring before us.
[*O.R.*, XIX, Part 1, p. 217.]

You will now follow the same route travelled by Hooker's First Corps
as it marched to the battlefield.

**Return to your car, turn around and go up the drive to Maryland
Route 34. Turn left onto that highway and drive 0.6 mile. Turn left on
the Keedysville Road at the base of the hill as you approach the edge
of Keedysville. You will then cross a narrow stone bridge and follow a
tributary down toward the Antietam, passing on your left an old mill
(Pry's Mill) on the tributary before the road turns sharply to the right
and then left across the Antietam on a larger old stone bridge. The
ford used by the divisions of Sedgwick and French of Sumner's Second Corps to cross the Antietam the following morning is about half a
mile downstream from the bridge, to your left.**

As you leave the bridge, take the right fork in the road. You will

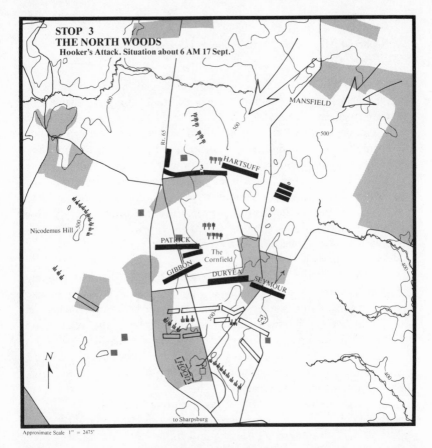

STOP 3
THE NORTH WOODS
Hooker's Attack. Situation about 6 AM 17 Sept.

MANSFIELD

Rt. 65

HARTSUFF

3

Nicodemus Hill

PATRICK

The
Cornfield

GIBBON

DURYEA

SEYMOUR

N

to Sharpsburg

Approximate Scale 1" = 2475'

have travelled 0.8 mile since leaving the highway. Continue on the
Keedysville road for a further 1.6 miles, then turn left on the Smoketown Road. After 0.4 mile you will encounter a small blue sign
pointing out the George Line House where General Mansfield died.
Do not turn left. Continue straight ahead, even though the Smoketown Road becomes narrower. The next mile should put you in the
mood of the nineteenth century. After a total distance on the Smoketown Road of about 1.8 miles you will come to a STOP sign at
Mansfield Monument Road. Turn right. You will pass the remnant of
the East Woods (on your left), and as the road turns to the west you
will encounter a line of monuments where the North Woods stood.
Slightly more than 0.5 mile from your turn at the STOP sign (and
after you have passed three major monuments in the line) you will
come to a parking area. Stop there and dismount. The Park Service
map at this site will help you to orient yourself.

STOP 3, THE NORTH WOODS

Note that you are on the north edge of the North Woods. The Poffenberger farm northwest of your position was here at the time, as was the Miller farm, the roofs and silo of which are visible to the southwest. At the time of the battle an orchard was located on the high ground to the left of the Miller Farm; between the orchard and the East Woods, which can be seen today well to the left, the ground was in pasture. The farm that stands so prominently beyond The Cornfield was not here at the time of the battle.

If you look west-southwest, you will see the open green slope of Nicodemus Hill with trees beyond. There were no trees there in 1862. The cavalry and reinforced artillery of *Jeb Stuart* held this critical terrain throughout the battle of Antietam. From Nicodemus Hill the Confederate guns could fire against the flank of Hooker's forces as they emerged from the North Woods and advanced astride the Hagerstown Pike, which ran through the valley between Nicodemus Hill and the ridge you occupy.

Nicodemus Hill was important for another reason. Because the Potomac River takes an eastward bend a short distance beyond Nicodemus Hill—not quite as far from the hill, in fact, as the position where you now stand—*Stuart's* command protected the Confederate left. Had Hooker been able to seize the hill *Lee's* entire position would have been compromised. On the other hand, because of a concentration of Union artillery on the high ground around the Poffenberger farm, *Lee* had no opportunity to move around Hooker's right flank, which is something he contemplated during the afternoon of the battle. From here, at the time of the battle, Union artillery could control the ground to the north of Nicodemus Hill as far as the bend in the Potomac.

Report of Major Geneneral George G. Meade, USA, Commanding Third Division, I Corps, Army of the Potomac

On the afternoon of the 16th . . . the division, constituting the advance of Hooker's Corps, moved . . . across the country, advancing on what was understood to be the enemy's left flank. Soon after leaving the road, the cavalry advance reported having been fired upon, when, by direction of the general commanding the corps, the regiment of First Pennsylvania Rifles (Bucktails) was advanced as skirmishers to a piece of woods on our left [East Woods], and four companies of the Third Regiment Pennsylvania Reserves were deployed as skirmishers and sent into a piece of woods on our right [North Woods], the main column formed of battalions in mass, division front, with the artillery moving over the open ground for a high ridge in front.

The Bucktails' skirmishers finding the enemy, General Seymour with the First Brigade, was directed to advance to their support. This was promptly done, and soon Seymour was closely engaged with the enemy's infantry and artillery. . . . In the mean time I had gained the crest with the head of the column, and entered a piece of woods [the North Woods], which proved to be in its direction perpendicular to the line along which Seymour had advanced [in the East Woods]. On entering these woods, the enemy's battery could be plainly seen in a corn-field, playing on Seymour's column in their front. The masses of his infantry deployed around the battery, and the fact that only one regiment—the head of my column—was deployed, deterred me from the endeavor to capture the battery by a charge. I, however, immediately ordered up Ransom's battery of light 12-pounders, who promptly came to the front and in battery at the edge of the [North] woods, opening on the enemy's battery and infantry a destructive enfilading fire, which soon caused him to withdraw his guns to an eminence in the rear, from which he commenced shelling the woods we occupied. . . .

In the mean time Magilton's and Anderson's brigades came up, and were deployed in line of battle to support Ransom's battery. After driving the enemy from the woods, Seymour held his own, and, darkness intervening, the contest closed for the night. [*O.R.*, XIX, Part 1, pp. 268–69.]

Report of Major General Joseph Hooker, USA, Commanding I Army Corps, Army of the Potomac

We all slept on our arms that night. The cleared space between the forests necessitated a change in my front from a division to a brigade, and Seymour's command held the advance when night overtook us, and bivouacked in advance of my corps when operations were suspended.

The night becoming dark and drizzly, I sought shelter in Miller's [Poffenberger's?] barn, a few yards to the left of the Hagerstown pike (facing the south), and directly in the rear of Seymour's brigade. Desultory firing was kept up between the pickets almost throughout the night, and about 9 o'clock p.m. I visited them in order to satisfy myself concerning this firing, and found that the lines of pickets of the two armies were so near each other as to be able to hear each other walk, but were not visible to each other. I found Seymour's officers and men keenly alive to their proximity to the enemy, and seemed to realize the responsible character of their service for the night. Indeed, their conduct inspired me with the fullest confidence, and on returning to the barn I immediately dispatched a courier informing the commanding general of my surroundings, and assuring him that the battle would be renewed at the earliest dawn, and that re-enforcements should be ordered forward in season to reach me before that moment.

General Mansfield, with his corps, did cross the creek that night, and encamped his command about 1 mile in rear of my own, and in the morning participated actively in the battle. We were now 3 or 4 miles in advance of where we had crossed the Antietam Bridge.

At daylight we were fully prepared to renew our march, which lay through orchards, corn-fields, and over plowed ground, skirted on either side by forests [East and West Woods], the cleared space between which averaging not more than 400 or 500 yards in width, the field and the object in view narrowing my front to quite a limited degree. Doubleday's division was posted on the right, Ricketts' on the left, and Meade's in reserve. . . . Gibbon's and Hartsuff's brigades were thrown forward, supported with the brigades of their respective divisions, while Meade followed them up in the center, instructed to spring to the assistance of either, as circumstances might require. Seymour continued to hold the advance . . . until our troops had passed him. With these dispositions completed, the battle was soon renewed on the morning of the 17th.

My object was to gain the high ground nearly three-quarters of a mile in advance of me, and which commanded the position taken by the enemy . . . to prevent which he had been re-enforced by *Jackson's* corps during the night, and at the same time had planted field batteries on high ground on our right and rear [Nicodemus Hill], to enfilade our lines when exposed during the advance.

We had not proceeded far before I discovered that a heavy force of the enemy had taken possession of a corn-field . . . a thirty-acre field in my immediate front, and from the sun's rays falling on their bayonets projecting above the corn could see that the field was filled

with the enemy, with arms in their hands, standing apparently at
"support arms." Instructions were immediately given for the assem-
blage of all of my spare batteries, near at hand . . . to spring into
battery on the right of this field, and to open with canister at once. In
the time I am writing every stalk of corn in the northern and greater
part of the field was cut as closely as could have been done with a
knife, and the slain lay in rows precisely as they had stood in their
ranks a few moments before. It was never my fortune to witness a
more bloody, dismal battle-field. Those that escaped fled . . . and
sought refuge behind the trees, fences, and stone ledges nearly on a
line with the Dunker Church, etc., as there was no resisting this
torrent of death-dealing missives [sic]. . . . My command followed the
fugitives closely until we had passed the corn-field a quarter of a mile
or more, when I was removed from my saddle in the act of falling out
of it from loss of blood, having previously been struck without my
knowledge. While my wound was being examined by the surgeon,
Sumner's corps appeared upon the field on my immediate right, and I
have an indistinct recollection of having seen Sedgwick's division pass
to the front. [*O.R.*, XIX, Part 1, pp. 218–19.]

Return to your car and continue westward on MANSFIELD
AVENUE. Turn left on the HAGERSTOWN PIKE. At 0.6 mile you
will reach the intersection with CORNFIELD AVENUE: turn left
and park in the turnout immediately to your left. En route you will
see the MILLER FARM on your left, and a short distance beyond, on
higher ground on your right, two 12-pounder Napoleon guns that
mark the positions of Battery B, Fourth U.S. Artillery.

Dismount and cross CORNFIELD AVENUE to the Massachusetts monument, which will give you a good view of the terrain
defended by *Jackson's* division.

STOP 4, THE CORNFIELD

The fields west of the Hagerstown Pike were fields also in 1862, and
the woodline at the west end of the field was approximately the same
then. Further to the south you will see a number of hardwood trees
surrounding the Philadelphia Brigade monument. These were planted
when the monument was erected; at the time of the battle this too was
open field. A park fence a few hundred feet south of the Philadelphia
Brigade monument marks the northern edge of the West Woods where it
extended to the Hagerstown Pike. The ridgeline behind you, where a

house and barn erected since the battle are located, is the position where *Jackson's* forces initially deployed.

Brigadier General Jubal A. Early describes the terrain:

[The west woods] runs along the Hagerstown road for several hundred yards, entirely on the left hand side as you proceed from Sharpsburg. Then there is a field, the edge of which runs at right angles to the road for about 200 yards, making thus an elbow in the woods, and then turns to the right and runs along the woods parallel to the Hagerstown road for a quarter of a mile, and the woods again turns square to the left and extends back about half a mile. . . . The woods is about 400 yards through, where it runs along the road, and back of it is a plantation road [near the present route 65 by-pass] running by a house and a barn and through the long elbow in the woods on the left. The field between the woods and the Hagerstown road forms a plateau, nearly level and on higher ground than the woods, which slopes down abruptly from the edge of the plateau. This woods is full of ledges of limestone and small ridges, affording excellent cover for troops. [*O.R.*, XIX, Part 1, p. 969.]

Looking to the north you will see the Miller Farm. A lane that ran up the ravine from a position just south of the modern silo to the EAST WOODS, to your right, marked the north edge of the Cornfield at the time of the battle. There is a fence along that lane now, as there was then, but it may not be visible if the crops are tall at the time of your visit. Two brigades from Meade's division deployed along that fence. The high ground behind the fence provided massed Union artillery with a good field of fire. The south edge of the cornfield was several rods north of Cornfield Avenue.

HOOKER'S ATTACK

Report of Maj. Gen. Thomas J. Jackson, CSA, Commanding Jackson's Corps, Army of Northern Virginia

By a severe night's march we reached the vicinity of Sharpsburg on the morning of the 16th. By direction of the commanding general, I advanced on the enemy, leaving Sharpsburg to the right, and took position to the left of *General Longstreet*, near a Dunkard church, *Ewell's* division (*General Lawton* commanding) forming the right, and *Jackson's* division (*General J. R. Jones* commanding) forming the left of my command. *Major-General Stuart*, with the cavalry, was on my left.

Jackson's division . . . was formed partly in an open field and

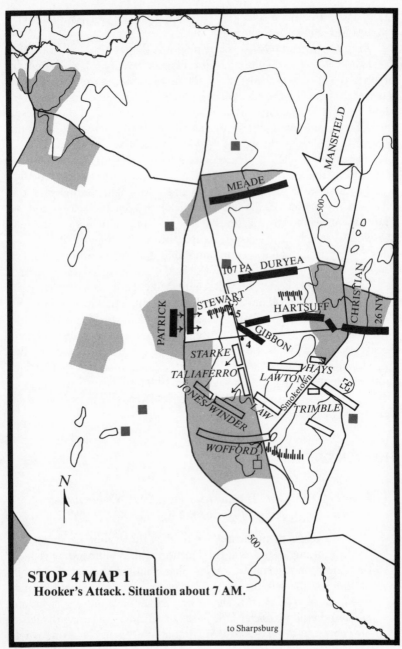

STOP 4 MAP 1
Hooker's Attack. Situation about 7 AM.

to Sharpsburg

Approximate Scale 1″ = 1666′

partly in the woods, with its right resting upon the Sharpsburg and Hagerstown turnpike; *Winder's* and *Jones'* brigades being in front, and *Taliaferro's* and *Starke's* brigades a short distance in their rear, and *Poague's* battery on a knoll in front. *Ewell's* division followed that of *Jackson* to the woods on the left of the road near the church. *Early's* brigade was then formed on the left of the line of *Jackson's* division, to guard its flank, and *Hays'* brigade was formed in its rear. *Lawton's* and *Trimble's* brigades remained during the evening with arms stacked near the church. A battery of the enemy, some 500 yards to the front of *Jackson's* division, opening fire upon a battery to the right, was silenced in twenty minutes by a rapid and well-directed fire from *Poague's* battery. Other batteries of the enemy opened soon after upon our lines, and the firing continued until after dark.

About 10 p.m. *Lawton's* and *Trimble's* brigades advanced to the front to relieve the command of *Brigadier-General Hood*, on the left of *Maj. Gen. D. H. Hill*, which had been more or less engaged during the evening. *Trimble's* brigade was posted on the right, next to *Ripley's*, of *D. H. Hill's* division, and *Lawton's* on the left.

The troops slept that night upon their arms, disturbed by the occasional fire of the pickets of the two armies, who were in close proximity to each other.

At the first dawn of day skirmishing commenced in front, and in a short time the Federal batteries, so posted on the opposite bank of the Antietam as to enfilade my line, opened a severe and damaging fire. This was vigorously replied to by the batteries of *Poague, Carpenter, Brockenbrough, Raine, Caskie,* and *Wooding.*

About sunrise the Federal infantry advanced in heavy force to the edge of the wood on the eastern side of the turnpike [the North Woods], driving in our skirmishers. Batteries were opened in front from the wood with shell and canister, and our troops became exposed for nearly an hour to a terrific storm of shell, canister, and musketry. *General Jones* having been compelled to leave the field, the command of *Jackson's* division devolved upon *General Starke*. With heroic spirit our lines advanced to the conflict, and maintained their position, in the face of superior numbers, with stubborn resolution, sometimes driving the enemy before them, and sometimes compelled to fall back before their well-sustained and destructive fire. Fresh troops from time to time relieved the enemy's ranks, and the carnage on both sides was terrific.

At this early hour *General Starke* was killed. *Colonel Douglass,* commanding *Lawton's* brigade, was also killed. *General Lawton,* commanding division, and *Colonel Walker,* commanding brigade, were severely wounded. More than half of the brigades of *Lawton* and *Hays* were either killed or wounded, and more than a third of *Trimble's,* and all the regimental commanders in those brigades, except two [13 out of 15], were killed or wounded. Thinned in their ranks and exhausted of their ammunition, *Jackson's* division and the brigades of *Lawton, Hays,* and *Trimble* retired to the rear, and *Hood,* of *Longstreet's* command, again took the position from which he had been before relieved. [*O.R.,* XIX, Part 1, pp. 955–56.]

Report of Maj. H. J. Williams, CSA, Fifth Virginia Infantry, Commanding Winder's Brigade, Jackson's Division, Army of Northern Virginia

At early dawn . . . the terrible struggle began in earnest, and the direction of their fire indicated plainly the design of the enemy to turn our left flank: Their heaviest field pieces were brought to bear upon us with wonderful rapidity and fearful precision, front and enfilading fires. Their infantry, advancing, compelled *Raines'* howitzers and *Poague's* Napoleon, under command of *Lieutenant Brown,* to withdraw to our rear, and soon our skirmishers became hotly engaged.

About 6 a.m. the advance column of the enemy approached our front, and the front line (*Winder's* and *Jones'* brigades), which had been ordered to lie down for concealment and protection, rose at the command of their intrepid leader and poured in a staggering volley, which stopped his advance. For three-quarters of an hour the front line, numbering less than 400 men, maintained the unequal contest, holding their ground and doing good work. Heavy re-enforcements advancing to the enemy's support, the front line was ordered to retire to the edge of the [West] wood where, in conjunction with the reserve brigade of the division, it remained for half an hour exposed to a terrific storm of grape, canister, and shell. At the end of this time, our line advanced into the open field and encountered the enemy upon the ground which we had previously held. The firing was fierce and incessant, the enemy standing firm for a time. Unable to withstand the resolute valor of our troops, he retired in considerable disorder. [*O.R.,* XIX, Part 1, p. 1012.]

Report of Brig. Gen. Jubal A. Early, CSA, Commanding Early's Brigade, Ewell's Division, Army of Northern Virginia

Shortly after dawn. . . . *General Jackson* in person ordered me to move my brigade to the left, along a route which he pointed out, to support some pieces of artillery which *Major-General Stuart* had in position to the left of our line. I immediately commenced this movement, and was thus separated from the rest of the division. . . . I found *General Stuart* about a mile from the position I had moved from, with several pieces of artillery in position on a hill, and engaged with some of the enemy's guns. At his suggestion I formed my line in rear of this hill and remained here for about an hour, when *General Stuart*, having discovered a body of the enemy's troops making their way gradually between us and the left of our main line, determined to shift his position to an eminence nearer our line and a little to the rear [Hauser Ridge]. He gave the instructions accordingly, and I moved back. . . .

Just as I was getting into line, *General Stuart* informed me that *General Lawton* had been wounded, and that *General Jackson* had sent for me to carry my brigade back and take command of the division. Leaving the Thirteenth Virginia Regiment, numbering less than 100 men, with *General Stuart*, at his request, I then moved to the rear of this woods around a corn-field, as the enemy had gotten into the woods to my right, and as I came near the position at which my brigade had been posted the night before, I found *Colonels Grigsby* and *Stafford*, of *Jackson's* division, rallying some 200 or 300 men of that division at the point at which *Stark's* brigade had been in position the night before. A body of the enemy, perhaps only skirmishers, had gotten into the woods to the left and was firing upon our men, being held in check by a scattering fire. This was the same body of woods at which the Dunkard church . . . is located. . . .

A portion of the enemy . . . had gotten into the farther end of this woods, where the field is between it and the road, and, as I came up, *Colonels Grigsby* and *Stafford* commenced to advance upon this body, and I immediately formed my brigade in line and advanced along in their rear, the enemy giving way as the advance was made. I halted my brigade on a ridge in this woods, and *Colonels Grigsby* and *Stafford*, at my suggestion, formed their men on my left. My line when thus formed was perpendicular to the Hagerstown road, and the right rested near the edge of the plateau above mentioned but was concealed and protected by the rise in the ground. A considerable

STOP 4 MAP 2
Hood's Counterattack.
Situation about 7:15 AM.

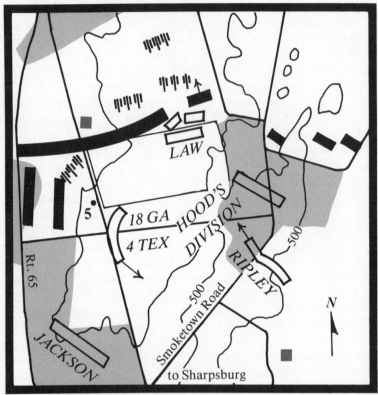

Approximate Scale 1" = 1000'

body of the enemy's troops was seen in the field in my front . . . which was evidently endeavoring to make a movement on our flank and rear. I directed *Colonel Smith,* of the Forty-ninth Virginia Regiment, to take command of the brigade and to resist the enemy at all hazards, and then rode in the direction of the position at which the rest of the brigades had been engaged, for the purpose of taking command of them and ascertaining their condition. . . . These brigades had fallen back some distance to the rear for the purpose of reorganizing, and . . . they were probably not in a condition to go into the fight again. [*O.R.*, XIX, Part 1, pp. 967–69.]

HOOD'S COUNTER ATTACK

*Report of Brig. Gen. John B. Hood, CSA, Commanding Division,
Longstreet's Corps, Army of Northern Virginia*

Arriving on the heights . . . near the town about 12 m. on the
15th . . . I was ordered . . . to move to the extreme left. . . . The
enemy [on the 16th] . . . made an attack upon the left flank of our line
of battle, the troops of this division being the only forces, on our
side, engaged. We succeeded in checking and driving back the enemy
a short distance when night came on, and soon the firing ceased. . . .
The officers and men of my command having been without food for
three days, except a half ration of beef for one day, and green corn,
General Lawton [commanding *Ewell's* division], with two brigades,
was directed to take my position, to enable my men to cook.

On the morning of the 17th . . . about three o'clock, the firing
commenced along the line occupied by *General Lawton.* At 6 o'clock I
received notice from him that he would require all the assistance I
could give him. A few minutes after, a member of his staff reported to
me that he was wounded, and wished me to come forward as soon as
possible. Being in readiness, I at once marched out on the field in line
of battle and soon became engaged with an immense force of the
enemy, consisting of not less than two corps of their army. It was here
that I witnessed the most terrible clash of arms, by far, that has
occurred during the war. The two little giant brigades of this division
wrestled with this mighty force, losing hundreds of their gallant
officers and men but driving the enemy from his position and forcing
him to abandon his guns on our left. The battle raged with the
greatest fury until about 9 o'clock, the enemy being driven from 400
to 500 yards. Fighting, as we were, at right angles with the general
line of battle, and *General Ripley's* brigade being the extreme left of
General D. H. Hill's forces and continuing to hold their ground,
caused the enemy to pour in a heavy fire upon the rear and right
flank of *Colonel Law's* brigade, rendering it necessary to move the
division to the left and rear into the woods near the Saint Mumma
[Dunker] church, which we continued to hold until 10 a.m. when
General McLaws arrived with his command. . . . I am thoroughly of
the opinion [that] had *McLaws* arrived by 8.30 a.m. our victory on
the left would have been as thorough, quick, and complete as upon
the plains of Manassas on August 30. [*O.R.*, XIX, Part 1, pp. 922–23.]

Report of Col. W. T. Wofford, CSA, Commanding Hood's Texas Brigade, Hood's Division, Longstreet's Corps

Our brigade was moved forward, at sunrise, to the support of *General Lawton.* . . . Moving forward in line of battle in the regular order of regiments, the brigade proceeded through the woods into the open field toward the corn-field, where the left encountered the first line of the enemy. Seeing *Hampton's* Legion and Eighteenth Georgia moving slowly forward, but rapidly firing, I rode hastily to them, urging them forward, when I saw two full regiments, one in their front and the other partly to their left. Perceiving at once that they were in danger of being cut off, I ordered the First Texas to move by the left flank to their relief, which they did in a rapid and gallant manner. By this time, the enemy on our left having commenced falling back, the First Texas pressed them rapidly to their guns, which now poured into them a fire on their right flank, center, and left flank from three different batteries, before which their well-formed line was cut down and scattered; being 200 yards in front of our line, their situation was most critical. Riding back to the left of our line, I found the fragment of the Eighteenth Georgia Regiment in front of the extreme right battery of the enemy [Battery B, Fourth U.S. Artillery], located on the pike . . . which now opened upon our thinned ranks a most destructive fire. The men and officers were gallantly shooting down the gunners, and for a moment silenced them. At this time the enemy's fire was most terrific, their first line of infantry having been driven back to their guns, which now opened a furious fire, together with their second line of infantry, upon our thinned and almost annihilated ranks.

By this time, our brigade . . . [had] suffered so greatly, I was satisfied they could neither advance nor hold their position without reinforcements. . . . I ordered them back under cover of the woods to the left of the church, where we halted and waited for support, none arriving. . . .

During the engagement . . . I was drawn to the left of our line, as it first engaged the enemy, who had succeeded in flanking us on the left, and, to escape from being surrounded, changed the direction to left-oblique, thus causing large intervals between the regiments on the left and right of the line. The Fifth Texas . . . moved with spirit across the field and occupied the woods on our right, where it met the enemy and drove and held them back until their ammunition was exhausted, and then fell back to the [West] woods with the balance of the brigade. The Fourth Texas . . . which, in our line of battle, was between the Fifth and First Texas, was moved by *General Hood* to the extreme left of our line on the pike road, covering our flank by holding the enemy in check.

This brigade went into the action numbering 854, and lost, in killed, wounded, and missing, 560 – over one half. [*O.R.*, XIX, Part 1, pp. 928–29.]

Report of Lieut. Col. S. Z. Ruff, CSA, Eighteenth Georgia Infantry, Wofford's Brigade, Hood's Division

About 7. a.m., the brigade was ordered to move forward in the direction of the firing. Advancing, about a quarter of a mile through the timber, we came upon the enemy posted in front of a piece of corn, and immediately opened fire upon them. After one or two rounds they gave way, and fell back to a considerable distance in the corn. Advancing, with the left of the regiment resting on the right of the [*Hampton*] legion, which had its left upon the turnpike, we drove the enemy in fine style out of the corn and back upon their supports. At the far edge of the corn, the ranks of the retreating line of the enemy unmasked a battery, which poured a round or two of grape into our ranks with terrible effect; but it was soon silenced by our riflemen, and the gunners ran away. At this moment we discovered a fresh line of the enemy advancing on our left flank in an oblique direction, threatening to cut us off, and our ranks being reduced to less than one third their original strength, we found it necessary to fall back. At the edge of the woods we met supports and rallied on them a part of our men; but the regiment was too much cut up for further action, and in a short time, in connection with the whole brigade, was taken from the field.

We carried 176 men into the action, and lost 101 in killed, wounded and missing; most of the missing are either killed or wounded. [*O.R.*, XIX, Part 1, p. 930.]

Report of Lieut. Col. B. F. Carter, CSA, Fourth Texas Infantry, Wofford's Brigade, Hood's Division

Soon after daylight the brigade formed line of battle in regular order, the Fifth Texas being on my right and First Texas on my left, and, about 7 a.m., were ordered to advance. I received no order as to which was the directing battalion, but, advancing diagonally to the right through the [West] woods, we entered the open field on the right of the turnpike. . . .

Here the fire upon us became severe, and, owing to our troops being in front of us and the dense smoke pervading, we were unable to return the fire or see the enemy clearly. Still advancing, I came directly behind the Eleventh Mississippi [*Law's* Brigade], when I received the order from *Captain Sellers* for the Texas Brigade to halt. Halting, I ordered the men to lie down. At the same moment the Eleventh Mississippi was ordered to advance, and a portion of two companies on my right, mistaking the order, advanced with them. After a moment I received an order from *General Hood* to move to the left until the left of my regiment rested on the crest, in advance, next to the turnpike road. Moving left-oblique in double quick, I occupied the position indicated, and was then ordered by *General Hood* to move directly up the hill on the left of the troops then advancing. The enemy then occupied the hill [the farm house to the South] in strong force, which receded before our steady advance.

Arriving at the top of the hill, at the intersection of the cornfield with the turnpike, I found the enemy not only in heavy force in the corn-field in front, but occupying a ravine in the field on the left of the turnpike, from which position they poured a destructive fire upon us. I discovered at once that the position was untenable, but if I fell back the troops on my right who had entered the corn-field would be surrounded; so, wheeling my regiment to the left, I posted the men along the fence on either side of the turnpike, and replied as best we could to the tremendous fire of the enemy.

We held this position for some time until the troops in the corn-field on my right were falling back, when I ordered the regiment to move along the line of fence by the left flank. This movement, however, exposed us so much that we fell back directly under the hill. Here I ordered the regiment to halt and form, but at the same moment received an order from *General Hood* to move by the left flank into the [West] woods. Forming here, I advanced on the left of the turnpike up to the fence at the edge of the field, and rested in this position until I was ordered by *Colonel Wofford* to fall back to the point we started from in the morning, where the remnant of the brigade was formed. . . . I carried into action about 200 men, and you will see how heavy our loss was (107 men) [*O.R.*, XIX, Part 1, pp. 811, 934–35.]

Narrative of a Courier on the Staff of Brig. Gen. Law

The regiments had become scattered by the long charge, and were now in a corn field, where a new alignment was impossible. Retreat became necessary, and the order was given to "fall back." There was no rout, no frantic rushing to the rear, though the fire of musketry and cannon was fearful. The men fell back in squads—often stopping to replenish their empty cartridge boxes from those of the dead and wounded, and then turning and returning the deadly fire of the overwhelming numbers before whom they were slowly and doggedly retiring.

When they reached the woods from which they had debouched about two hours before 4,000 strong, only 700 could be mustered to form a new line. . . . Out of nine regiments but one field officer besides *Col. Law* reported for duty . . . a major of a Texas regiment. Rev. J. S. Johnston, "A Reminiscence of Sharpsburg," *Southern Historical Society Papers*, VIII (January, 1880), 526–27.

Hood's men probably did not understand all of the reasons why their counterattack succeeded beyond all reasonable expectation. General Meade provides one possible explanation.

Report of Brig. Gen. George G. Meade, USA, Commanding Third Division, I Corps

Seymour and Ricketts advancing through one piece of woods, and Doubleday, on their right, advancing along the Hagerstown pike, left an open space between, in which was a plowed field and an orchard; beyond this was a corn-field, the possession of which the enemy warmly disputed.

Ransom's battery was advanced into the open ground between the two advancing columns, and played with great effect on the enemy's infantry and batteries. The brigades of Anderson and Magilton on reaching the corn-field were massed in a ravine extending up to the pike. Soon after forming, I saw the enemy were driving our men from the corn-field. I immediately deployed both brigades, and formed line of battle along the fence bordering the corn-field, for the purpose of covering the withdrawal of our people and resisting the farther advance of the enemy. Just as this line of battle was formed, I received an order from the general commanding the corps to detach a brigade to re-enforce our troops in the woods on the left. I directed Magilton's brigade to move in that direction, which order was promptly executed, notwithstanding the brigade, moving by the flank, was subjected to a warm fire from the corn-field.

Anderson's brigade still held the fence on the right, but the gap made by the withdrawal of Magilton was soon filled by the enemy, whose infantry advanced boldly through the corn-field to the woods. Seeing this, I rode up to Ransom's battery and directed his guns on their advancing column, which fire, together with the arrival of Magilton's brigade, in connection with Seymour and Ricketts, drove the enemy back, who, as they retreated, were enfiladed by Anderson, who eventually regained the crest of the ridge in the corn-field. At this time, about 10 a.m., my division had been engaged for five hours, and their ammunition was being exhausted. I therefore welcomed the arrival of Banks' XII Corps, the left column of which . . . moved up to our support in the woods on the left, and a column under General Williams moved up to the woods on the right by the turnpike. . . .

Between 11 and 12 a.m. . . the corps had the misfortune to lose the services of its skillful and brave commander . . . who did me the honor to direct me to assume the command of the corps on his leaving the field. I directed the various divisions to be withdrawn as soon as they were relieved, and to be assembled and reorganized on the ridge in our rear. By 2 p.m. the division of the Pennsylvania Reserves, now commanded by General Seymour, were organized on this ridge, supplied with ammunition, and held in readiness to repel an attack if the enemy should attempt one on our right flank, and assist in any advance we might make. [*O.R.*, XIX, Part 1, pp. 269–70.]

Leave your car where it is and walk to the STOP sign where the CORNFIELD AVENUE intersects with the old Hagerstown Turn-pike. Turn right and walk north along that road for about 60 yards to the gun position. Be careful of the traffic.

STOP 5, STEWART'S BATTERY, HOOKER'S ATTACK

Report of Brig. Gen. Abner Doubleday, USA, Commanding First Division, I Corps, Army of the Potomac

At dawn of day . . . the battle was opened with great spirit by the enemy's batteries, which were promptly answered by those of my division. Soon after I was directed by General Hooker to have my brigades in readiness to be sent as circumstances might require. I had previously designated Gibbon's brigade to take the advance, to be followed in succession by Phelps', Patrick's, and Hofmann's brigades. The latter, however, was left as a guard to our batteries in rear, which were opposing the attempt of some rebel batteries [on Nicodemus Hill] to enfilade our lines. Hofmann's brigade was ordered forward at a later period . . . but General Hooker directed it to remain, as the guns there were doing excellent service in silencing the enemy's artillery. . . .

I now sent General Gibbon's brigade forward to commence the attack . . . followed by Phelps' brigade, as a support, and about twenty minutes afterward Patrick's brigade was also sent forward, by order of General Hooker. Gibbon advanced in column of division on the left of the Hagerstown turnpike until he reached an open space. He then deployed the Sixth Wisconsin Volunteers on the right and the Second Wisconsin Volunteers on the left, and threw them forward into a corn-field in his front. A section of Campbell's battery, under Lieutenant Stewart, was also brought into action on an eminence in rear, to fire over the heads of the troops, in answer to the enemy's batteries in front. The two regiments pushed gallantly forward, supported by the Seventh Wisconsin . . . and the Nineteenth Indiana Volunteers.

After a short engagement, General Gibbon saw that his line would probably be flanked on the right from the woods which extended down in that direction. To meet this contingency, he ordered up a section of Campbell's battery, and directed the Seventh Wisconsin and Nineteenth Indiana Regiments to cross the road, deploy on the right of the others, and push forward rapidly into the woods. His entire brigade soon became hotly engaged.

In the mean time Phelps' brigade had followed . . . Gibbon, and when it reached the open space . . . beyond the [North] woods where Campbell's battery was posted, it moved by the flank and deployed forward into a corn-field in rear of Gibbon's command. . . . As soon as Gibbon's brigade became engaged, Phelps moved his line up, and formed about 25 paces in his rear. Observing that the enemy's line now formed a crotchet, which partially flanked Gibbon's line, Colonel Phelps ordered Colonel Post, who was in command of the Second Regiment of U.S. Sharpshooters, to move to the right and front, advance his left, and engage that portion of the enemy's line that flanked ours. In this engagement the Sharpshooters suffered severely [43%] . . . after capturing two battle-flags from the enemy.

While this was going on, I sent Patrick's brigade to follow the two others. It advanced, and for a short time took post in the same corn-field as a support. A strong enfilading fire . . . came from the woods against our troops in the corn-field. To meet this, I directed General Patrick to occupy and hold the woods, detaching, however, one of his regiments to support Campbell's battery, a section of which had moved forward to the road in the vicinity of a barn and some haystacks. . . .

The Seventh Wisconsin . . . and Nineteenth Indiana [Gibbon's brigade] . . . moved into the woods to drive off the enemy, who were acting against our right flank. This movement was simultaneous with that of Patrick's brigade, all crossing the road and moving forward into the woods at the same time. The two regiments . . . took position in advance of, and parallel to, the rest of Gibbon's line. Patrick's three regiments had scarcely taken position in the woods before a body of the enemy appeared on their right, guarding a battery of light guns they had posted there. General Hooker directed that one of Patrick's regiments be sent to watch this battery, and the Twenty-third New York Volunteers . . . was detached for that purpose. The two remaining regiments . . . closed up on the Seventh Wisconsin and Nineteenth Indiana, and all moved forward together.

The enemy previous to this had kept up a brisk fire, but was sheltered by a series of rocky ledges, which afforded them almost perfect security; they poured in heavy volleys of musketry. To meet this increase of fire, Patrick's two regiments were thrown forward in the first line.

To all appearance the enemy had been strongly re-enforced [by Hood's division] and they not only resisted our farther advance, but moved to try and capture Campbell's battery and regain possession of the corn-field. This charge was handsomely repulsed by the fire of the Second Wisconsin and Sixth Wisconsin, . . . by the rapid discharges of the battery, which fired double canisters, and by the flank fire of the Seventh Wisconsin and Nineteenth Indiana Regiments, of Gibbon's brigade, and the Twenty-first New York and Thirty-fifth New York Volunteers, of Patrick's brigade, these four regiments having taken up a position perpendicular to their former one, which enabled them to pour in a heavy fire upon the flank of the charging column. Patrick could not have changed position in this way under ordinary circumstances, but it was evident that a large part of the troops that had been in his front were detached to aid in the charge. These united agencies drove the enemy back, saved the guns, and gave us a renewed possession of the corn-field. General Patrick now pushed his regiments up to the road, which he held firmly for some time. . . . [*O.R.*, XIX, Part 1, pp. 223–25.]

Report of Lieut. Col. Edward S. Bragg, USA, Sixth Wisconsin Infantry, Fourth [Gibbon's] Brigade, First Division, I Corps

Early on the morning . . . the Sixth Wisconsin Volunteers . . . supported by the brigade, commenced the attack upon the enemy's left flank. No sooner was the column in motion than the enemy opened fire on us with artillery, and so accurate was his range that the second shell exploded in the ranks, disabling 13 men. . . . Not withstanding this shock, the column moved steadily forward until it reached the wood, when, by direction of General Gibbon, Company I was deployed to the left and Company C to the right in front of the line as skirmishers, and the regiment immediately deployed and advanced to their support.

The skirmishers soon found the enemy lodged in a corn-field and his advance concealed along fences and under cover, but rapidly drove in his advance, and the regiment moved up steadily in support, the right and center on and to the right of the Hagerstown turnpike, and the left across a corn-field. . . . The portion of the line in the corn-field. . . . was soon under heavy fire, and drove the enemy from his cover.

The advance of the right wing did not discover the enemy until it reached a rise of ground in front of the barn and stacks to the right of the road when the enemy's skirmishers lying along the edge of a wood running down in a point to the right of the barn, where they were lying undisturbed—the right of my line of skirmishers having failed to advance, either from a failure to hear or heed commands. . . . I discovered the enemy in force, lying in line of battle along the fence and across the field to the wood, at right angles with the road, his line being then within musket range. At the same time he increased his fire from the woods on the right flank. This rendered the advance impracticable, and I ordered the company in the road to lie down under cover of the fence. . . . The regiment remained in the front of the fight until they had expended nearly their last round of ammunition. The enemy broke and ran before their advance . . . and the regiment pursued, and only retired again in the presence of a host that it would have been madness to have opposed with a handful of men. . . . The loss of the regiment in the engagement was . . . 152. [*O.R.*, XIX, Part 1, pp. 254–56.]

Report of Col. Walter Phelps, Jr., USA, Twenty-second New York Infantry, Commanding First Brigade, First Division, I Corps

At 5.30 a.m. . . . the enemy's batteries opened upon our lines, and I was ordered by General Doubleday to move to the support of Gibbon's brigade, which had already advanced to attack the enemy's lines. Advancing through a belt of woods, in which Major-General Hooker and staff were stationed, and which was directly in rear of Campbell's battery, I was ordered by General Hooker, who in person designated the position for this brigade to occupy, to move by flank through the open field in which this brigade had taken position, and, passing into a corn-field, to form line of battle and support Gibbon's brigade, which I observed was steadily advancing to the attack. The direct and cross artillery fire from the enemy's batteries playing upon this field was very heavy, but my brigade was moved without loss to a position some 90 paces in advance of Campbell's battery, where I deployed column, and in line of battle moved steadily forward some 50 paces in rear of Gibbon's infantry, who at this time had not engaged the enemy, but were cautiously advancing through the corn-field. . . . Gibbon's brigade having engaged the enemy, who were posted in the road behind a line of fence, and sheltered by woods, I moved this brigade forward, and halted about 25 paces in rear of his line, ordering the men to lie down, and was prepared to move to his support when necessary.

Having ascertained that the enemy's line was formed with their left advanced, making a crotchet, and that they were in position to partially enfilade our lines, I ordered the Second U.S. Sharpshooters, Colonel Post, to move to the right and front, advancing his left, and to engage the enemy at that point. I immediately advised General Doubleday . . . of the enemy's position . . . on my right, and of the disposition of the . . . Sharpshooters. General Doubleday . . . ordered a brigade to their right. . . .

The effect of the engagement between the Sharpshooters and the enemy was to draw a very heavy fire from their advanced line, and I ordered the brigade forward to the support of the line in front. The musketry fire at this point was very heavy, but the two brigades appeared to hold their position easily. The loss of the . . . Sharpshooters . . . was severe [66 men]. The entire brigade suffered heavily in wounded . . . but, with General Gibbon's regiments, held their position until relieved by General Sedgwick's division, when I fell back slowly and in good order some 80 paces in the rear of the cornfield, and again formed line of battle.

The brigade went into the action . . . with about 425 officers and men, and their loss . . . is a fraction over 43 percent of those engaged. Their loss . . . at South Mountain was a fraction less than 25 per cent. of those engaged. [*O.R.*, XIX, Part 1, pp. 233–34.]

Report of Lieut. James Stewart, USA, Battery B, Fourth U.S. Artillery, Gibbon's Brigade

I was ordered by General Gibbon to bring my section [2 guns] forward [through the North wood and into the open ground beyond] and place it in position, about 75 yards . . . to the left of the turnpike, for the purpose of shelling the woods, distant from 800 to 900 yards, directly in my front. After shelling for some time, General Gibbon ordered the section to be still farther advanced to a position in front of some straw-stacks, about 30 yards to the right of the turnpike [near the other 12-pounder Napoleon that you can see at the northern end of the field, this side of the barn].

As soon as I came into battery in this position, I observed large bodies of the enemy from 400 to 500 yards distant, and ordered the guns to be loaded with spherical case, 1/4 and 1/2 seconds, because the ground was undulating, and not suitable for canister. After firing two or three rounds from each gun, the enemy partially broke, ran across a hollow in front of the section, crossed to the left of the turnpike, entered a corn-field, and, under cover of the fences and corn, crept close to our guns, picking off our cannoneers so rapidly that in less than ten minutes there were 14 men killed and wounded in the section.

About this time Captain Campbell, commanding the battery, brought the other four guns into battery on the left of my section, and commenced firing canister at the enemy in the corn-field, on the left of the turnpike. In less than twenty minutes Captain Campbell was severely wounded . . . and the command of the battery devolved upon me.

General Gibbon was in the battery, and, seeing the advantage which the enemy had, ordered one of the guns which was placed on the turnpike to be used against the enemy's infantry [Wofford's brigade of Hood's division] in the corn-field, General Gibbon acting both as cannoneer and gunner at this piece. The fire was continued by the entire battery for about ten minutes longer in this position, the enemy part of the time being but 15 or 20 yards distant. The loss of the entire company whilst in this position was 1 captain wounded, 3 sergeants, 4 corporals, 32 privates killed and wounded, and 26 horses killed and 7 wounded. While in this position the battery was supported by General Gibbon's brigade and a part of the Twentieth New York Volunteers.

General Gibbon ordered me to limber to the rear and place the battery in battery in the same position my section first occupied in the morning. [*O.R.*, XIX, Part 1, pp. 229–30.]

Battery B was also supported by two regiments from Patrick's brigade, as the following account makes clear.

Report of Brig. Gen. Marsena R. Patrick, USA, Commanding Third Brigade, First Division, I Corps

We marched across the open field and into the [North] wood beyond, through the plowed field and orchard into a corn-field, where Gibbon's brigade lay, and where my own was placed in its support. We could not have remained here more than from five to seven minutes, when I received an order from General Doubleday to march my brigade rapidly across the [Hagerstown] road, and hold the woods at a little distance on the right of the road. This movement was rapidly executed, but while in progress an order from General Doubleday directed me to send a regiment to protect a battery in the corn-field near the straw-stack. The Twentieth Regiment New York State Militia . . . was instantly countermarched, and reported to General Gibbon, at Battery B, Fourth U.S. Artillery, where it remained until the battery was withdrawn, some hours after. The Seventh Wisconsin Regiment crossed the road at the same time with my brigade, and took position in the wood parallel with and in advance of the lines, on the other side of the road beyond the battery, where it joined the Nineteenth Indiana, which had preceded it by only a very few minutes.

Scarcely had my three regiments reached the woods when a body of the enemy was discovered filing off to our right and rear . . . and, on reporting the fact to General Hooker, he directed that one of my regiments should be detached to watch and check the movement. Colonel Hoffman, with the Twenty-third Regiment, was dispatched to the right to head off the enemy in that direction, and the Twenty-first and Thirty-fifth moved forward into the wood, closing upon the two regiments of Gibbon's brigade, whose skirmishers were now at the brow of the little eminence above the low grounds, in front of which was a corn-field [where you now stand], from which came the enemy's fire.

The fire of the enemy up to this time was brisk, not heavy, but on reaching this point a most galling fire was poured in from the enemy, strongly posted behind the rocks on our left, and my two regiments . . . were thrown forward into the first line to meet it. The troops on the opposite side of the road and fields and along the edge of the woods were now being rapidly driven back, and to check this advantage of the enemy, as well as to protect Battery B, on my left, I threw my whole command, including the Seventh Wisconsin and Nineteenth Indiana, across the open space and under the rocky ledge, perpendicular to my former position and parallel to the road, when I was joined at double quick by the Twenty-third, now relieved on the right by General Meade.

The rocky ledge, a 'breastwork' prepared by nature better than it could have been made by man, is immediately behind the line of trees a few hundred feet west of where you now stand. You will pass it later in the tour, as you descend STARKE AVENUE on your way to STOP 9.

We remained but a few minutes here before we had checked the enemy's advance sufficiently to push our lines up to the road, which we held firmly for some time, the Thirty-fifth regiment capturing the colors of the rebel regiment advancing on our battery. [In this action the First Texas lost its colors in addition to 170 men killed and wounded and 12 others missing. [O.R., XIX, Part 1, p. 933.] Rallying once more, the enemy drove us back to the rocky ledge, which we held until our ammunition being almost exhausted and the line attacked in flank and rear on the right, I directed my command to fall back to a line of rock at right angles to the road and about 15 rods

Today's view north from vicinity of Visitor Center. The East Woods is on the right. (HWN)

from the woods to hold there until ammunition and re-enforcements could be obtained. We remained here between the fires of our own and the enemy's batteries long enough for the men to make coffee, they having moved so early as to fail of breakfast. [*O.R.*, XIX, Part 1, pp. 243–44.]

Report of Brig. Gen. Abner Doubleday, USA, Commanding First Division, I Corps

General Williams, of Mansfield's corps, now came up with re-enforcements. He sent a regiment at my request to watch the rebel force that supported the enfilading battery which was acting against the right of Patrick's line. The other regiments that he brought up with him were notified of the nature of the ground and of the position of the enemy, and were instructed by General Patrick as to the position they ought to assume to enfilade the enemy's line and drive him from his strong position, near the Dunker Church, which seemed to be the key of the battlefield. The re-enforcements sent us did not attack in the right place, and they were swept away by a terrific fire against their left and front from an enemy behind the rocks they could not see. Their line gave way, and the main body of the rebels advanced. We had no troops to stem the shock. My own command had been fighting since daylight, and being out of ammunition was obliged to fall back. Patrick's brigade covered our retreat, resisting the enemy gallantly and retiring in perfect order. Campbell's battery . . . was no longer in a condition for active service, and was compelled to retire behind the supports of Sedgwick's division. It was soon followed by Gibbon's and Phelps' brigades, exhausted as they were by long-continued fighting, nearly out of ammunition, and too few in number to keep back the overpowering forces that were advancing. . . . The division fell back in perfect order to a new line of defense. . . . Thirty guns had been concentrated on the right flank . . . and my division was directed to join the remains of General Sumner's corps as a support to these guns. . . . [O.E., XIX, Part 1, pp. 225–26.]

Return to your car. Drive east on CORNFIELD AVENUE to the next parking area. Park and Dismount. You are now in the middle of what was the East Woods at the time of the battle. The western edge of the old East Woods was just short of the two 12 pounder Napoleon guns 30 yards to the west. At the time of the battle the East Woods extended southward to the Smoketown Road.

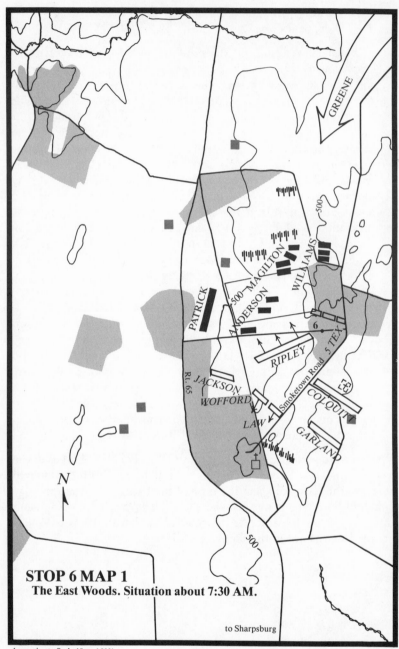

STOP 6 MAP 1
The East Woods. Situation about 7:30 AM.

to Sharpsburg

Approximate Scale 1″ = 1666′

STOP 6, THE EAST WOODS

The National Park Service map positioned at this site will help keep you oriented. Note that the East Woods in 1862 were far more extensive, covering the meadow north and south of this position and extending nearly to the line of guns that crosses the road west of this stop. A short distance east of your present position the old SMOKETOWN ROAD crosses CORNFIELD AVENUE, which was constructed by the U.S. Army when it laid out the military park some thirty-five years after the battle. This segment of the Smoketown Road would have been completely enveloped by the East Woods at the time of the battle.

If you walk west toward the line of guns to the sign marking the western edge of the East Woods, you will get a good insight into the way in which accidents of terrain influence a battle. Looking south toward the Visitor's Center, you can see only the top portion of the flagpole — Confederate artillery posted there could not detect Union forces in this position. The position is similarly masked from Nicodemus Hill. But you should also note the low ground stretching to the south. It protected counterattacking Confederate infantry from the heavy artillery east of the Antietam.

The 31st Georgia regiment, of *Lawton's* brigade, occupied the higher ground a short distance south of your present position at first light on the 17th.

Report of Maj. J. H. Lowe, CSA, Thirty-first Georgia Infantry, Commanding Lawton's Brigade, Ewell's Division

At dawn, when the enemy could be seen, heavy skirmishing commenced and continued for an hour. The skirmishers, after their ammunition was nearly exhausted, were ordered to retire . . . with their brigade. At that time the enemy commenced advancing, and soon a general engagement ensued. While the brigade was engaged with the enemy's infantry, it was under a heavy fire from their batteries on our right, killing and wounded many of our men. After a severe engagement, the brigade was compelled to fall back a short distance. Re-enforcements then came, and with them we made a charge in the most gallant manner. . . . Before the charge the brigade lost its commander, and nearly every regiment lost its regimental commander; also the greater portion of the different companies lost their company commanders. After the charge the brigade fell back, and, in taking off the wounded, a great many were lost for a short time from their regiments. [*O.R.*, XIX, Part 1, p. 975.]

Trimble's brigade, on the right of *Jackson's* line, was posted some 400–500 yards to the south west, in front of and parallel to the present road leading from the Smoketown Road to the MUMMA FARM.

Report of Col. James A. Walker, CSA, Thirteenth Virginia Infantry, Commanding Trimble's Brigade, Ewell's Division

My pickets were posted in the edge of a wood, which was occupied but a short distance farther in by the enemy, and my main body was placed in a plowed field, connecting with *Lawton's* brigade on my left and with *Ripley's* brigade, of *D. H. Hill's* division, on my right, the latter forming a right angle with my line. . . . At daylight heavy skirmishing commenced between the pickets, and was kept up without intermission until about sunrise, when the enemy's line of battle was advanced, driving my pickets in. Soon after daylight the enemy opened fire from a battery which was posted on a hill across the Antietam, and which consequently enfiladed our position, and, as my command was exposed to full view of their gunners and had no shelter, this fire was very annoying, but less destructive than I at first apprehended it would be.

About the time my skirmishers were driven in, the enemy also opened on us from the front with artillery, The line of infantry which they brought up first, advanced to the edge of the woods where my skirmishers had been posted, and opened fire upon us, to which my men replied with spirit and effect, holding them in check. The whole force of the enemy opposed to my regiments occupied the shelter of the wood, except that portion which confronted the left of my line, where the Twelfth Georgia regiment was posted [some 250 yards south of your present position].

Observing that the cool and deliberate fire of this tried and veteran regiment was annoying that portion of the enemy's line very greatly, I ordered the Twenty-first Georgia and Twenty-first North Carolina Regiments to wheel to the left, and, taking shelter under a low stone fence running at right angles to their former line, direct their fire upon the wavering Yankee regiment, with the view of breaking the enemy's line at this point. They did so promptly, and a few rounds from them had the desired effect, and the enemy's line was entirely broken.

At this opportune moment, fresh troops came up to the assistance of *Lawton's* brigade, which was hotly engaged on our left, and I ordered my command to advance, which they did, but the fresh troops, which were advancing in such good order at first, gave way under the enemy's fire and ran off the field before they had been halted by their officers and almost before they had fired a gun. Being thus left without support on our left, my men could advance no farther with safety, and halted. I tried to hold the advanced position thus gained until troops came to our support, but the enemy was first re-enforced, and we were compelled to fall back to our original line.

About this time the officers of the brigade began to report that their companies were out of ammunition. I directed them to gather what they could from the cartridge-boxes of the dead and wounded, and we were thus enabled to keep up the fight. (I would state here that our supply of ammunition had been heavily drawn upon by the long-continued and heavy skirmishing; the pickets had fired all in their boxes, and I had to divide the ammunition of the men in line with them before they were driven in.) Being thus left without ammunition, when a fresh brigade came to my support, I ordered . . . the commandants of regiments to bring back what men were still left with them to a designated point in rear of the village of Sharpsburg, where they could be supplied with ammunition, and ordered the other staff officers of the brigade to gather up the stragglers from the different regiments of the command and carry them to the same point. . . . Out of less than 700 men carried into action, the brigade lost 228 in killed and wounded. [O.R., XIX, Part 1, pp. 976–78.]

The fight was now taken up by *Hood's* small division of two brigades, "marching out on the field in line of battle" from the woods behind the Dunker Church.

HOOD'S COUNTER ATTACK

Report of Col. E. M. Law, CSA, Fourth Alabama Infantry, Commanding Brigade, Hood's Division, Longstreet's Corps

The battle had lasted about an hour and a half, when I was ordered to move forward [from the Dunker Church] into the open field across the turnpike. On reaching the road, I found but few of our troops on the field, and these seemed to be in much confusion, but still opposing the advance of the enemy's dense masses with determination. Throwing the brigade at once into line of battle, facing northward, I gave the order to advance. The Texas Brigade, *Colonel Wofford*, had in the mean time come into line on my left, and the two brigades now moved forward together. The enemy, who had by this time advanced half-way across the field and had planted a heavy battery at the north end of it, began to give way before us, though in vastly superior force. The Fifth Texas Regiment (which had been sent over to my right) and the Fourth Alabama pushed into the [East] wood . . . and drove the enemy through and beyond it. The other regiments of my command continued steadily to advance in the open ground, driving the enemy in confusion from and beyond his guns. So far, we had been entirely successful and everything promised a decisive victory. It is true that strong support was needed to follow up our success, but this I expected every moment.

At this stage . . . a powerful Federal force (ten times our number) of fresh troops was thrown in our front. Our losses up to this time had been very heavy; the troops now confronting the enemy were insufficient to cover properly one-fourth of the line of battle; our ammunition was expended; the men had been fighting long and desperately, and were exhausted from want of food and rest. Still, they held the ground, many of them using such ammunition as they could obtain from the bodies of . . . the dead and wounded. It was evident that this state of affairs could not long continue. No support was at hand. To remain stationary or advance without it would have caused a useless butchery, and I adopted the only alternative—that of falling back to the [West] wood. . . . The enemy followed very slowly and cautiously. Under direction of General Hood I reformed my brigade in the rear of Saint Mumma's Church, and, together with the Texas Brigade, which had also retired, again confronted the enemy, who seemed to hesitate to enter the woods. During this delay re-enforcements arrived, and the brigade was relieved for the purpose of obtaining ammunition. [*O.R.*, XIX, Part 1, pp. 937–38.]

As *Hood's* men fell back from their exposed positions in the Cornfield, reinforcements began to arrive from *Maj. Gen. D. H. Hill's* division, which occupied the center of *Lee's* original line. *Ripley's* brigade initially was deployed along the slopes east of the Visitor's Center about 200 yards west of *Trimble's* division and "in full view" of Union batteries across the Antietam.

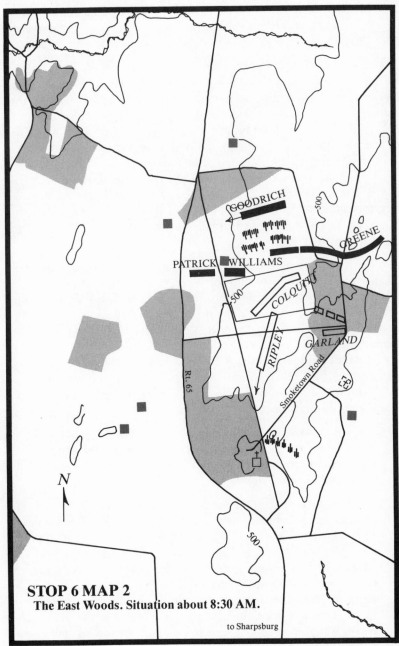

STOP 6 MAP 2
The East Woods. Situation about 8:30 AM.

to Sharpsburg

Approximate Scale 1″ = 1666′

Report of Brig. Gen. Roswell S. Ripley, CSA, Commanding Brigade, D. H. Hill's Division, Jackson's Corps, Army of Northern Virginia

The enemy from his batteries on the eastern bank . . . opened a severe enfilading fire on the troops of my command. . . . This fire inflicted serious loss before the troops were called into positive action, the men lying under it, without flinching, for over an hour, while the enemy plied his guns unceasingly. During this while, a set of farm buildings in our front [Mumma farm] were set on fire to prevent them being made use of by the enemy.

At about 8 o'clock I received orders to close in to my left and advance. The troops sprung to their arms with alacrity and moved forward through the burning buildings in our front, reformed on the other side, and opened a rapid fire upon the enemy. [*O.R.*, XIX, Part 1, pp. 1032–33.]

Ripley's brigade replaced *Trimble's* brigade *[Walker]*, which withdrew to the rear. Advancing forward to the edge of the East Woods, it then obliqued across the southwest-tip of the woods to replace *Hood's* troops just south of the Cornfield, along the present Cornfield Avenue. *Ripley's* brigade then fell back to the ridge west of the Hagerstown turnpike, behind what soon was to become known as the "Bloody Lane."

Colquitt's brigade followed *Ripley* and at least a portion of it reached the fence at the northern edge of the Cornfield, where it ran into fresh troops from Mansfield's Twelfth Corps advancing through the East Wood and the northeast corner of the Cornfield.

Report of Col. A. H. Colquitt, CSA, Sixth Georgia Infantry, Commanding Brigade, D. H. Hill's Division, Jackson's Corps, Army of Northern Virginia

About 7 o'clock in the morning my brigade entered the fight. It was moved [from the western end of the Sunken Road] to the front and formed on the right of *General Ripley's* brigade, which was then engaged. After a few rounds had been discharged, I ordered an advance, and at the same time sent word to the regiments on my left to advance simultaneously. The order was responded to with spirit by my men, and, with a shout, they moved through the corn-field in front, 200 yards wide, and formed on the line of the fence. The enemy was near and in full view. In a moment or two his ranks began to break before our fire, and the line soon disappeared under the crest of the hill upon which it had been established. It was soon replaced by another, and the fire opened with renewed vigor.

In the mean time *Garland's* brigade, which had been ordered to my right, had given way, and the enemy was advancing, unchecked. The regiments upon my left having also failed to advance, we were exposed to a fire from all sides and nearly surrounded. I sent in haste to the rear for re-enforcements, and communicated to *General Hill* the exposed condition of my men. With steady supports upon the right we could yet maintain our position. The support was not at hand and could not reach us in time. The enemy closed in upon the right so near that our ranks were scarcely distinguishable. At the same time his line in front advanced. My men stood firm until every field officer but one had fallen, and then made the best of their way out.

In this sharp and unequal conflict I lost many of my best officers and one-half of the men in the ranks. If the brigades upon the right and left had advanced, we should have driven the enemy from the field. He had at one time broken in our front, but we had not strength to push the advantage. [*O.R.*, XIX, Part 1, pp. 1053–54.]

Garland's brigade left its position on the Hagerstown road to support *Colquitt* about 10 o'clock. From the following reports it would seem that the men of the brigade were still unsettled from their recent experience at South Mountain, where they were outflanked in the woods and lost their commander.

Report of Col. D. K. McRae, CSA, Commanding Garland's Brigade, D. H. Hill's Division, Jackson's Corps, Army of Northern Virginia

We moved by the left flank, until we reached a point near the woods, when line of battle was formed and the advance begun. Some confusion ensued, from conflicting orders. When the brigade crossed the fence, it was halted and formed and again advanced. Coming in sight of the enemy, the firing was commenced steadily and with good will, and from an excellent position, but, unaccountably to me, an order was given to cease firing—that *General Ripley's* brigade was in front. This produced great confusion, and in the midst of it a force of the enemy appearing on the right, it commenced to break, and a general panic ensued. . . . In vain . . . the field and most of the company officers exerted themselves to rally it. The troops left the field in confusion, the field officers, company officers, and myself bringing up the rear. [*O.R.*, XIX, Part 1, p. 1043.]

Report of Capt. Thomas M. Garrett, CSA, Fifth North Carolina Infantry, Garland's Brigade, D. H. Hill's Division, Jackson's Corps

The brigade was halted upon the left of the "burning house," and formed in line of battle. While halted here for a few minutes, and while passing to our position, we were subjected to a very severe cross-fire from the enemy's artillery. . . . The regiment, being formed in line on the right of the brigade, was moved forward rapidly across the open field and over a fence into the woods in front. Here a state of confusion ensued which it is difficult to portray. Various conflicting orders (mere suggestions, perhaps, taking that shape), were passed down the line, the men in ranks being allowed by the officers to join in repeating them, so that it became utterly impossible to understand which emanated from the proper authority.

The regiment, following the movements of the brigade, which were vacillating and unsteady, obliquing to the right and left, came upon a ledge of rock and earth, forming a fine natural breastwork. Under the cover of this the regiment, following the example of those on the left, fell down and sought shelter. Seeing a regiment of the enemy coming up in the open field in our front and . . . flank, and the breastwork turning where the right of the regiment rested in such a manner as to expose a few files of men of my regiment, I ordered these to deploy as flankers to the right and take shelter behind the trees.

At this moment, and while directing this movement, *Captain Thomson*, Company G, came up to me, and in a very excited manner and tone cried out to me, "They are flanking us! See, yonder's a whole brigade." I ordered him to keep silence and return to his place. The men before this were far from being cool, but, when this act of indiscretion occurred, a panic ensued, and, despite the efforts of file-closers and officers, they began to break and run. I have employed this language in regard to *Captain Thomson's* conduct because he remained upon the ground and exerted himself to rally the men, and, while it manifests clearly a want of capacity to command, my observation of him did not produce a conviction that it proceeded from a cowardly temper.

I gave an order to the few men who remained—not more than 10 in number—to retire, and called upon the few officers who were around me to rally behind the fence in our rear. A few rallied by the example of *Lieut. Isaac E. Pearce,* commanding Company B, who acted with great spirit, and all of the men belonging to my company present in the regiment rallied to my side. With them I made a stand at the fence, and ordered the men to fire upon the advancing enemy. This they did with coolness and deliberation. I observed, however . . . that all the brigade on the left were retreating in disorder, and had already passed the fence without halting. I retired with the few men behind the fence, toward the town. . . . Here I met *General Lee* in the street, and reported to him the misfortune . . . and asked for directions. He ordered me to rally all the stragglers I could, without regard to what command they belonged, and report with them to *General Evans.* Only about 50 of my regiment could be found. . . . [*O.R.,* XIX, Part 1, pp. 1043–44.]

Published Union reports from Ricketts' division of fighting in the East Woods and Cornfield are sparse and lacking in detail. Ricketts himself described the action in one brief paragraph.

The division gained the outer edge of the wood, and kept up a fearful fire for four hours, until, the ammunition being exhausted and the supports coming up, it was compelled to retire to refill boxes, after which the division joined the rest of the corps on the right, near the turnpike and . . . was not employed again during the day. . . . Out of 3,158 taken into action, 1,051 were killed and wounded. [*O.R.,* XIX, Part 1, p. 259.]

None of Ricketts' brigade commanders published official reports of the battle. Brigadier General Abram Duryea, commanding the lead brigade, lost a third of his men in 30 minutes, which may explain why only one of his subordinates—a captain—filed a report. Duryea's brigade initially deployed along the fence bordering the northern edge of the Cornfield—the same position that Meade later occupied.

Report of Capt. James MacThomson, USA, One Hundred Seventh Pennsylvania Infantry, Duryea's Brigade, Ricketts' Division, I Army Corps

At early dawn . . . I moved the One hundred and seventh Regiment by the flank to the field on the right. Here, forming column by divisions, we moved forward through a narrow strip of timber, gained the night previous, into a plowed field, in which, [on the] opposite side, Thompson's Pennsylvania battery had just gotten into position. Advancing half way across the field to within easy supporting distance of the battery, we halted for about five minutes, the enemy's shell and round shot flying about us like hail, killing and wounding some of our poor fellows, but not injuring the *morale* of the regiment in the least. Shortly we were again advancing and passing the battery, and over a clover field reached the . . . corn-field.

Deploying into line, we entered the field and pushed rapidly through to the other side. Here we found, in different positions, three full brigades of the enemy. We opened fire immediately upon those in front, and in fifteen minutes compelled them to fall back. Receiving re-enforcements, however, he soon regained his position, and an unequal conflict of nearly three quarters of an hour resulted in forcing us back through the corn-field. Our brigade had, however, done its work. We had held at bay a force of the enemy numerically five times our superior for considerably more than an hour, and at one time driving them. We were now relieved by re-enforcements coming up [probably Meade's two brigades], and retired to the rear. During the balance of the day we were constantly on the *qui vive*, but were not again called into action save to support batteries. [*O.R.*, XIX, Part 1, p. 262.]

Brigadier General George L. Hartsuff, commanding the Third Brigade, was severely wounded at the outset while examining the ground in his front. Hartsuff's brigade subsequently advanced through the East Woods toward this position to tangle with *Hays'* Confederate brigade, coming up from the second line of *Lawton's* division. Unfortunately the *Official Records* contain no reports from Hartsuff's brigade, which suffered 599 casualties in the Cornfield and this portion of the East Woods.

Col. William A. Christian, commanding the Second Brigade, completely lost his composure, broke for the rear and resigned his commission two days later. His four regiments, however, fought their way through the woods and fields to a point in the woods where the white house 40 yards to the east now stands.

Report of Lieut. Col. Richard H. Richardson, USA,
Twenty-sixth New York Infantry, Christian's Brigade, Ricketts'
Division, I Corps

Marched at daylight . . . under orders, across the fields, formed line of battle, occupying the left of the brigade, and halted some 400 or 500 yards from the [East] wood, beyond which the enemy lay in position. I was directed to deploy in column by division, which I did, and advanced obliquely toward the wood under a heavy fire of shot and shell, and halted, as directed, 100 yards in rear of the brigade of General Duryea, that brigade moving to the right. I was ordered to advance in support of General Hartsuff, and did so. Under direction of General Seymour [commanding First Brigade, Meade's Division] we deployed in line of battle along the fence. . . .

The enemy were in sight, about 350 yards, engaged with Hart-suff's brigade. I gave the command to commence firing by file, and the battalion continued firing evenly and carefully for some 30 rounds, average, when the command ceased firing, saving ammunition. This cessation brought the enemy out more plainly in view on the open ground, and we again opened fire, driving the enemy again behind the fence, and under cover of the corn-field. I again gave orders to cease firing, being nearly out of ammunition, and sent word twice to the colonel commanding the brigade [Colonel Peter Lyle had assumed command after Christian's erratic behavior] for ammunition or relief. We resumed our firing until every round of cartridge was expended, when, the relieving column advancing, we retired in good order to the point indicated for supplying the men. [*O.R.*, XIX, Part 1, p. 263.]

INTERVENTION OF THE XII CORPS

The "relieving column" came from the XII Corps, which two days previously had been placed under command of Brigadier General Joseph K. F. Mansfield. The Twelfth Corps had bivouacked the previous night about a mile and a half behind Hooker's First Corps, and at the first sound of cannon at daylight on the 17th it had resumed its movement "each regiment, by order of General Mansfield, marching in column of companies, closed in mass . . . over ground of intermingled woods, plowed fields, and corn-fields."

Report of Brig. Gen. Alpheus S. Williams, USA, Commanding XII Corps

Before reaching the position of General Hooker's corps, information was brought that his reserves were all engaged and that he was hard pressed by the enemy. The columns were hastened up and deployed in line of battle with all the rapidity that circumstances would permit. Five of the regiments of the First Division were new and wholly without drill.

The massed battalions had been moved with such haste that the proper intervals for deployment had not been carefully attended to. The old regiments, however, deployed promptly, and the new regiments (both officers and men of which behaved with marked coolness) soon got into line of battle, with more promptitude than could have been expected.

While the deployment was going on, and before the leading regiments were fairly engaged, it was reported to me that the veteran and distinguished commander of the corps was mortally wounded. I at once reported to Major-General Hooker on the field, took from him such directions as the pressing exigencies would permit, and hastened to make a disposition of the corps to meet them. Crawford's brigade was directed to deploy to the right, its right regiment extending to the [Hagerstown] . . . stone pike. Gordon held the center, while Brigadier-General Greene's division, following the first division in column, was directed to the ridge on the left, extending its line from the lane on Gordon's left to the burned buildings [Mumma farm] a few rods northerly of the brick church.

While General Greene was moving into position, I was strongly solicited by Brigadier-General Gibbon to send re-enforcements to the right to support General Doubleday's position. I accordingly detached the Third Brigade [Goodrich] of General Greene's division, with orders to report to any general officer found on the field indicated. At the same time I ordered the One hundred and twenty-fourth Pennsylvania Volunteers (Crawford's brigade) to push forward past the farm-house of Mr. Miller, cross the pike into the [West] woods beyond, and hold the ridge as long as practicable.

In the mean time the whole line had formed in good order, and were pushing the enemy from the woods and open fields. The requisitions made upon the corps would permit of no reserves, and . . . to cover the points threatened or pressed, every regiment (save Thirteenth New Jersey, held in reserve for a while by General Gordon) was, as early as 6.30 to 7 o'clock a.m. engaged with the enemy.

The enemy at this time had pushed his columns into the open fields in advance of a strip of woods, a few hundred yards wide, which extended along a gentle ridge from the brick church, on the Sharpsburg road, to the farm-house of J. Miller. . . . In the rocky ravines of these woods, and in a considerable valley in the rear of them, the enemy covered his supports and brought up his re-

The Dunker Church and battle aftermath. (USAMHI)

enforcements. A prominent hill [Hauser Ridge] beyond was a strong position for his artillery. Into these woods, after a severe struggle of [nearly] . . . two hours' duration, we drove the enemy. A line of high post-and-rail fence on each side the public road between the church and the [Miller] farm house . . . , a few rods from and nearly parallel with the inner edge of the woods, proved a great obstruction to our rapid pursuit, checking up our line until the enemy could bring up his strong re-enforcements.

All the regiments of this corps were engaged, and had been under arms from daylight, without food; still, they held their position, exposed part of the time to an enfilading fire from an enemy's battery on the right, and all the time to a tremendous fire of musketry and artillery in front. In the mean time Brigadier-General Greene, on the left, with two small brigades of his division, numbering only about 1,700 men, had successfully resisted several attacks, and at about 8 o'clock a.m., making a dash, had seized the woods where they abut upon the road at the brick church. . . . These he gallantly held for several hours. [O.R., XIX, Part 1, pp. 475–76.]

STOP 7
Dunker Church: Greene's Attack

KERSHAW

GREENE 9:30 A.M.

GREENE
11:00 A.M

Rt. 65

7

N

to Sharpsburg

Approximate Scale 1" = 1000'

Turn right onto the SMOKETOWN ROAD. As you drive along this ridge you will get a better understanding of the terrain over which *D. H. Hill's* three brigades moved and fought. Keep in mind that the East Woods extended some little distance to your immediate left before the road bends to the right. The road marks the southernmost edge of the East Woods for about 200 yards beyond the bend.

Greene's Division fought its way through the woods along this ridge, then dropped off to the low ground north of the Mumma Farm on your left, and remained there for an indeterminate time to reorganize and resupply ammunition. It subsequently advanced to the crest of the hill immediately east of the Visitor's Center to support several batteries of artillery firing into the West Woods, where *McLaws'* Confederate division was advancing northward to hit the flank of Sedgwick's column of brigades.

Continue on the Smoketown Road until you reach the Hagerstown Pike at the Dunker Church. Stop short of the intersection and read Greene's report.

STOP 7, THE DUNKER CHURCH

Williams was in error when he stated that Greene's division seized the Dunker Church "at about 8 o'clock a.m." He was not in a position personally to witness Greene's fight, since he obviously had elected to remain near his own division, and Greene's official report is ambiguous with respect to the passage of time.

Report of Brig. Gen. George S. Greene, USA, Commanding Second Division, XII Corps

The division was carried into action about 6.30 a.m., under the orders of Brigadier-General Mansfield. As we were going into action the Third Brigade was detached to the right, leaving under my command the First and Second Brigades, with an aggregate of 1,727.

The division encountering the enemy in the first woods in our front drove them before it, and, entering the open ground partly covered with corn, moved to the left and took position on the right of the post and rail fence enclosing the field on the right of the burned [Mumma] house. There was a battery of brass guns at our left, which we protected. This battery getting out of ammunition for long range was replaced by another.

While in this position the enemy formed in strong force in the woods to the right of the white brick church and advanced on our line. The line was advanced to the axle-trees of the guns, and delivered their fire when the enemy were within 70 yards. They immediately fell back, having suffered immense loss. The division advanced, driving the enemy from the woods near the church and occupying the woods. . . . The position . . . in the advanced woods was very critical. We were in advance of our line on the right and left of us. Sumner's corps [French's division], which had advanced on our left, had retired, as had also the troops on our right [Sedgwick's division]. Guns were sent for, and a section of Knap's battery arrived, and were ordered to take position on our left. The ground on our left and front was broken and wooded, and concealed the movements of the enemy. I placed the division in line, with the right thrown back, and sent forward skirmishers and sought re-enforcements from General Williams. None were at the time available, and the enemy advancing in large force, threatening to envelop the small command, they were forced to retire. They rallied in the second line of woods [East Woods]. They held the woods by the church nearly two hours, in advance of any other troops in their vicinity. They were in action from 6.30 a.m. to 1.30 p.m. After rallying our men we were ordered to fall back, to allow the men to rest and get water and clean their guns. [*O.R.*, XIX, Part 1, p. 505.]

Report of Maj. Orrin J. Crane, USA, Seventh Ohio Infantry, Commanding First Brigade, Greene's Division, XII Corps

The brigade . . . was formed at 5.30 a.m. in column of division, right in front. It was then marched in column about 1 mile to a point of woods, where the enemy were in force and had engaged our right, holding them in check.

At this point the order came to deploy column into line of battle, which was promptly executed. We then advanced a short distance into the [East] woods, where the enemy were formed under cover of a fence. The action commenced. After exchanging a few shots the engagement became general, which continued for an hour and a half of severe fighting, with great slaughter to the enemy, when the enemy gave way in confusion and disorder before the furious onset of our troops. We pursued them rapidly, capturing many prisoners, and strewing the ground with their dead and wounded.

After pressing them closely for a distance of one-half mile, we were obliged to slacken our fire, as our ammunition had given out, when, receiving a supply, we changed our line by the right flank, and marched to an elevation, where we awaited the advance of the enemy who was advancing in column of regiments. We then received orders to fall back under cover of the hill, and awaited the advance of the enemy; when within a short range our troops were quickly thrown forward to the top of the hill, where we poured into their advancing columns volley after volley. So terrific was the fire of our men that the enemy fell like grass before the mower . . . [and] retired in great disorder, . . . not being able to rally their retreating forces.

We charged them in a heavy piece of woods, driving them out of it, capturing a large number of prisoners . . . and made terrible havoc in their ranks. . . . We gained the woods and held our position for two hours. We were then ordered to retire. . . . [*O.R.*, XIX, Part 1, p. 506.]

Most reports submitted in Greene's two brigades mention either that the division withdrew from the West Woods at about 1 p.m., or that it remained in the area of the Dunker Church for two hours, so Williams

View north from the Dunker Church vicinity. (USAMHI)

manifestly was in error in giving the time at 8 a.m. Had Greene's division in fact held that ground at that hour, it would had to have been overrun before the Confederate divisions of *McLaws* and *Walker* could reach Sedgwick's left flank in the West Woods.

The Confederates who attacked Greene and were subsequently pursued across the Hagerstown pike and into the West Woods came mostly from *Kershaw's* South Carolina brigade, *McLaws'* division, which had been ordered forward from the vicinity of *Lee's* Command post about 9 a.m. A Congressional Medal of Honor was awarded to a corporal in this action for capturing a flag allegedly belonging to the 7th South Carolina Infantry. [*O.R.*, XIX, Part 1, p. 510.]

Turn right at the intersection, continue on the Hagerstown Pike for slightly more than 0.1 mile, and TURN LEFT into the *cul de sac* around the Philadelphia Monument. Park here. Walk west to the fence and National Military Park markers to read the text and get the best view of the terrain described.

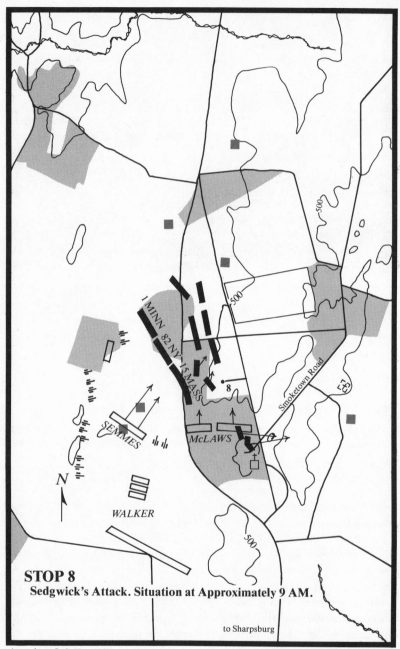

1 MINN
82 N.Y.
15 MASS

8

SEMMES

McLAWS

Smoketown Road

N

WALKER

to Sharpsburg

STOP 8
Sedgwick's Attack. Situation at Approximately 9 AM.

Approximate Scale 1″ = 1666′

STOP 8, SEDGWICK'S ATTACK, 9:00–9:30 A.M.

Contrary to the impression created by the presence of trees, you are *not* in the West Woods. Rather, you are standing at the western boundary of the field described by *General Early* [see above, p. 127], "the edge of which runs at right angles to the road for about 200 yards, making thus an elbow in the woods, and then turns to the right and runs along the woods parallel to the Hagerstown road for a quarter of a mile." The northern face of the West Woods described by General Early ran along the wire fence a few hundred feet to your left. The east face ran along the wire fence just west of this stop. It is necessary to keep in mind that for the most part what formerly was the West Woods is now open fields, while a significant portion of the field where *Jackson's* division initially deployed is now dotted with trees planted by survivors of the Philadelphia Brigade.

If you look to the west through the trees you will discern an extended ridge some 500 yards to the west. Known today as HAUSER'S RIDGE, this was an important Confederate artillery position by this stage of the battle. Once Williams' troops had entered the West Woods near the Dunker Church, *Stuart* could no longer fire his guns from Nicodemus Hill without endangering Confederate troops. Accordingly *Stuart*

> withdrew the batteries to a position farther to the rear, where our own line could be seen, and ordered *General Early* to rejoin his division, with the exception of the Thirteenth Virginia Infantry . . . which was retained as a support for the artillery. The artillery opened from its new position, at close range, upon the enemy with still more terrible effect than before. [*O.R.*, XIX, Part 1, p. 820.]

This ground changed hands several times during the battle. *Jackson's* division had initially deployed partly in the field and partly in the woods to the west, before advancing into the Cornfield. When the remnants of the division fell back before Hooker's onslaught, *Early's* brigade was brought from Nicodemus Hill and posted immediately to the west of your present position: his right rested "near the edge of the plateau" where it could be "concealed and protected by the rise in the ground." [*O.R.*, XIX, Part 1, p. 969.] *Early* reported that "a considerable body" of Union troops then occupied the field to your rear and that a Union battery posted near the southeast corner of this field—where the woods extended to the Hagerstown pike—threatened to enfilade his line. Later elements of Williams' division reached the fences that lined the Hagerstown pike and held their ground until withdrawn upon the approach of Sedgwick's division, II Army Corps.

SEDGWICK'S ATTACK

About 600 yards to your left, slightly to the north and west of the Dunker Church, you can see two conspicuous monuments. One of these marks the location of the 125th Pennsylvania, of Williams' division, and the other the position of the 34th New York, the left regiment in Sedgwick's front line. The right regiment, the 1st Minnesota, would have crossed the Hagerstown Pike on the high ground a short distance this side of the Miller Farm.

Hooker's corps had fought through the East Woods and the Cornfield before it was repulsed and driven back by *Hood's* counterattack and reinforcements from *D. H. Hill's* division, and Williams' division in turn had driven the Confederates back into the West Woods. One of Williams' regiments, the 125th Pennsylvania, had even advanced into the woods just north of the Dunker Church, where it held its ground until the arrival of Sedgwick's division, about 9 a.m.

Report of Maj. Gen. Edwin V. Sumner, USA, Commanding II and XII Army Corps

On the evening of the 16th . . . I received an order at Keedysville to send the Twelfth Corps (Banks') to support General Hooker, and to hold my own, the Second Corps, in readiness to march for the same purpose an hour before daylight. Banks' corps, under General Mansfield, marched at 11.30 p.m., and my own corps was ready to move at the time ordered, but did not receive from headquarters the order to march till 7.20 a.m. on the 17th. I moved Sedgwick's division immediately in three columns on the receipt of the order, followed by French's division in the same order. Richardson was ordered to move in the same direction by the commanding general about an hour later.

On arriving at the place where Hooker had been engaged, I found him wounded, and his corps . . . repulsed. Banks' corps, under the immediate command of General Mansfield, had gone into battle on Hooker's left, and was engaged when I came upon the field. . . .

My First Division (Sedgwick's) went into battle in three lines. After his first line had opened fire for some time, the enemy made a most determined rush to turn our left, and so far succeeded as to break through the line between Banks' corps and my own until they began to appear in our rear. In order to repel this attack from the rear, I immediately faced Sedgwick's third line about, but the fire at that moment became so severe from the left flank that this line moved off in a body to the right [north], in spite of all the efforts that could be made to stop it. The first and second lines after some time followed this movement, but the whole division was promptly rallied, took a strong position, and maintained it to the close of the battle. [*O.R.*, XIX, Part 1, pp. 275–76.]

Report of Brig. Gen. Oliver O. Howard, USA, Commanding Second [Sedgwick's] Division, II Corps

The division, consisting of General Gorman's, General Dana's, and General Burns' brigades, commanded by myself, left camp near Keedysville about 7 a.m. and proceeded in three lines, moving by the right flank in a westerly direction, forded the Antietam [near the Pry house], ascended a gentle slope, continuing in the same direction for about a quarter of a mile beyond. At this point the lines were fronted, and established from 60 to 70 paces apart, facing toward . . . Sharpsburg. General Gorman commanded the front line, General Dana the second, and I the rear line. The advance was ordered for the three lines simultaneously.

The three moved forward with very little wavering, under a fire from the enemy's batteries, which at first were concealed from us by a skirting of woods. The left of the third line was slightly disordered by fences, woods, and our own batteries. We passed through a large corn-field, skirting of woods, then a plowed field, a second skirting of woods more extended than the first, where I was ordered by an aide from General Sumner to detach a regiment to the support of General Mansfield. I halted the Seventy-first Pennsylvania . . . in the place indicated, on the right of the third line.

At this point the musketry fire began to tell upon us, and I received an order from General Sedgwick to move up my entire line. I delayed the third line for the detached regiment to come up, and then moved on across the Sharpsburg turnpike. Just after passing the turnpike, I noticed confusion on the left, and quite a large body of men falling back. I judged them to be troops that our division was relieving. To what brigade they belonged I did not know. I pushed the third line on a little farther, and into the woods beyond the turnpike, preserving about the distance first indicated. In these woods the first line had passed to the south opening, and near a dirt road [now the by-pass] engaged the enemy, formed in line of battle not more than 60 yards distant. The second and third lines, so far as I could observe from my position near the center of the latter, were lying down as ordered.

Nearly the whole of the first line in good order stood and fired some 30 or 40 rounds per man, when word came that the left of our division had been completely turned by the enemy, and the order was given by General Sumner in person to change the position of the third line. He afterward indicated to me the point where the stand was to be made, where he wished to repel a force of the enemy already in our rear. The noise of musketry and artillery was so great that I judged more by the gestures of the general as to the disposition he wished me to make than by the orders that reached my ears.

The troops were hastily faced about, and moved toward the rear and right in considerable confusion, but at about 100 yards from the right of where the first line was engaged, and nearly perpendicular to the turnpike, a portion of General Gorman's brigade, with one regiment of Dana's brigade, was first halted in line, and by a sharp fire repulsed the enemy advancing at that point. On the left of the turnpike regiments of the second and third lines were rallied, facing in the same direction toward Sharpsburg, and here they fired.

General Gorman's brigade was a second time established on the right of the turnpike and behind a stone wall, where they remained until drawn in to the left, taking a new position, in conjunction with the rest of the division. In the mean time Kirby's battery . . . was placed in position by General Sedgwick himself, and the enemy receiving the combined musketry and artillery fire, were not only checked but driven back with great slaughter. At this time—about 11 a.m., I should judge—General Sedgwick having been severely wounded, and having remained on the field for upward of an hour afterward, until he was so weak he could scarcely stand, turned over the command of the division to me.

The next hour was spent by officers of every grade . . . in rallying and reorganizing their commands, all having suffered more or less confusion in the change of position. Meanwhile the batteries of the Pennsylvania Reserves, located on a high plat of ground near the house of Joseph Poffenberger, opened fire, and checked several attempts of the enemy to establish batteries in front of our right and turn our right flank. . . . General Dana's brigade was sent . . . to the left, to assist in supporting batteries of Smith's division [VI Army Corps]. The rest of the division I posted as strongly as possible near the house of Joseph Poffenberger, with instructions to hold this point at all hazards. This portion of the general line of battle was now very quiet, except an occasional attempt of the enemy to locate a battery on a high point beyond the turnpike, near a corn-field. . . .

The total loss of the division is . . . 355 killed, 1,577 wounded [and] 321 missing. . . . a record of almost unparalleled loss during a single battle. They have poured out their blood like water. . . . [*O.R.*, XIX, Part 1, pp. 305–8.]

Report of Brig. Gen. Willis A. Gorman, USA Commanding First Brigade, Second Division, II Army Corps

After crossing the Antietam Creek and arriving at an open field about three-quarters of a mile from the enemy's position, three lines of battle were formed, my brigade being in the advance and front. The First Minnesota Regiment, Colonel Sully, occupied the right of the brigade; the Eighty-second New York Volunteers, Colonel Hudson, on their left; the Fifteenth Massachusetts Volunteers, Lieutenant-Colonel Kimball, next, and the Thirty-fourth New York Volunteers, Colonel Suiter, on the extreme left. In my rear about 50 yards was the second line (General Dana's brigade), and about the same distance in their rear General Howard's . . . brigade.

In this order we began the advance upon the enemy at a rapid pace, the lines being at a distance of 50 yards apart. Before we had advanced 50 yards, the enemy opened a rapid and well-directed fire upon us from one or more batteries, but, moving directly on, they retired rapidly before our advancing columns. Passing through a strip of timber, we entered a large open field, which was strewn with the enemy's dead and wounded, and passed over it at a rapid charge into an open woods, where the enemy's heavy lines of infantry first came into view, the front of which retired in considerable disorder before our advance. We pursued them until we passed the strip of woods and emerged into the edge of a field, where the Fifteenth . . . Massachusetts . . . of my brigade, captured . . . a battle-flag. . . . Instantly my whole command became hotly engaged, giving and receiving the most deadly fire it has ever been my lot to witness. Although the firing was not so rapid, it was most deadly, and at very close range. We also had to stand the most terrific fire of grape and canister, which told fearfully on the three right regiments of the brigade.

After we had expended from 40 to 50 rounds at the enemy, it became evident that he was moving in large force on our left, where his firing became terrific. On our left, in the woods, there was a force that told me they belonged to General Crawford's brigade [125th Pennsylvania], that were posted there when we first entered it. They fought handsomely until the heavy force of the enemy turned their left, when they retired rapidly, and by this movement in five minutes the enemy's fire came pouring hotly on our left flank and rear. Being in front, and without orders of any kind from any one, and finding that the two rear lines were changing position and had already moved from their original place, I gave an order, which reached no one but Colonel Sully, to move quietly by the right flank so as to unmask the second and third lines, to enable them to direct their fire to check the rapid advance of the enemy on my rear, and to enable them to fire without endangering my left regiment.

Shortly before this, I heard Major General Sumner directing the third line to face about, in order to repel the enemy, which had broken our left, supposing the design to be to take up a better position than the one just previously occupied, I having informed the general that my left must be supported or I could not hold the position. The attack of the enemy on that flank was so sudden and in such overwhelming force that I had no time to lose, for my command could have been completely enveloped and probably captured, as the enemy was moving not only upon my left flank but also forcing a column toward my right, the two rear lines having both moved from their position before either of my three right regiments changed theirs.

Perceiving this, after moving a short distance, my command faced about again toward the enemy and gave him another fire, which to some extent checked his advance. After moving a short distance farther, his forces were perceived moving to our right, when the First Minnesota faced toward him and delivered another fire, which again checked his movement. I then ordered that my force be formed behind a stone wall at a distance of about 200 yards to the right and slightly to the rear of our first position. I was then ordered by General Sumner to hold the woods on the left and east of the turnpike, where I formed the entire brigade at a distance of about 400 yards from the original position. The Thirty-fourth New York, being upon the extreme left in the front line of battle, after having withstood a most terrible fire, and having lost nearly one-half the entire regiment in killed and wounded, was ordered by Major-General Sedgwick . . . to retire and take up a new position behind a battery to the right and rear. I immediately ordered them to reform on the left of the brigade, which they did.

In this terrible conflict . . . the Fifteenth Massachusetts, Thirty-fourth and Eighty-second New York Volunteers, lost nearly one-half their entire force engaged. The position of the First Minnesota was more favorable, owing to the formation of the ground. The coolness and desperation with which the brigade fought could not be surpassed. . . . Captain Saunders' company of sharpshooters, attached to the Fifteenth Massachusetts Volunteers, together with the left wing of that regiment, silenced one of the enemy's batteries and kept it so, driving the cannoneers from it every time they attempted to load, and for ten minutes fought the enemy in large numbers at a range of from 15 to 20 yards, each party sheltering themselves behind fences, large rocks, and straw stacks. The first Minnesota Regiment fired with so much coolness and accuracy that they brought down three several times one of the enemy's flags, and finally cut the flag-staff in two. . . . The three right regiments of the brigade kept their front clear and the enemy from advancing during the time they were engaged. [*O.R.*, XIX, Part 1, pp. 311–12.]

The following report describes the fighting some 150 yards in front of where you now stand. The right wing of the 15th Massachusetts extended a short distance across the present bypass. The buildings mentioned in the report belonged to A. Poffenberger and are a short distance to the south and just west of the bypass.

Report of Lieut. Col. John W. Kimball, USA, 15th Massachusetts Infantry, First Brigade, Second Division, II Army Corps

We . . . moved forward in line under a severe artillery fire about one mile . . . passing fences, fields, and obstacles of various descriptions, eventually occupying a piece of woods, directly in front of which, and well covered by the nature of the ground, field of grain, hay-stacks, buildings, and a thick orchard, were the enemy in strong force.

At this time we were marching by the right-oblique, in order to close an interval between my command and . . . [the] Eighty-second New York Volunteers, and as we gained the summit of a slight elevation my left became hotly engaged with the enemy . . . at a distance of not more than 15 yards. A section of the enemy's artillery was planted upon a knoll immediately in front of and not more than 600 yards distant from my right wing. This was twice silenced and driven

back by the fire of my right wing, concentrated upon it. The engagement lasted between twenty and thirty minutes, my line remaining
unbroken, the left wing advancing some 10 yards under a most terrific
infantry fire.

Meanwhile the second line of the division, which had been
halted some 30 or 40 yards in our rear, advanced until a portion of
the Fifty-Ninth Regiment New York Volunteers . . . had closed upon
and commenced firing through my left wing on the enemy. Many of
my men were by this maneuver killed by our own forces, and my
most strenuous exertions were of no avail either in stopping this
murderous fire or in causing the second line to advance to the front.
At this juncture General Sumner came up, and his attention was
immediately called by myself to this terrible mistake. He immediately
rode to the right of the Fifty-ninth, . . . ordered the firing to cease
and the line to retire, which order was executed in considerable
confusion.

The enemy soon appeared in heavy columns, advancing upon
my left and rear, pouring in a deadly cross-fire on my left. I immediately and without orders ordered my command to retire, having first
witnessed the same movement on the part of both the second and
third lines. We retired slowly and in good order, bringing off our
colors and a battle-flag captured from the enemy, reforming by the
orders of General Gorman in a piece of woods [North woods] some
500 yards to the rear, under cover of our artillery. . . .

My entire regiment behaved most gallantly during the engagement, evincing great coolness and bravery, as my list of casualties will
show. [Total killed, wounded and missing, 348]. Although suffering
terribly from the fire of the enemy, it was with great surprise that
they received the order to retire, never entertaining for a moment any
idea but that of complete success, although purchased at the cost of
their lives. The order forbidding the carrying wounded men to the
rear was obeyed to the very letter. [*O.R.*, XIX, Part 1, p. 313.]

Report of Brig. Gen. Jubal A. Early, CSA, Commanding Ewell's Division, Jackson's Corps

A very heavy column of [Union] infantry . . . was . . . within 200
yards of my right flank. This made me aware of the fact that our
troops which I had seen giving way had fallen back, leaving the
enemy entire possession of the field in front. . . . My condition . . .
was exceedingly critical, as another column was advancing in my

front and had reached the woods in which I was. I saw the vast importance of maintaining my ground, for, had the enemy gotten possession of this woods, the heights immediately in rear, which commanded the rear of our whole line, would have fallen into his hands. I determined to wait for the re-enforcements promised by *General Jackson,* hoping that they would arrive in time to meet the columns on my right. I, however, threw my right flank back quietly under cover of the woods, so as not to have my rear exposed in the event of being discovered. I kept an anxious eye on the column on my right, as well as on the one moving up in my front, and very soon I saw the column on my right move into the woods in the direction of the church. I looked to the rear for the re-enforcements and could not see them coming. I was thus cut off from the main body of our army on the right, and a column was moving against me from the left. There was no time to be lost, and I immediately ordered my brigade to move by the right flank parallel to the enemy, and directed *Colonel Grigsby,* who commanded the body of troops he and *Colonel Stafford* had rallied, to move his command back in line, so as to present front to the enemy, who were coming up on the flank. I moved back along the rear of the woods until I caught up with the enemy, who had the start on me. I was, however, concealed from his view, and it was evident that my presence . . . was not suspected. Passing from behind a ridge that concealed my brigade . . . we came in full view of his flankers, who . . . were made aware of my presence by a fire which I directed the leading regiment to pour into them. They immediately ran into the main body, which halted, and I continued to move by the flank until my whole force was disclosed.

Just at this time, I observed the promised re-enforcements coming up toward the woods at the farther end. I ordered the brigade to face to the front and open fire, which was done in handsome style and responded to by the enemy. I did not intend to advance to the front, as I observed some of the troops which had come up to re-enforce me preparing to advance into the woods from the direction of my right flank, and was afraid of exposing my brigade to their fire, and that the two movements would throw us into confusion as they would have been at right angles. Moreover, the other column was advancing on my flank, held in check, however, by *Colonels Grigsby* and *Stafford,* with their men, and by the Thirty-first Virginia Regiment, which was on my left. The enemy in front, however, commenced giving way, and the brigade, which I have always found difficult to restrain, commenced pursuing, driving the enemy in front entirely out of the woods. Notwithstanding my efforts to stop my men, they advanced until my left flank and rear became exposed to a fire from the column on the left, which had advanced past my former position. I also discovered another body of the enemy moving across the plateau on my left flank, in double-quick time, to the same position, and I succeeded in arresting my command and ordered it to retire, so that I might change front and advance upon this force. Just as I reformed my line, *Semmes'*, *Anderson's*, and part of *Barksdale's* brigades, of *McLaws'* division, came up, and the whole, including *Grigsby's* command, advanced upon this body of the enemy, driving it with great slaughter entirely from and beyond the woods. . . . As soon as this was accomplished, I caused the regiments of the brigade to be reformed and placed in position as before. [*O.R.*, XIX, Part 1, pp. 970–71.]

Report of Maj. Gen. Lafayette McLaws, CSA, Commanding Division, Longstreet's Corps

On the morning of September 16, my command . . . marched through Harper's Ferry . . . and halted near Halltown . . . a short distance from the road . . . toward Shepherdstown . . . on the way to Sharpsburg, to which place I had been directed to march by orders from *General Lee*. . . . The entire command was very much fatigued. . . . A large number had no provisions, and a great portion had not had time or opportunity to cook what they had. All the troops had been without sleep during the night previous, except while waiting in line for the wagon trains to pass over the pontoon bridge at Harper's Ferry. . . . I . . . started the command at 3 p.m. Halted after dark . . . within 2 miles of Shepherdstown, when, receiving orders to hasten forward, again commenced the march at 12 o'clock that night, many of the regiments still without provisions. . . .

On the morning of the 17, about sunrise, the head of my column reached the vicinity of *General Lee's* headquarters near Sharpsburg. I rode on to the town, looking for *General Lee*, and on my return, not finding him, met *General Longstreet*, who directed me to send *General Anderson's* division direct down the road to the hill beyond Sharpsburg, where he would receive orders. I learned from him where *General Lee's* camp was, and reported to *General Lee* for orders. He directed me to halt my division near to his headquarters. . . . About an hour after this my division was ordered to the front by an aide-de-camp of *General Lee, Major Taylor*.

In about 1 mile we came in rear of the position, which was pointed out by *Major Ratchford*, of *General D. H. Hill's* staff, as the one the division was to occupy. I was, of course, entirely ignorant of the ground and of the location of the troops. *General Hood*, however, who was present, pointed out the direction for the advance, and my line of battle was rapidly formed, *General Cobb's* brigade on the right, next *General Kershaw's*, *Generals Barksdale* and *Semmes* on the left. Just in front of the line was a large body of woods, from which parties of our troops, of whose command I do not know, were seen retiring, and the enemy, I could see, were advancing rapidly, occupying the place.

My advance was ordered before the entire line of *General Kershaw* could be formed. As the enemy were filling the woods so rapidly, I wished my troops to cross the open space between us and the woods before they were entirely occupied. It was made steadily and in perfect order, and the troops were immediately engaged, driving the enemy before them in magnificent style at all points, sweeping the woods with perfect ease and inflicting great loss on the enemy. They were driven not only through the woods, but over a field in front of the woods, [your present location] and over two high fences [bordering the Hagerstown pike] beyond, and into another body of woods [North woods] over half a mile distant.

From the commencement of the fight, the men were scattered, by the engagement, through the woods where the enemy made their only stand, and, there being no immediate support, the several brigades fell back into the woods, and the line, to maintain the position, was formed by the brigades of *Generals Ransom (Walker's* division) and *Armistead (General Anderson's* division), which had been sent to my support; of *General Early*, which was already in position, and the brigades of *Generals Barksdale* and *Kershaw*. *Captain Read's* battery had been placed in position on the right of the woods, which we had entered, and did most excellent service, but it was exposed to such a severe fire, *General Kershaw* ordered it back after losing 14 officers and men and 16 horses. Another battery, *Captain Carlton's*, which I had ordered into position in the woods in front of *General Ransom's* brigade, was so severely cut up in a short time by the direct and cross-fires of numerous batteries that I ordered it to retire.

The enemy did not make an attempt to retake the woods after they were driven from them . . . but kept up a terrific fire of artillery. There was an incessant storm of shot and shell, grape and canister, but the loss inflicted by the artillery was comparatively very small.

Fortunately, the woods were on the side of a hill, the main slope of which was toward us, with numerous ledges of rocks along it. Thus it was, our men, although under this fire for hours, suffered so little from it.

I could do nothing but defend the position my division occupied. The line was too weak to attempt an advance. There were not men enough to make a continuous single line. In some places for considerable distance there were no men at all, while just beyond us, across an open field, about 400 or 500 yards distant, were the lines of the enemy, apparently double and treble, supporting numerous batteries, which crossed fire over every portion of the ground. The artillery of the enemy was so far superior to our own in weight of metal, character of guns and numbers, and in quality of ammunition, that there was but very little to be gained by opposing ours to it, and I therefore did not renew the attempt after the first experiments. . . .

The losses in the different brigades were . . . 39.5 percent [of those] carried into action. [*O.R.*, XIX, Part 1, pp. 857–60.]

Report of Brig. Gen. John G. Walker, CSA, Commanding Division, Longstreet's Corps

The division . . . after participating in the capture of . . . Harper's Ferry, crossed the Blue Ridge, the Shenandoah, and the Potomac . . . at Shepherdstown, and reached the neighborhood of Sharpsburg . . . on the 16th, where I reported to *General Lee*. In accordance with his instructions, at daylight the next morning I placed the division on the extreme right of our position and about 1-1/2 miles south of Sharpsburg . . . in such way as to cover the ford over the Antietam . . . and to be within supporting distance of the command of *Brigadier-General Toombs*, which lay in front of the [Burnside] bridge. . . .

Soon after 9 a.m. I received orders from *General Lee*, through *Colonel Long*, of his staff, to hasten to the extreme left, to the support of *Major General Jackson*. Hastening forward, as rapidly as possible, along the rear of our entire line of battle, we arrived, soon after 10 o'clock, near the woods where the commands of *Generals Hood* and *Early* were struggling heroically to hold but gradually and sullenly yielding to the irresistible weight of overwhelming numbers. Here we at once formed line of battle, under a sharp artillery fire, and, leaving the Twenty-seventh North Carolina and Third Arkansas Regiments to hold the open space between the [West] woods and *Longstreet's* left, the division . . . advanced in splendid style, firing and cheering as they went, and in a few minutes cleared the woods, strewing it with the enemy's dead and wounded. *Colonel Manning*, with the Forty-sixth and Forty-eighth North Carolina and Thirtieth Virginia, not content with the possession of the woods, dashed forward in gallant style, crossed the open fields beyond, driving the enemy before him like sheep, until, arriving at a long line of strong post and rail fences, behind which heavy masses of the enemy's infantry were lying, their advance was checked; and it being impossible to climb over these fences under such a fire, these regiments, after suffering a heavy loss, were compelled to fall back to the woods. . . . [This] enabled the enemy to temporarily reoccupy the point of woods. . . . [around the Dunker Church].

In the mean time *Brigadier-General Ransom*, whose brigade was farther on the left, having driven the enemy through and from the [West] woods, with heavy loss, continued . . . to hold it for the greater portion of the day, notwithstanding three determined infantry attacks, which each time were repulsed with great loss to the enemy, and against a most persistent and terrific artillery fire, by which the enemy hoped . . . to drive us from our strong position – the very key of the battlefield. . . . For eight hours our brave men lay upon the ground, taking advantage of such undulations and shallow ravines as gave promise of partial shelter, while this fearful storm raged a few feet above their heads, tearing the trees asunder, lopping off huge branches, and filling the air with shrieks and explosions, realizing to the fullest the fearful sublimity of battle. . . .

The division suffered heavily, particularly *Manning's* command . . . which at one time sustained almost the whole fire of the enemy's right wing. Going into the engagement, as it was necessary for us to do, to support the sorely pressed divisions of *Hood* and *Early*, it was, of course, impossible to make dispositions based upon a careful reconnaissance of the localities. The post-and-rail fences stretching across the fields lying between us and the enemy's position, I regard as the fatal obstacle to our complete success on the left. . . . Of the existence of this obstacle none of my division had any previous knowledge, and we learned it at the expense of many valuable lives. [*O.R.*, XIX, Part I, pp. 914–17.]

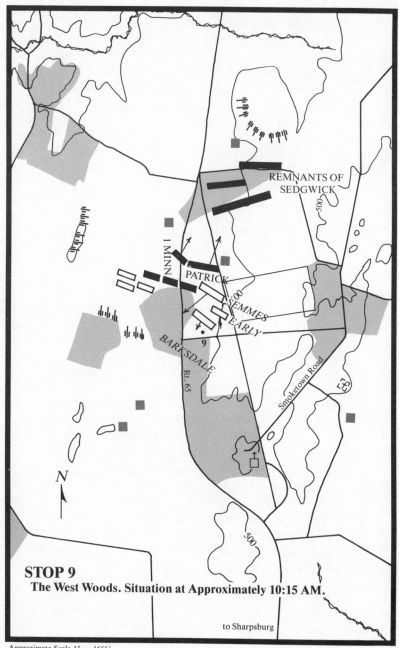

REMNANTS OF
SEDGWICK

1 MINN

PATRICK

SEMMES

EARLY

BARKSDALE

Rt. 65

9

Smoketown Road

500

500

500

N

STOP 9
The West Woods. Situation at Approximately 10:15 AM.

to Sharpsburg

Approximate Scale 1″ = 1666′

Return to your car. Drive to the Hagerstown pike, turn left and proceed only about 0.1 mile until you reach the first intersection. TURN LEFT on STARKE AVENUE, proceed about 300 yards, and stop by the historical markers that you will see on your right before reaching the bypass.

STOP 9, THE WEST WOODS

The woods that you see ahead of you is all that remains of the original West Woods, although the area immediately around the car was open field at the time of the battle. In the initial Union assault, the 19th Indiana worked its way into the woods to your front, where it halted until the Confederates attempted to take Battery B. The regiment then changed front forward so as to threaten the flank of enemy forces that might move north astride the turnpike.

Later the regiment, together with the 7th Wisconsin and two regiments of Patrick's brigade, crossed the field to your right to take position behind the stone outcroppings to your right-rear, which served nicely as natural breastworks for the troops supporting Battery B. Later they charged across the field beyond to the Hagerstown Pike, losing the regimental commander of the 19th Indiana in the vicinity of the modern white house on the high ground some 400 yards to your left-rear. Patrick finally was forced to give up this position when Early's brigade moved in from your left and threatened to take him in reverse.

Later the right regiment of Sedgwick's division, the 1st Minnesota, would have had to divide ranks and step around your car as it advanced ahead into the West Woods some 200 yards beyond the bypass. One has to walk into those woods and to the far side, where Sedgwick's first line was stopped by Confederate artillery and small arms fire at least 20 minutes or so *before McLaws* struck the Union left flank, to appreciate the sense of isolation and confusion that the men of the first line must have felt when they heard all hell break loose on the high ground behind them.

Report of Col. Alfred Sully, USA, First Minnesota Regiment, First Brigade, Second Division, II Army Corps

We were formed on the right of the front line of battle . . . and advanced . . . into a woods close to the enemy and in front of our line of battle. Here we were posted behind a rail [today a wire] fence. The enemy soon appeared in force on the left of the brigade, opened a very severe fire of musketry on us, while some of their artillery in front of us also opened on us. Our loss here was very heavy, yet the men bravely held their position, and did not leave it until after the two brigades in rear had fallen back and the left regiments were moving, when they received the order to retire.

Retiring in line of battle, we again halted outside the woods, to hold the enemy in check while the rest were retiring. Here the Eighty-second New York with their colonel and colors reported to me, and formed on my right. The Nineteenth Massachusetts also reported, and formed on my left. We were soon again engaged with the enemy, but, seeing that the enemy were turning my right, I ordered the line to fall back in line of battle. The regiment here also suffered greatly in killed and wounded. We again made a stand near some farm-house [Nicodemus] for a short time, and here took up a strong position about 100 yards back, behind a stone fence, when a section of artillery was sent to assist us. We kept the enemy in check till they brought a battery of artillery on our flank, which compelled me to order the regiments back to join our line of battle [near the North woods]. . . . We marched into the action with 435 . . . [and lost] . . . total enlisted men killed, wounded, and missing, 118. [*O.R.*, XIX, Part 1, pp 314–15.]

Semmes' brigade from *McLaws'* division would have overrun your car as the remnants of Sedgwick's division fought their way back to the shelter of the North woods and the Union artillery concentrated around the John Poffenberger farm. Crossing Starke Avenue, which was built by the U.S. Army when the battlefield was developed in the 1890's, *Semmes'* brigade pushed up this valley nearly as far as the buildings on the Miller farm, to your right, before it was stopped.

Report of Brig. Gen. Paul J. Semmes, CSA, Commanding Brigade, McLaws' Division, Longstreet's Corps

Moving forward by the flank in the direction of the enemy, before coming in view, two brigades were met retiring from the front apparently badly cut up. An incessant current of wounded flowed to the rear, showing that the conflict had been severe and well contested. Coming in full view of the enemy's line, *Major-General McLaws*, in person, ordered me to move forward in line to the support of *Major-General Stuart*, on our extreme left. Immediately the order was given "by company into line," followed by "forward into line," both of which movements were executed, in the presence of the enemy, under a fire occasioning severe loss in killed and wounded.

The brigade advanced steadily for 200 yards under fire before the order was given to commence firing. This order was then given at long range for most of our arms, for the purpose of encouraging our troops and disconcerting the enemy. The troops . . . needed little encouragement. Their officers had already inspired them with enthusiasm, and they continued to advance with vivacity. The effect on the enemy's fire . . . was distinctly visible in the diminished numbers of killed and wounded.

The enemy at first met our advance by a corresponding one. Our troops continued to press steadily forward, pouring a deadly fire into his ranks, and he, after advancing 100 yards, gave way; and we continued to drive him from position to position, through wood and field for a mile, expending not less than 40 rounds of ammunition. My brigade was thrown farther to the front than the troops on my right by about 300 yards, and for a time was exposed to a terrible front and enfilading fire, inflicting great loss. . . . Had it been possible to have strengthened it by a supporting force of 2,000 or 3,000 men, there was not then, nor is there now, a doubt in my mind that the enemy's right, though in vastly superior numbers, would have been driven upon his center and both, in confusion, on his left, utterly routing him. . . .

The loss in killed and wounded was, of the Fifty-third Georgia Volunteers, 30 per cent; Thirty-second Virginia, 45 per cent; Tenth Georgia, 57 per cent; Fifteenth Virginia, 58 per cent. . . . Thirty-six prisoners . . . were captured at a farm-house, [Miller] the most advanced position held by my brigade. . . .

The colors of the Tenth Georgia received forty-six shots, and the pike was once hit and twice cut in two. [*O.R.*, XIX, Part 1, pp. 874–75.]

Report of Lieut. Gen. Thomas J. Jackson, CSA, Commanding Corps, Army of Northern Virginia

No further advance, beyond demonstrations, was made by the enemy on the left. In the afternoon, in obedience to instructions from the commanding general, I moved to the left with a view of turning the Federal right, but I found his numerous artillery so judiciously established in their front and extending so near to the Potomac, which here makes a remarkable bend . . . as to render it inexpedient to hazard the attempt. In this movement *Major General Stuart* had the advance and acted his part well. This officer rendered valuable service throughout the day. His bold use of artillery secured for us an important position, which, had the enemy possessed, might have commanded our left. [*O.R.*, XIX, Part 1, pp. 956–57.]

Report of Maj. Gen. William B. Franklin, USA, Commanding VI Corps, Army of the Potomac

General Smith's division led the column, and its head arrived at the field of battle about 10 a.m. [and] . . . was ordered to go to the assistance of General Sumner, forming on his left . . . Slocum's division arrived on the field about 11 o'clock. Immediately after its arrival two of his brigades were formed in column of attack, to carry the wood in the immediate vicinity of the white church. . . . About the same time General Sumner arrived on the spot, and directed the attack to be postponed, and the enemy at once proceeded to fill the wood with infantry, and planted a battery there, which opened a severe fire upon us. Shortly afterward the commanding general came to the position and decided that it would not be prudent to make the attack, our position on the right being then considerably in advance of what it had been in the morning. The division, therefore, held its place until it was finally removed on the 19th. [*O.R.*, XIX, Part 1, pp. 376–77.]

Continue on Starke Avenue until you reach the bypass. Turn left, and as you drive along, try to imagine Confederate soldiers to your left hugging the ground behind rock ledges, seeking refuge from Union artillery. Try also to envision Sedgwick's front line as it encountered Confederate troops and artillery on Hauser Ridge to your right.

The old farm that you will see on your right was also owned by a family named Poffenberger. *Semmes'* brigade fought here for 10 or 15 minutes before resuming the advance for nearly another half mile, "crossing two fields and across four fences" before they reached the house, barn and other outbuildings of the Miller Farm.

When you reach the sign marking the entrance to Visitor's Center, TURN LEFT: this could be a good time to view the displays and use the facilities in the Visitor's Center, which you will pass on your right. Whether you stop at the Visitor's Center or prefer to go direct to STOP 10, drive north (from here and also from the Visitor's Center)

Ruins of the Mumma Farm. (USAMHI)

along the Hagerstown Turnpike until you reach the intersection with the SMOKETOWN ROAD, opposite the Dunker Church.

TURN RIGHT: proceed about 0.2 mile on the Smoketown Road to the first intersection and turn right again. After turning you will crest a rise with the Visitor's Center on your right and the Mumma farm and cemetery to your left. You may want to pause at the turnout near the cemetery to view the position of *Trimble's* brigade, *Ewell's* division, which anchored the right of *Jackson's* original line.

Trimble initially deployed his regiments on line between the Smoketown Road and the Mumma farm, parallel with the park road where you are parked and a short distance on this side of the Mumma family cemetery that you see on the higher ground to your left. According to *Early's* report this brigade, commanded in this battle by Colonel *James A. Walker*, "suffered terribly, his own horse was killed under him, and he had himself been struck by a piece of shell." [*O.R.*, XIX, Part 1, p. 968.] For *Walker's* report of this action see above, pp. 150–51.

When *Trimble's* brigade was forced to fall back *Ripley's* brigade from *D. H. Hill's* division, which had been deployed a few hundred yards to your right, moved forward about 7 a.m. to occupy this line.

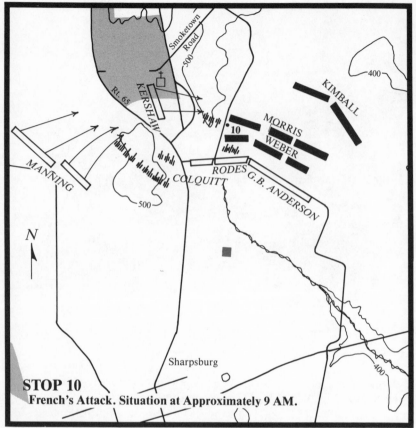

French's Attack. Situation at Approximately 9 AM.

Approximate Scale 1″ = 1666′

After *Ripley's* regiments advanced into the East Woods and thence, by moving by the left flank, into the Corn Field this position was occupied (about 7:30 a.m.) by *Colquitt's* brigade, also of *Hill's* division. When *Colquitt* moved by the left flank along the western edge of the East Woods to support *Ripley* in the Cornfield, *Garland's* brigade, also of *Hill's* division, passed through this position as it moved into the East Woods, where it quickly broke and fell back "in panic" when a portion of *Greene's* division unexpectedly appeared on its right flank [*O.R.*, XIX, Part 1, p. 1043].

After fighting its way through the East Wood, Greene's division stopped in the low ground "on the right of the post and rail fence enclosing the field on the right of the burned house" (see above, p. 163) to reorganize and resupply ammunition, before moving forward to the crest of the hill where the Visitor's Center is located to support Tompkins' battery.

Continue for about 0.3 mile to the next turnout on your left. From this site you can look east toward the Antietam across the line of French's attack and view the high ground around the Sharpsburg cemetery to the south, a key to *Lee's* defensive position.

STOP 10, FRENCH'S ATTACK

Report of Brig. Gen. William H. French, USA, Commanding Third Division, II Corps, Army of the Potomac

My division, composed of Brig. Gen. Max Weber's and Kimball's brigades, and three regiments of new levies under the command of Col. Dwight Morris (Fourteenth Connecticut), having been in readiness since daybreak on the 17th . . . was put in motion by orders of the general commanding the corps at about 7.30 o'clock a.m. The Antietam creek was forded by the division, marching in three columns of brigades; Max Weber on the left, the new regiments in the center, and Kimball's brigade on the right. When my left flank had cleared the ford a mile, the division faced to the left, forming three lines of battle adjacent to and contiguous with Sedgwick's, and immediately moved to the front.

The enemy, who was in position in advance, opened his batteries, under which fire my lines steadily moved until the first line, encountering the enemy's skirmishers, charged them briskly, and entering a group of houses on Roulette's farm [about 600 yards to your left-rear], drove back the force, which had taken a strong position for defense. Whilst Max Weber was clearing his front and driving before him the enemy's first line, a sudden and terrible fire was opened upon his right by the troops, which had succeeded in breaking the center division of the line of battle. At the same time a heavy column endeavored at turn my left and rear. [*O.R.*, XIX, Part 1, pp. 323–24.]

Weber's brigade was deployed a short distance in front of your car, with the right resting on the road about 150 yards ahead. The Confederate attack against Weber's right was made by the 8th South Carolina, the right regiment in Kershaw's brigade line, which extended about as far north as the Dunker Church. His other regiments surged across the Hagerstown turnpike to attack the right section of Tompkins' battery. *Walker's* brigade of *Walker's* division, commanded by *Col. Van H. Manning*, likewise made a determined attack through the West Woods until it encountered "two heavy panel fences, running obliquely" along the Mumma lane. Most of the brigade did not advance farther, but fell back to the West Woods where it took shelter behind "a breastwork of rails" found just in front of the woods, where they were "well protected" and "in short range of the enemy." Two of these regiments, the 48th North Carolina and the 30th Virginia, at one time attempted to charge over the fences and up the slope of the hill, but "found themselves so massed up that they were compelled to lie down in the face of the enemy and under a withering fire. . . . They suffered severely, and in a short time were compelled to retire" in some disorder, although they probably "behaved as well as any troops could who were in such an exposed and fatal position." [*O.R.*, XIX, Part 1, p. 918.]

At this time the western bend of the sunken road was held by *Rodes'* brigade and returning fragments of the three brigades that *Hill* had sent earlier into the East Woods, while *G. B. Anderson's* brigade prolonged the line southeast of the intersection with the Roulette lane. Later the division of *Maj. Gen. R. H. Anderson*, of *Longstreet's* Corps, comprising some 2,000–4,000 men, arrived and formed in the cornfield immediately behind *D. H. Hill's* line.

Report of Col. John W. Andrews, USA, First Delaware Infantry, Third Brigade, Third Division, II Corps, Army of the Potomac

The first Delaware Infantry, forming the right of Brig. Gen. Max Weber's brigade, after fording Antietam Creek, marched in column for a mile, then, facing to the left, advanced in line of battle, forming the first line of General French's division. The enemy's batteries now opened a severe fire. Having advanced steadily through woods and corn-fields, driving all before us, we met the enemy in two lines of battle, posted in a road or ravine 4 feet below the surface of the adjoining field, with a third line in a corn-field in the rear, the ground gradually rising so that they were able to fire over the heads of those in the ravine; our right was also exposed to the sudden and terrible fire from the troops who succeeded in breaking the center division [Sedgwick] of the line of battle. We were at this time about 20 paces off the enemy, and returned their fire for some time with much coolness and effect. A charge was then ordered and attempted, but our second line, composed of new levies, instead of supporting our advance, fired into our rear. We had now lost one-third of our men, and 8 officers commanding companies were either killed or wounded. Under these circumstances we fell back gradually to a stronger position until relieved by our third line, composed of veterans under General Kimball. This was our first battle. . . . [*O.R.*, XIX, Part 1, p. 337.]

When Weber was wounded Col. Andrews assumed command of the Third brigade, which "continued fighting until their ammunition was expended." He reported capturing about 300 prisoners at a cost of 582 casualties for the three regiments in the brigade. [*Ibid.*, pp. 193, 336.]

French's second line at this stage of the fight comprised three regiments "hastily raised and without drill" [*Ibid.*, p. 334] commanded by Col. Dwight Morris. The 14th Connecticut (the monument in the field to your left) was deployed a short distance in front of your present position, with the right flank extending to the Mumma lane, where it was exposed to "a severe cross-fire" until ordered to withdraw to a stone wall about 90 yards to the rear. The 130th Pennsylvania, in line to the left of the 14th Connecticut (and slightly to the rear of the black monument that you see on the crest further to your left), received the fire of Confederates in the sunken lane and of a force "on the right" which was probably some portion of *Manning's* brigade and the 8th South Carolina. As the commander of the 130th described it,

> About this time a force of the enemy advanced on a battery posted on our right, which was withdrawn. The enemy then changed front, and advanced on our right to the fence bounding the field in which we were posted. Changing our front to meet his advancing lines, we held him in check until a charge was made by a brigade on our right, which drove the enemy back in great disorder. [*O.R.*, XIX, Part 1, p. 336.]

Report of Brig. Gen. William H. French, USA, Commanding Third Division, II Corps, Army of the Potomac, continued:

At this moment Captain Sumner communicated to me, from the general commanding the corps [General Sumner], that his right divisions were being severely handled, and directed me to press the enemy with all my force. Appreciating the necessity of the order, without waiting for the new regiments to recover from the disorder incident to their long march in line through woods, corn-fields, and over fences, I left them in reserve and ordered Kimball to charge to the front. With an unsurpassed ardor this gallant brigade, sweeping over all obstacles, soon crowned the crests of the hills on our left and right. . . . General Kimball . . . brought his veterans into action, and fought the enemy on the front and either flank with such desperate courage and determination as to permit the arrival of the re-enforcements, which reached the field three hours after my division had sustained the conflict. After the arrival of re-enforcements, the exhaustion of ammunition brought my line from the crests it had carried to the second line, which, being supplied, my troops were ready to continue the action. Richardson's division supported me with that success which always distinguished that noble corps. Brooke's brigade was particularly conspicuous. . . .

The conduct of the new regiments must take a prominent place in the history of this great battle. Undrilled, but admirably armed and equipped, every regiment, either in advance or reserve, distinguished itself . . . according to the energy and ability of their respective commanders. . . . My loss was 1,817. . . . [*O.R.*, XIX, Part 1, p. 324.]

For several hours French was supported by Tompkins' Battery [to your immediate right], which belonged to Sedgwick's division. This battery had accompanied the First Corps when it crossed the Antietam the previous day, and had been ordered by Hooker to take position "on a knoll on the left of the road, directly in front of some burning ruins."

Report of Capt. John A. Tompkins, USA, Battery A,
First Rhode Island Light Artillery,
Second Division, II Corps, Army of the Potomac

My battery . . . . opened fire about 9 o'clock upon a battery directly in front of my position. At 9.30 the enemy appeared upon my right front with a large column, apparently designing to charge the battery. I was not aware of their approach until the head of the column [*Kershaw*] gained the brow of a hill, about 60 yards from the right gun of the battery. The pieces were immediately obliqued to the right, and a sharp fire of canister opened upon them, causing them to retire in confusion, leaving the ground covered with their dead and wounded, and abandoning one of their battle-flags, which was secured by a regiment which came up on my right [probably the 28th Pennsylvania, where a corporal received the Medal of Honor for capturing a flag supposed to belong to the 7th South Carolina] after the enemy had retreated. The enemy now opened a fire upon us from a battery in front, and also from one on the right, near the white school-house [Dunkard Church]. Two guns were directed to reply to the battery on the right, while the fire of the rest was directed upon the guns in front, which were silenced in about twenty minutes, and one of their caissons blown up.

On my left the troops of General French were engaged with the enemy, who occupied a corn-field, in front of which was a line of fence-rails. About 10.30 the enemy were re-enforced [by *Anderson's* division], and advanced their line to the edge of the corn-field. I at once ordered the battery to open on them with shell and case-shot, using 1-1/2-seconds and 2-seconds fuses. Twice they advanced their flag to the edge of the field, but were forced to retire by the rapid and destructive fire of the battery. At 11.30, finding my ammunition running low, I sent to General Sumner for orders, and at 12 m. was relieved by Company G, First Rhode Island Light Artillery. [*O.R.*, XIX, Part 1, pp. 308–9.]

The last and most desperate attempt by the Confederates to dislodge French's right flank occurred about 12.30, when *Hill's* troops had already been driven from the Sunken Road and had reformed in the area of the Piper Farm. *Longstreet* ordered *Col. J. R. Cooke* to take his own regiment, the 27th North Carolina, and the 3rd Arkansas (both of *Manning's* brigade), which plugged the gap between *Colquitt's* left flank at the western end of the Sunken Road and the rest of *Walker's* division in the West Woods, to attack. Advancing from their position at the fence line near the top of the slope directly ahead, the two small regiments stormed across the turnpike opposite the Visitor's Center, and rushed down the slope on your right.

Report of Brig. Gen. John G. Walker, CSA, Commanding Division, Longstreet's Corps, Army of Northern Virginia, continued

This order was promptly obeyed in the face of such a fire as troops have seldom encountered without running away, and with a steadiness and unfaltering gallantry seldom equalled. Battery after battery, regiment after regiment opened their fire upon them hurling a torrent of missiles through their ranks, but nothing could arrest their progress, and three times the enemy broke and fled before their impetuous charge. Finally they reached the fatal picket-fences before

Dead along the fences on Hagerstown Pike. (USAMHI)

alluded to [see above, p. 179]. To climb over them, in the face of such a force and under such a fire, would have been sheer madness to attempt, and their ammunition, being now almost exhausted, *Colonel Cooke*, very properly, gave the order to fall back, which was done in the most perfect order, after which the regiments took up their former position, which they continued to hold until night. [*O.R.*, XIX, Part 1, pp. 915–16.]

By this time Tompkins' battery had been replaced by Owen's First Rhode Island artillery. As Owens proceeded toward the brow of the hill to engage Confederate infantry,

then in plain sight from that position . . . a noise from my right attracted my attention, and I saw our infantry retreating in disorder toward me, and then about 150 yards off, closely followed by the rebels. I limbered up quickly and started on the trot into the road

Dead in the Bloody Lane. (USAMHI)

leading direct from the [Mumma] ruins, and when the last caisson left the ground the enemy were close upon us. I halted when a few hundred yards to the rear, and, after replenishing the ammunition in the gun-limbers, took the pieces alone of the right section and proceeded up behind the advance that retook the field, but the infantry was quite unsteady on the right and broke the second time, and not deeming it prudent to risk even the section under such circumstances, I withdrew and reported to General Sumner for orders. [*O.R.*, XIX, Part 1, p. 326.]

After a quick terrain appreciation, continue driving to a STOP sign at the "T" intersection. The Piper Farm is in the valley ahead. TURN LEFT and drive to the first parking area, near the Sunken Road. Park and dismount. Use the asphalt walk and stairs to descend into the Sunken Road and then walk to your left (west) to the small grove near the top of the hill.

STOP 11A
The Bloody Lane. Situation at Approximately 10:30 AM.

Approximate Scale 1″ = 1666′

STOP 11-A, THE BLOODY LANE

You are now standing in one of the most celebrated corners of any Civil War battlefield—the Bloody Lane. This old sunken road was so washed by rain over the years that it formed a natural "breastwork" or "rifle pit," and was so described in many Union reports. Behind the sunken road a cornfield stood where the parking lot is today, while beyond, on the crest of the hill, was a conspicuous orchard.

D. H. Hill was responsible for the center of the Confederate line, extending from the Boonsborough turnpike (nearly three-quarters of a mile to the south) to the junction with the Hagerstown turnpike (about 0.2 mile to the west).

When Hooker commenced his attack, *Hill* sent three brigades north into the East Woods and the Cornfield. By the time the fighting flared up here the remnants of these brigades had been driven back and were reforming under *Colquitt* along the Sunken Road to the west. *Rodes'* brigade held the Sunken Road from *Colquitt's* right to the bend near your present location. *G. B. Anderson's* brigade, which initially was deployed on Hill's right, astride the Boonsborough turnpike, moved by the left flank about 8:30 a.m. to occupy the sunken road from *Rodes'* right flank to a point about two-thirds of the way to the tower. Soon afterwards *R. H. Anderson's* division, which had followed *McLaws* from Harper's Ferry, advanced in column across the fields from the vicinity of *Lee's* headquarters to a position between the Piper farm and the Hagerstown Turnpike and subsequently was sent forward to support and extend *Hill's* line in the sunken road. *Anderson* was soon wounded and *Brig. Gen. Roger A. Pryor* assumed command of the division. For reasons that are not clear, no official reports of this battle from any commands in *Anderson's* division are contained in the *Official Records*.

Report of Maj. Gen. Daniel H. Hill, CSA, Commanding Division, Jackson's Corps, Army of Northern Virginia

My ranks had been diminished by some additional straggling, and the morning of the 17th I had but 3,000 infantry. I had, however, twenty-six pieces of artillery of my own and near fifty [five?] pieces of *Cutts'* battalion, temporarily under my command. Positions were selected for as many of these guns as could be used; but all the ground in my front was completely commanded by the long-range artillery of the Yankees on the other side of the Antietam, which concentrated their fire upon every gun that opened and soon disabled or silenced it. . . .

It was now apparent that the Yankees were massing in our front, and that their grand attack would be made upon my position, which was the center of our line. I sent several urgent messages to *General Lee* for re-enforcements, but before any arrived a heavy force . . . advanced in three parallel lines, with all the precision of a parade day, upon my two brigades. . . . [*O.R.*, XIX, Part 1, pp. 1022–23.]

Report of Brig. Gen. R. E. Rodes, CSA, Commanding Brigade, D. H. Hill's Division, Jackson's Corps, Army of Northern Virginia

My brigade was not engaged until late in the forenoon. About 9 o'clock I was ordered to move to the left and front to assist *Ripley, Colquitt,* and *McRae,* who had already engaged the enemy, and I had hardly begun the movement before it was evident that the two latter had met with a reverse, and that the best service I could render them and the field generally would be to form a line in rear of them and endeavor to rally them before attacking or being attacked. *Major-General Hill* held the same view, for at this moment I received an order from him to halt and form line of battle in the hollow of an old and narrow road just beyond the [Piper] orchard, and with my left about 150 yards . . . east of the Hagerstown road. In a short time a small portion of *Colquitt's* brigade formed on my left, and I assumed the command of it. This brought my left to the Hagerstown road. *General [G. B.] Anderson's* brigade, occupying the same road, had closed up on my right.

A short time after my brigade assumed its new position, and while the men were busy improving their position by piling rails along their front, the enemy deployed in our front in three beautiful lines, all vastly outstretching ours, and commenced to advance steadily. Unfortunately, no artillery opposed them in their advance. *Carter's* battery [at the tower] had been sent to take position in rear, by me, when I abandoned my first position [immediately west of the tower], because he was left without support, and because my own position had not then been fully determined. Three pieces, which occupied a fine position immediately on my front, abandoned it immediately after the enemy's skirmishers opened on them.

The enemy came to the crest of the hill overlooking my position, and for five minutes bravely stood a telling fire at about 80 yards, which my whole brigade delivered. They then fell back a short distance, rallied, were driven back again and again, and finally lay down just back of the crest, keeping up a steady fire, however. In this position, receiving an order from *General Longstreet* . . . I endeavored to charge them with my brigade and that portion of *Colquitt's* . . . on my immediate left. The charge failed, mainly because the Sixth Alabama Regiment, not hearing the command, did not move forward with the others, and because *Colquitt's* men did not advance far enough. That part of the brigade which moved forward found themselves in an exposed position, and, being outnumbered and unsustained, fell back before I could . . . get the Sixth Alabama to move. Hastening back to the left, I arrived just in time to prevent the men from falling back to the rear of the road we had just occupied. It became evident to me then that an attack by us must, to be successful, be made by the whole of *Anderson's* brigade, mine, *Colquitt's*, and any troops that had arrived on *Anderson's* right. My whole force at this moment did not amount to over 700 men. . . .

About this time I noticed troops *[R. H. Anderson]* going in to the support of *[G. B] Anderson* or to his right, and that one regiment and a portion of another, instead of passing on to the front, stopped in the hollow immediately in my rear and near the orchard. As the fire on both sides was, at my position at least, now desultory and slack, I went to the troops referred to and found that they belonged to *General Pryor's* brigade. Their officers stated that they had been ordered to halt there by somebody, not *General Pryor.* Finding *General Pryor* in a few moments, and informing him as to their conduct, he immediately ordered them forward.

Returning toward the brigade, I met *Lieutenant-Colonel [J. N.] Lightfoot*, of the Sixth Alabama, looking for me. Upon his telling me that the right wing of his regiment was being subjected to a terrible enfilading fire, which the enemy were enabled to deliver by reason of their gaining somewhat on *Anderson*, and that he had but few men left in that wing, I ordered him to hasten back, and to throw his right wing back out of the old road. . . .

The right wing of the 6th Alabama stood at the bend in the sunken road: the 2nd North Carolina of *G. B. Anderson's* brigade held the road from the bend to the Roulette lane, with the rest of *Anderson's* brigade prolonging the line about two-thirds of the way to the tower. The brigades of *Wilcox* and *Wright*, of *R. H. Anderson's* division, extended the line to the tower while the rest of the division occupied the cornfield and the Piper Orchard.

Obviously *Rodes* hoped that by refusing his right wing and deploying it on the high ground behind the sunken road he could more effectively resist the advance of Richardson's Union division, which had come up to the left of French and from the high ground immediately to the north of the tower could enfilade this portion of *Rodes'* line.

Report of Brig. Gen. Rodes, continued.

Instead of executing the order . . . *[LTC. Lightfoot]* moved briskly to the rear of the regiment and gave the command, "Sixth Alabama, about face; forward march." *Major Hobson,* of the Fifth, seeing this, asked him if the order was intended for the whole brigade; he replied, "Yes," and thereupon the Fifth, and immediately the other troops on their left, retreated. I did not see their retrograde movement until it was too late for me to rally them, for . . . just as I was moving on after *Lightfoot,* I heard a shot strike *Lieutenant Birney* . . . immediately behind me. Wheeling, I found . . . that he had been struck in the face. . . . He could walk after I raised him, though he thought a shot or piece of shell had penetrated his head just under the eye. I followed him a few paces, and watched him until he had reached a barn, a short distance to the rear, where he first encountered some one to help him. . . . As I turned toward the brigade, I was struck heavily by a piece of shell on my thigh. At first I thought the wound was serious, but finding, upon examination, that it was slight, I again turned toward the brigade, when I discovered it . . . retreating in confusion. I hastened to intercept it at the Hagerstown road. I found, though, that with the exception of a few men . . . not more than 40 in all, the brigade had completely disappeared from this portion of the field. This small number, together with some Mississippians . . . and North Carolinians, making in all about 150 men, I rallied and stationed behind a small ridge leading from the Hagerstown road eastward toward the [Piper] orchard . . . and about 150 yards in rear of my last position. . . .

In this engagement the brigade behaved very handsomely and satisfactorily, and, with the exception of the right wing of the Sixth Alabama (where *Colonel [John B.] Gordon,* while acting with his customary gallantry, was wounded desperately, receiving five wounds), had sustained almost no loss until the retrograde movement began. It had, together with *Anderson's* troops, stopped and foiled the attack of a whole corps of the enemy for more than an hour, and finally fell back only when, as the men and officers supposed, they had been

ordered to do so. We might have been compelled to fall back afterward (for the troops on my right had already given way when we
began to retreat), but . . . for the unaccountable mistake of *Lieutenant-Colonel Lightfoot*, the retreat would not have commenced at this
time, if at all. . . .

My force at the beginning of the fight was less than 800 effective
men. The loss was . . . 203. [*O.R.*, XIX, Part 1, pp. 1036–38.]

Writing forty years later, the commander of the Sixth Alabama
remembered vividly the fighting at this spot before he was wounded and
his successor had failed to comprehend *Rodes'* intent.

*Reminiscences of Col. John B. Gordon, CSA, Sixth Alabama, Rodes'
Brigade, D. H. Hill's Division, Jackson's Corps, Army of Northern
Virginia*

The day was clear and beautiful, with scarcely a cloud in the sky.
The men in blue . . . formed in my front, an assaulting column four
lines deep. The front line came to a "charge bayonets," the other lines
to a "right shoulder shift." The brave Union commander, superbly
mounted, placed himself in front, while his band in rear cheered
them with martial music. It was a thrilling spectacle. The entire force,
I concluded, was composed of fresh troops from Washington or some
camp of instruction. So far as I could see, every soldier wore white
gaiters around his ankles. The banners above them had apparently
never been discolored by the smoke and dust of battle. Their gleam-
ing bayonets flashed like burnished silver in the sunlight. With the
precision of step and perfect alignment of a holiday parade, this
magnificent array moved to the charge, every step keeping time to the
tap of the deep-sounding drum. . . .

Mars is not an aesthetic god. . . . Every act and movement of the
Union commander in my front clearly indicated his purpose to dis-
card bullets and depend upon bayonets. He essayed to break through
. . . by the crushing weight and momentum of his solid column. It
was my business to prevent this. . . . To oppose man against man . . .
was impossible; for there were four lines . . . to my one. . . . My first
impulse was to open fire upon the compact mass as soon as it came
within reach of my rifles, and to pour into its front an incessant hail-
storm of bullets during its entire advance across the broad, open
plain; but . . . that plan, . . . was rejected because, during the few
minutes required for the column to reach my line, I could not hope

to kill and disable a sufficient number of the enemy to reduce his strength to an equality with mine.

The only remaining plan was . . . . to hold my fire until the advancing Federals were almost upon my lines, and then turn loose a sheet of flame and lead into their faces. I did not believe that any troops on earth, with empty guns in their hands, could withstand so sudden a shock. . . . All horses were sent to the rear, and my men were at once directed to lie down upon the grass and clover. They were quickly made to understand, through my aides and line officers, that the Federals were coming upon them with unloaded guns; that not a shot would be fired at them, and that not one of our rifles was to be discharged until my voice should be heard from the centre commanding "Fire!". . . . I would stand at the centre, watching the advance, while they were lying upon their breasts with rifles pressed to their shoulders, and . . . they were not to expect my order to fire until the Federals were so close upon us that every Confederate bullet would take effect.

There was no artillery at this point upon either side, and not a rifle was discharged. The stillness was . . . oppressive, as in close order, with the commander still riding in front, this column of Union infantry moved majestically to the charge. . . . Some of my impatient men asked permission to fire. "Not yet. . . . Wait for the order."

Soon they were so close that we might have seen the eagles on their buttons; but my . . . eager boys still waited for the order. Now the front rank was within a few rods of where I stood. . . . With all my lung power I shouted "Fire!"

My rifles flamed and roared in the Federals' faces. . . . The effect was appalling. The entire front line, with few exceptions, went down in the consuming blast. The gallant commander and his horse fell in a heap near where I stood—the horse dead, the rider unhurt. Before his rear lines could recover from the terrific shock, my exultant men were on their feet, devouring them with successive volleys. Even then these stubborn blue lines retreated in fairly good order. . . .

The result, however . . . did not satisfy the intrepid Union commander. Beyond the range of my rifles he reformed his men into three lines, and on foot led them to the second charge, still with unloaded guns. This advance was also repulsed; but again and again did he advance in four successive charges . . . with . . . bayonets. Finally his troops were ordered to load. He drew up in close rank and easy range, and opened a galling fire upon my line. . . . The fire . . . at close quarters now became furious and deadly. . . . I was not at the front when . . . the awful carnage ceased, but one of my officers long afterward assured me that he could have walked on the dead bodies of my men from one end of the line to the other. . . . The statement did not greatly exaggerate the shocking slaughter. [General John B. Gordon, *Reminiscences of the Civil War* (New York: Charles Scribner's Sons, 1903), pp. 84–88.]

Report of Brig. Gen. Nathan Kimball, USA, Commanding First Brigade, Third Division, II Corps, Army of the Potomac

My brigade . . . was formed into line of battle on the left of General Sedgwick's division, and in the third line, Generals Weber's and Morris' forming the first and second lines. In this position I moved directly forward about three-fourths of a mile, when General Weber encountered the enemy's pickets and drove them back, and soon came upon the enemy in force, posted in a strong position in an orchard, corn-field, ditches, and upon the hill-sides. At this moment, in obedience to your order, I moved my brigade forward and formed my line in front on the left of General Weber. My right wing, consisting of the Fourteenth Regiment Indiana Volunteers . . . and the Eighth Regiment Ohio Volunteers . . . was posted on the hill-side in front of the [Piper] orchard, their left resting on a lane running in the direction of Sharpsburg [Roulette lane]; my left wing, consisting of the Seventh Regiment Virginia Volunteers . . . and the One hundred and thirty-second Regiment Pennsylvania Volunteers . . . resting on an extension of the same line, their right resting on the [Roulette] lane . . . and their left extending toward the creek.

Directly on my front, in a narrow road running parallel with my line, and, being washed by water, forming a natural rifle-pit between my line and a large corn-field, I found the enemy in great force, as also in the corn-field in rear of the ditch. As my line advanced to the crest of the hill, a murderous fire was opened upon it from the entire force in front. My advance farther was checked, and for three hours and thirty minutes the battle raged incessantly, without either party giving way. The enemy, having been re-enforced, made an attempt to turn my left flank by throwing three regiments [probably from Wright's brigade, near the tower] forward entirely to the left of my line, which I met and repulsed, with loss, by extending my left wing, Seventh Virginia and One hundred and thirty-second Pennsylvania, in that direction. Being foiled in this, he made a heavy charge on my center, thinking to break my line, but was met by my command and repulsed with great slaughter. I then, in turn, ordered a charge, which was promptly responded to, and which resulted in driving the enemy entirely from the ditches, etc., and some distance into the corn-field beyond. In this charge my command captured about 300 prisoners. . . .

At this time a brigade of General Richardson's division [Meagher] advanced to my relief on the left of my line, securing that flank from further assaults. In the mean time, the line on my right having been abandoned, the enemy [3rd Arkansas and 27th North Carolina] made an attempt to turn that flank, and by that to gain my rear, and succeeded in gaining a corn-field directly on my right. To repulse them, a change of front was made by the Fourteenth Indiana and Eighth Ohio Volunteers, which resulted in driving the enemy from my right, and restored the line, which was afterward occupied by Smith's division of General Franklin's corps.

For four hours and a half my command was under most galling fire, and not a man faltered or left the ranks until the field was left . . . in our possession, those who were sent with the wounded to the rear quickly returning to their places in line. For three and a half hours of this time we were upon the field, and maintained our position without any support whatever. My men having exhausted all their ammunition, the fight was maintained for some time with the supplies stripped from the bodies of their dead and wounded comrades. . . .

The battle was fought under your own eye, general, and I need not tell you how terrible was the conflict. The loss in my command [631 killed and wounded, 8 missing] is a lasting testimony of the sanguinary nature of the conflict, and a glance at the position held by the rebels tells how terrible was the punishment inflicted on them. The corn-fields on the front are strewn with their dead and wounded, and in the ditch first occupied by them the bodies are so numerous that they seem to have fallen dead in line of battle, for there is a battalion of dead rebels. [*O.R.*, XIX, Part 1, pp. 193, 327–28.]

Report of Lieut. Col. Vincent M. Wilcox, USA,
One Hundred and Thirty-Second Pennsylvania Infantry,
First Brigade, Third Division, II Army Corps

We were brought under fire a little before 8 o'clock, and although ours was a new regiment, not yet organized a month and never before in sight of the enemy, still they behaved like veterans and well-disciplined troops. We brought into action 750 men, and brought out 364, exclusive of officers. . . .

General, you directed me to hold the eminence in front of the rifle-pit at all hazards, and not to fall back until ordered by you, and I am happy to say that it was done, although at a fearful sacrifice. The men were supplied with 60 rounds of ammunition, and exhausted their supply, and took the cartridges from the dead and wounded, and kept up the fire against the enemy. He tried upon several occasions to outflank us, but the sure and deadly aim of our men drove him back to his rifle-pits in disorder. . . . When our men were nearly exhausted of strength and ammunition, you directed me to fix bayonets and charge upon the rifle-pits, but at this moment the Irish Brigade [Meagher] came up and joined our men in the charge. They drove the enemy from their stronghold. . . . [O.R., XIX, Part 1, p. 331.]

You should now proceed to STOP 11-B, which is by the metal markers across the road from the tower. If you walk up the 'Bloody Lane,' you will see at once how well concealed were the men of *G. B. Anderson's* brigade until Kimball broke through the place vacated by the 5th and 6th Alabama regiments, and Richardson's division beyond the tower. The upended cannon barrel is where *Brig. Gen. G. B. Anderson* was mortally wounded. What he was doing here is obvious—it was the only place along his battle line where he could see anything.

Should you prefer to drive, you can park at the tower. If you have time, a walk to the top of the tower would give you an excellent view of the surrounding terrain and especially of the ridges east of the Antietam where the Union artillery found a commanding position.

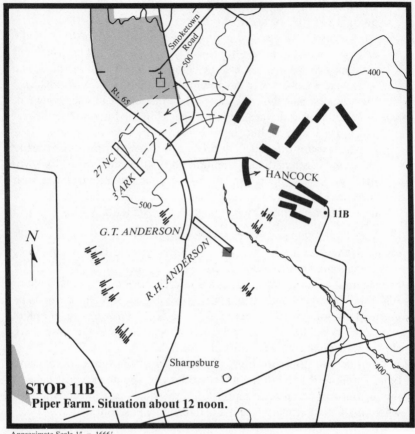

STOP 11B
Piper Farm. Situation about 12 noon.

Approximate Scale 1″ = 1666′

STOP 11-B, THE PIPER FARM

Report of Col. R. T. Bennett, CSA, Fourteenth North Carolina Infantry, Commanding [G. B.] Anderson's Brigade, D. H. Hill's Division, Jackson's Corps, Army of Northern Virginia

The command of this brigade devolved upon me after the disabling and death of the ranking officers. . . . The enemy, soon after the [sunken] road had been taken by *Anderson's* brigade, came into the field in front of us from the direction of the locality of *Garland's* brigade. Their advance was beautiful in the extreme, and great regularity marked their column. As the center was unmasked by the right and left flanks, this precision of movement was preserved by the lines until a space not exceeding 50 yards separated the combatants. Then . . . a well-directed fire sent them in disorder some 50 paces rearward. Recovering, however, they charged our position with the same result . . . with the addendum of wild confusion. The bravery of a field officer apparently checked the spreading symptoms of panic, and once more their courage was brought to the test. Poor return, indeed, they made for the gallantry of their leader. Confusion that seemed remediless followed.

At this juncture the colonel commanding gave orders for bayonets to be fixed, preparatory to an advance of the line. However, two fresh columns of the enemy were seen double-quicking to the relief of the shattered ranks of the foe, and stern necessity bade us be satisfied with simple holding of our ground. During all this time the Fourth Brigade appeared perfectly self-possessed. . . .

Shortly after, . . . word came for the command to keep a lookout on the extreme right. While directing ourselves to that point, masses of Confederate troops in great confusion, portions of *Major-General Anderson's* division as we then knew, for the Sixteenth Mississippi [*Featherston's* brigade] and Second Florida [*Pryor's* brigade] of that command, coming to our succor, broke beyond the power of rallying after five minutes' stay. In this stampede . . . the Fourth North Carolina State Troops and Thirtieth North Carolina troops participated.

The hour of 1 p.m. had arrived. *Anderson's* division had gone to the rear. Two regiments (Fourth and Thirtieth) of our own brigade were missing. The dark lines of the enemy had swept around our right, and were gradually closing upon the ground of *Rodes'* brigade. They having gone to resist the lines in front was an easy task, to contend against front and rear attacks we were totally inadequate, and the bare alternative of retreat was presented. The command was ordered to make the retreat by the right-oblique, with frightful loss in some regiments. . . . The task was achieved. The command was reformed at the road leading to Sharpsburg, and participated in all the skirmishes of the afternoon.[*O.R.*, XIX, Part 1, pp. 1047–48.]

In reading the following reports, it would be helpful to keep in mind that the 14th North Carolina held that portion of the sunken road where it was joined by the Roulette lane, and the 30th North Carolina was at the right of the line, about where *Brig. Gen. Anderson* was wounded.

Report of Captain A. J. Griffith, CSA, Commanding Fourteenth Regiment, North Carolina Troops, Anderson's Brigade, D. H. Hill's Division, Jackson's Corps

The regiment . . . formed line of battle [in front of Sharpsburg]. . . . About 8 o'clock received orders to move by the left flank, passing through a corn-field into an old road; filed to the left, and took position in front of the enemy . . . well protected by banks. The enemy advanced immediately, and a heavy fire opened on both sides. At this position it drove the enemy back three times, disorganizing their lines, with heavy loss.

About 11 o'clock received orders from the right that a new line of the enemy was advancing in the rear. The regiment fell back to a road [Hagerstown turnpike] and took position behind a stone fence, losing many men while changing position. Having but few men, it rallied with other regiments and drove the enemy back, and remained in line in front of the enemy until late at night; then marched a short distance to the rear to rally. . . .

The casualties were 213 killed, wounded, and missing, including *Col. R. T. Bennett*, blown up by a shell (severely shocked). [*O.R.*, XIX, Part 1, p. 1050.]

Report of Maj. William W. Sillers, CSA, Thirtieth
North Carolina Infantry, Anderson's Brigade,
D. H. Hill's Division, Jackson's Corps

Our line was formed in a road which, by the wear of travel, had been let down to the depth of a foot or more into the earth. In front of the right wing of our regiment, and at a distance of not more than 50 paces, there was a ravine which, extending diagonally to the left, gradually narrowed down the level space in front until in front of the extreme left of the Thirtieth there was not more than 30 paces of level ground.

Our position was taken, I suppose, about 8.30 a.m. In the space of half or three-quarters of an hour the enemy made his appearance, crossed the ravine, and began his advance up the hill. A well-directed fire broke his line and drove him back.

Up to this time, as far as the eye could reach to the right (300 yards), there was no support to our brigade; but about this time *Brigadier-General Wright's* brigade came up. The enemy continued to make his appearance, first on one hill, then another, but always at long range. The line was ordered to advance, and halted on the edge of the ravine. Here a hot fire was kept up for a few minutes. Soon the line was ordered to take its first position, and did so. In a very short time *Colonel Parker* passed me, retiring, seriously wounded, from the field. From this time, about 11.30 a.m., the regiment was under my command.

A desultory fire was kept up for some time, the enemy making demonstrations in front of the brigade on our right. Our fire at this point was not very effective, the range being too great and a fence intervening. Soon my attention was called to our right, which was again unsupported. Almost immediately my attention was called to the opposite flank (the left), which was uncovered as far as I could see. I sent a captain to the left to see if any one was there, and he reported no one. I then gave the order to fall back. We retired about 300 yards. Here we made a stand. Twice we advanced from this point, and twice we fell back to it. A short time before sunset the enemy advanced. We joined a charge against them and drove them so effectually that they did not appear again. In our last position we were under a pretty severe fire from artillery. . . .

The regiment before the fight numbered about 250, all told. We lost . . . a total of 76. I brought off from the fight 159. [*O.R.*, XIX, Part 1, pp. 1051–52.]

Maj. Gen. Israel B. Richardson, USA, commanding the First Division in the Second Army Corps, was mortally wounded in the fight for the Sunken Road and the Piper Farm, so his perspective of what happened is not known. He was replaced early in the afternoon by Brig. Gen. Winfield S. Hancock, commanding the First Brigade, Second Division, of VI Army Corps, which had just arrived upon the field. McClellan, who was in the area of the East Woods at that time, directed Hancock in person to take command of Richardson's division "and to command the center of our forces." [*O.R.*, XIX, Part 1, p. 407.] His report of events here is the most complete available.

Report of Brig. Gen. Winfield S. Hancock, USA, Commanding First Division, II Corps, Army of the Potomac

About 9.30 o'clock a.m. . . . the division . . . crossed the Antietam at the ford constructed by our engineers; then moved forward on a line nearly parallel to the creek, and formed line of battle by brigades in a ravine behind the high ground overlooking Roulette's house, the Second Brigade [Meagher] . . . on the right . . . the Third [First] brigade . . . [Caldwell], on his left and the [Third] brigade commanded by Colonel Brooke . . . in the rear. Meagher's brigade immediately advanced, and soon became engaged with the enemy, posted to the left and in front of Roulette's house. This brigade continued its advance under a heavy fire nearly to the crest of the hill overlooking Piper's house, the enemy being posted in strong force in a sunken road directly in its front.

A severe and well-sustained musketry contest then ensued, which, after continuing until the ammunition was nearly expended, this brigade, having suffered severely . . . was by direction of General Richardson relieved by the brigade of General Caldwell which had remained until this time in support. Caldwell's brigade advanced to within a short distance of the rear of Meagher's brigade. The latter then broke by companies to the rear, and the former by companies to the front, and in this manner passed their respective lines. Caldwell's brigade immediately advanced to the crest over-looking the sunken road and about 30 yards distant from it, and at once became engaged in a most desperate contest, the enemy then occupying that position in great strength, supported by other troops in their rear. . . . At this time Colonel Brooke's brigade formed a second line in support of Caldwell's brigade . . . Meagher's brigade retiring to the rear to replenish . . . ammunition, having received an order to that effect from General Richardson.

The enemy [27th North Carolina and 3rd Arkansas] having pierced the troops on the right of Roulette's house . . . Colonel Brooke . . . immediately led three regiments in that direction, and formed line of battle on the crest in front of Roulette's house and inclosures, sending one regiment . . . to dislodge the enemy, who had then gained a foothold in the corn-field in rear of those buildings. The enemy was promptly driven out by this regiment. . . . The other two regiments . . . were then led by Colonel Brooke to the support of General Caldwell's brigade, forming line on the same crest with it . . . a vacant space having been made in the line owing to the fact that the Fifth New Hampshire Volunteers had been moved to the left . . . to prevent a flank movement by the enemy toward our left. . . . A spirited contest arose between [this] . . . regiment and a force of the enemy, each endeavoring to be the first to gain the high ground to the left. . . .

The enemy was re-enforced by fresh troops during the contest, his first line having been driven off the field. Finally an advance was made from this position to Piper's house by the brigade of Caldwell and the two regiments under Colonel Brooke, under a heavy fire of musketry and artillery, the enemy having a section of brass pieces in the front firing grape and a battery to the right throwing shell. This advance drove the enemy from the field and gave us possession of the house and its surroundings—the citadel of the enemy at this position of the line, it being a defensible building several hundred yards to the rear of the sunken road. . . . This having been accomplished, the musketry firing at this point ceased. . . .

Having possession of Piper's house, by direction of General Richardson the line was withdrawn a short distance of take position on a crest, which formed a more advantageous line. Up to this time the division was without artillery, and in taking up the new position it suffered severely from artillery fire, which could not be replied to. A section of Robertson's battery of horse artillery (brass pieces) . . . then arrived on the ground and did excellent service. Subsequently a battery of brass guns of Porter's [V] corps . . . also arrived and was posted on the same line. A heavy fire then ensued between the enemy's artillery and our own, ours finally retiring, being unable to reach the enemy, who used rifled guns, ours being smooth-bores.

General Richardson was severely wounded, about this time, while . . . personally directing the fire of one of our batteries. General

Meagher's brigade having refilled their cartridge-boxes, returned . . .
and took its position in the center of the line. . . . Early in the
afternoon, after General Richardson had been removed, . . . I was
directed to take command of his division by Major-General McClellan in person. . . . My instructions were to hold that position. . . . I
found the troops occupying one line of battle in close proximity to
the enemy, who was then again in position behind Piper's house. The
Fourteenth Connecticut . . . and a detachment from the One hundred and eighth New York, under command of Col. Dwight Morris,
were in reserve, the whole command numbering about 2,100 men,
with no artillery. . . . I felt able . . . to hold the position as . . .
instructed . . . but was too weak to make an attack, unless an advance
was made on the right, as I had no reserves and the line was already
enfiladed from its forward position by the enemy's artillery in front of
our right wing, which was screened from the fire of our artillery on
the right by a belt of woods [West Woods]. . . .

Affairs remained in this position during the night. . . . Our loss
was . . . 207 killed, 940 wounded, 16 missing; total 1,163. [*O.R.*, XIX,
Part 1, pp. 277–81.]

*Report of Lieut. Gen. James Longstreet, CSA, Commanding
Army Corps, Army of Northern Virginia*

From this moment our center was extremely weak, being defended by but part of *Walker's* division and four pieces of artillery;
Cooke's [27th North Carolina] regiment, of that division, being without a cartridge. In this condition, again the enemy's masses moved
forward against us. *Cooke* stood with his empty guns, and waved his
colors to show that his troops were in position. The artillery played
upon their ranks with canister. Their lines began to hesitate, soon
halted, and after an hour and a half retired. Another attack was
quickly made a little to the right of the last. *Captain Miller,* turning
his pieces upon these lines and playing upon them with round shot
over the heads of *R. H. Anderson's* men, checked the advance, and
Anderson's division, with the artillery, held the enemy in check until
night. [*O.R.*, XIX, Part 1, p. 840.]

Report of Maj. Gen. Daniel H. Hill, CSA,
Commanding Division, Jackson's Corps

There were no troops near, to hold the center, except a few hundred rallied from various brigades. The Yankees crossed the old road which we had occupied in the morning, and occupied a corn-field and orchard in advance of it. They had now got within a few hundred yards of the hill which commanded Sharpsburg and our rear. Affairs looked very critical. I found . . . [*Boyce's* South Carolina] battery concealed in a corn-field and ordered it to move out and open upon the Yankee columns. . . . It moved out most gallantly, although exposed to a terrible direct and reverse fire from the long-range Yankee artillery across the Antietam. A caisson exploded, but the battery unlimbered, and with grape and canister drove the Yankees back.

I was now satisfied that the Yankees were so demoralized that a single regiment of fresh men could drive the whole of them in our front across the Antietam. I got up about 200 men, who said they were willing to advance to the attack if I would lead them. We met, however, with a warm reception, and the little command was broken and dispersed. . . . *Colonel Iverson*, Twentieth North Carolina; *Colonel Christie*, Twenty-third North Carolina [and] *Captain Garrett*, Fifth North Carolina [all from *Garland's* brigade] . . . had gathered up about 200 men, and I sent them to the right to attack the Yankees in flank. They drove them back a short distance, but in turn were repulsed. These two attacks, however, had a most happy effect. The Yankees were completely deceived by their boldness, and induced to believe that there was a large force in our center. They made no further attempt to pierce our center, except on a small scale. . . .

General Pryor had gathered quite a respectable force behind a stone wall on the Hagerstown road, and *Col. G. T. Anderson* had about a regiment behind a hill immediately to the right of this road. A Maine regiment [7th Maine, Third Brigade, Second Division, VI Corps] came down to this hill wholly unconscious that there were any Confederate troops near it. A shout and a volley informed them of their dangerous neighborhood. The Yankee apprehension is acute; the idea was soon taken in, and was followed by the most rapid running I ever saw.

The night closed in with our troops in the center, about 200 yards in rear of the position held in the morning. . . . The skulkers and cowards had straggled off, and only the bravest and truest men of my division had been left. . . . Hunger and exhaustion had nearly unfitted these brave men for battle. Our wagons had been sent off across the river on Sunday, and for three days the men had been sustaining life on green corn and such cattle as they could kill in the fields. In charging through an apple orchard . . . with the immediate prospect of death before them, I noticed men eagerly devouring apples. . . . The loss [in the division] in two battles, out of less than 5,000 engaged . . . was nearly two-thirds of the entire force. . . . 2,316 reported killed and wounded. . . .

Our artillery . . . could not cope with the superior weight, caliber, range, and number of the Yankee guns; hence it ought only to have been used against masses of infantry. On the contrary, our guns were made to reply to the Yankee guns, and were smashed up or withdrawn before they could be effectually turned against massive columns of attack. An artillery duel between the Washington Artillery and the Yankee batteries across the Antietam on the 16th was the most melancholy farce in the war. [*O.R.*, XIX, Part 1, pp. 1024–26.]

Return to your car and follow the road as it proceeds past the tower and winds east and south. Note the steeply rolling, cross-compartmented terrain.

Because of the nature of this terrain, because McClellan obviously had no intention of attacking this portion of the Confederate line in any strength, and also because *Lee* received urgent demands to send re-enforcements to meet pressures elsewhere, this portion of the line was lightly held. Throughout much of the morning a battery occupied the high ground immediately south of the tower. *Lee* massed his artillery on the hills to your right front—the old Sharpsburg cemetery and, across the Boonsborough turnpike, the site of the more recent National Cemetery.

East of the Antietam, Sykes' division of the Fifth Corps was in position immediately south of the Boonsborough pike and behind the hills overlooking the creek. Brig. Gen. Alfred Pleasonton, commanding the Cavalry Division of the Army of the Potomac, was directed soon after the commencement of Hooker's attack, to cross the Antietam with his cavalry and horse batteries "to some suitable position beyond the bridge." He advanced four batteries to the prominent ridge on your left, supported by a battalion of U.S. regular infantry. These guns fired for two hours in support of Union forces attacking *Hill* in the Sunken Road. Withdrawing to resupply their ammunition, the horse artillery returned to the ridge, this time supported by four additional battalions of infantry from Sykes' division.

*Report of Brig. Gen. Alfred Pleasonton, USA, Commanding
Cavalry Division, Army of the Potomac*

The fight was then renewed with increased vigor . . . the enemy's
batteries being soon driven from their position in front of us. At the
same time a heavy column of dust could be seen moving behind the
Sharpsburg Ridge toward Sumner's left. I directed the fire of the
batteries into this dust, and soon the development of the enemy's line
of battle, fully a mile long [probably *R. H. Anderson's* division], could
be seen bearing down upon Richardson's division on Sumner's left,
then commanded by Hancock. . . . The enemy's batteries were also
playing heavily upon this division. . . . I directed the fire of some
eighteen guns upon the enemy's line . . . for twenty minutes, when
we had the satisfaction of seeing this immense line first halt, deliver a
desultory fire, and then break and run to the rear in the greatest
confusion and disorder. A section of Tidball's battery was immediately advanced to the crest of a hill several hundred yards to the front.
. . . a most favorable position for operating on a battery then in full
play upon the center of Sumner's line. The fire from this section
contributed in no small degree toward silencing this battery. [*O.R.*,
XIX, Part 1, pp. 211–12.]

When you reach the STOP sign at the Boonsborough pike (Maryland #34), you will be about in the middle of the line of *G. B. Anderson's*
Confederate brigade before it moved northward to its position in the
Sunken Road. Later the 2nd and 10th battalions, US infantry, advanced to
approximately this position to take possession of some hay-stacks in the
field across the road. Skirmishers from this force reached the fence bordering "a lane running at right angles to the pike," – your present location.

Cross Maryland 34 and continue on the Park road. You may want to
pause at the top of the hill to read Col. B. C. Christ's report of his troubles
as he endeavored to attack Confederate infantry and artillery located in
what is now the National Cemetery to your right.

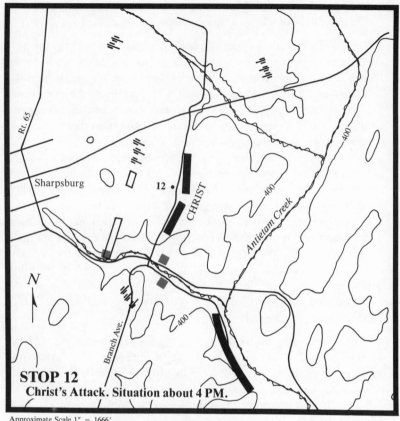

Sharpsburg

Rt. 65

12 •

CHRIST

Antietam Creek

400

400

400

N

Branch Ave.

STOP 12
Christ's Attack. Situation about 4 PM.

Approximate Scale 1″ = 1666′

STOP 12

Report of Col. Benjamin C. Christ, USA, Fiftieth Pennsylvania Infantry, Commanding First Brigade, First Division, IX Army Corps

During the afternoon I crossed the [Burnside] bridge and marched to the right, and parallel with the stream, for several hundred yards. I here deployed the Seventy-ninth New York Volunteers as skirmishers, supported by the [rest of the brigade] . . . and then moved forward in front of the enemy's battery (heavily supported by infantry), in the rear of a corn-field, on the right of the road. On reaching the crest of a hill, about 350 yards in front of the battery, I discovered that my support on my left had not come up. Deeming my force alone inadequate for the attack on both artillery and infantry, I was obliged to halt until supported on my left.

While halting under cover from the enemy directly in front, he opened a battery on my left which commanded my whole line . . . and for thirty minutes we were under a most severe fire of round shot, shell, grape, and canister, and suffered severely. It was impossible to move forward . . . (no place in the neighborhood that afforded any cover) and the alternative presented itself either to retire from a good position . . . or to wait patiently until some demonstration on the left would compel [the enemy] . . . to change the direction of his fire. . . . I could not get under cover without retiring at least 250 yards, in full view of the enemy, and if there would have been the least confusion the men might have retreated in disorder, and exposed a larger and more disordered front to his fire. . . . I chose the former. . . .

A demonstration on the left compelled the enemy to change the direction of his fire, and my supports coming, we moved to the front, where we engaged the enemy on his left, and in about one hour succeeded in driving both his artillery and infantry from the position. I charged on the battery with the Seventeenth Michigan Regiment . . . supported by the Fiftieth Pennsylvania and Twenty-eighth Massachusetts Volunteers, but when within 100 yards of his guns (and while he was covered by a hill which prevented my advance column from shooting either his horses or their riders), he limbered up his pieces and retired. I did not deem it prudent to advance after his artillery had retired, for . . . the woods were lined with his sharpshooters, and I would only have exposed my command to their fire without gaining

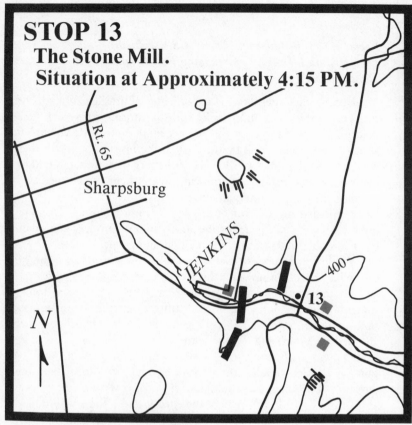

Approximate Scale 1" = 1000'

anything. I retired with my charging party to my line of battle, and maintained my position until ordered to take another farther down and near the bridge, where the men slept on their arms for the night. [*O.R.*, XIX, Part 1, pp. 438–39.]

Continue to the markers just short of the overpass above the Sherrick House (marked with a prominent Park Service sign on the left side of the road). Since this is a one-way road, you can stop here if you pull over well to the side on the hard surface.

STOP 13, THE STONE MILL

The stone house and mill in the ravine on your right are mentioned in several reports. The road to your left, on the other side of the overpass, leads to the Burnside bridge, and was a dangerous avenue of advance for Union troops of Willcox's division as they fought their way up the ravine some distance beyond this point.

Report of Brig. Gen. Orlando B. Willcox, USA, Commanding First Division, IX Army Corps

My orders . . . were to take the right of the corps in the attack on Sharpsburg.

After crossing the bridge, the road turns sharply to the right, runs up a stream about 200 yards, then to the left along an open hollow or ravine, which winds along to the village, overlooked by heights to the right and left. Once on the heights, the country is rolling and intersected with field fences, many of which are stone. The enemy's sharpshooters were posted behind these fences as well as hay-stacks, which also, with orchards and corn-fields, served to conceal their lines. A battery of field guns also commanded the road and hollow down to the river, and the whole plateau above was swept by cross-fire of artillery. Christ's brigade was . . . drawn up on the crest on the right of the road, his left resting near the road. . . .

The Second Brigade, under Colonel Welsh, formed on the heights to the left [south] of the road. . . . My division now formed part of a line which Generals Burnside and Cox were commanding, and all moved forward about 3 o'clock. We were under fire from the moment a man appeared at the crest of the plateau or crossed the hollow. [*O.R.*, XIX, Part 1, p. 430.]

Report of Col. Thomas Welsh, USA, Forty-fifth Pennsylvania Infantry, Commanding Second Brigade, First Division, IX Army Corps

In compliance with verbal instructions from Brigadier-General Willcox, I moved my whole command over a steep hill, immediately charging the enemy and driving them rapidly in the direction of Sharpsburg, my troops advancing to the edge of the town and capturing the rebel *Captain Twiggs* and several soldiers.

Discovering that we had advanced beyond our supporting forces on our right, and . . . left, I withdrew my command to an orchard directly on the left of Colonel Christ. . . . My command was exposed for several hours to a tremendous cross-fire from the artillery of the enemy, as well as a direct fire from their infantry and riflemen in our front, yet they advanced with steadiness and rapidity, driving the enemy at all points. . . . I had great difficulty in restraining the ardor of my troops, who seemed anxious to charge through the town and capture the batteries beyond. [*O.R.*, XIX, Part 1, p. 441.]

Report of Col. F. W. McMaster, CSA, Seventeenth South Carolina Infantry, Evans' Brigade, Hood's Division, Longstreet's Corps

In the afternoon [Tuesday, September 16], by order of *Colonel Stevens*, I took my regiment and the Holcombe Legion, in all about 100 men, and moved forward about half a mile to support the skirmishers of *Jenkins'* brigade and of a Georgia regiment.

About 1 o'clock Wednesday . . . the skirmishers were driven in, and, with the assistance of *Captain Twiggs* (a most noble and gallant officer), of the First Georgia Regiment [*G. T. Anderson's* brigade, *Jones'* division], I succeeded in rallying 40 or 50 of the skirmishers, and formed them on my left. In a short time I was informed by a lieutenant of a Louisiana artillery company that a battery of the enemy had proved quite destructive to his battery, and that he would be forced to discontinue firing unless it was silenced. I immediately sent out about 25 volunteers, who silenced the battery of the enemy for some time.

About 3 p.m. a brigade of the enemy flanked my command on the right, and, after firing a few moments, the Holcombe Legion and a few of the Seventeenth Regiment, in spite of my efforts, broke and ran. I then ordered the remainder of my command to retire to an apple orchard, about 200 yards in rear, where, with 40 or 50 men, made up mostly of my regiment and a few Georgians and Palmetto Sharpshooters, I fought the enemy for half an hour or more. Being flanked on both sides, I retired to a stone house adjoining, which I converted into a fort, and fought for some time, until *Drayton's* brigade, on the right, and *Jenkins'* brigade, on the left, had completely abandoned the ground, and the enemy had almost entirely surrounded my little band. When resistance on our part was entirely futile, I gave the order to retreat, and the enemy entered the house and took *Captain Twiggs* and 10 of my men prisoners in three min-

The Burnside Bridge. (B&L)

utes after I left. . . . After I retreated to Sharpsburg it was near night, and I could not assemble my men in sufficient numbers to do any good. As an evidence of the work we did this day, some of the men shot as high as 60 rounds. [*O.R.*, XIX, Part 1, pp. 945–46.]

As soon as you cross the overpass, turn left, following the marked route to Burnside's Bridge. This road was here at the time of the battle, and this was the ravine mentioned in the reports of Willcox and Welsh. At the time of the Civil War Centennial, a bypass was built to carry the traffic that normally would have used the famous Burnside bridge: you have just crossed over this bypass.

Remember that the road is now TWO-WAY. You will see the Antietam and the bridge on your left as you drive up the hill to the parking area on the heights. Park there and use the steps and walkway to approach the bridge. Cross the bridge and stand behind the stone wall to the left, facing the creek.

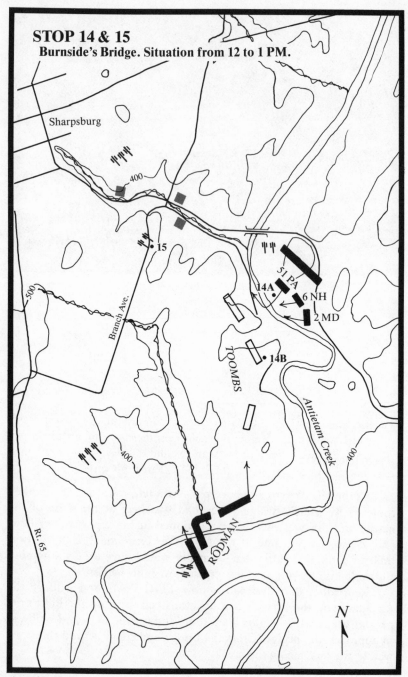

STOP 14 & 15
Burnside's Bridge. Situation from 12 to 1 PM.

Sharpsburg

400

51 PA

15

14A

6 NH

2 MD

Branch Ave.

TOOMBS

14B

500

Antietam Creek

400

400

Rt. 65

RODMAN

N

Approximate Scale 1″ = 1666′

STOP 14-A, BURNSIDE BRIDGE

You are now at one of the most photogenic sites of the Civil War. At the time of the battle the road ran between the post and rail fence and the creek. Quarry pits along the crest of the hill to the west overlooking the bridge served as field fortifications for the men of *Brig. Gen. Robert Toombs'* brigade, enabling them to command the approach to the bridge by the road, while Confederate batteries on nearby hills and also on the heights overlooking Sharpsburg were sited to cover any approach along the banks from the north.

Brig Gen. Jacob D. Cox, who was entrusted with the difficult task of seizing the bridge, describes the military problem that confronted him:

> The valley in which the stream runs is quite narrow, the steep slope on the right bank approaching quite to the water's edge. On this slope the roadway is scarped, running both ways from the bridge end, and passing to the higher land above by ascending through ravines above and below; the other ravine being some 600 yards above the bridge, the turn about half that distance below. On the hillside immediately above the bridge was a strong stone fence running parallel to the stream. The turns of the roadway were covered by rifle-pits and breastworks, made of rails and stone, all of which defenses as well as the woods which covered the slope, were filled with the enemy's infantry and sharpshooters. Besides the infantry defenses, batteries were placed to enfilade the bridge and all its approaches. The crest of the first hill above the bridge is curved toward the stream at the extremes, forming a sort of natural *tete-de-pont*. The next ridge beyond rises somewhat higher, though with less regularity, the depression between the two being but slight, and the distance varying in places from 300 to 700 yards. [*O.R.*, XIX, Part 1, p. 424.]

McClellan wrote two official reports of the Maryland campaign, the first on October 15, 1862 and a second and far more detailed report dated August 4, 1863. Because he was superseded in command of the Army of the Potomac by Burnside on November 7, 1862, his initial report was not influenced by subsequent events and therefore is assumed to be a more reliable source for his perceptions at the time of the battle and particularly of events that occurred here.

Report of Maj. Gen. George B. McClellan, USA, Commanding the Army of the Potomac

Burnside's corps, consisting of Willcox's, Sturgis', and Rodman's divisions, and Cox's Kanawha division, was intrusted with the difficult task of carrying the bridge across the Antietam . . . and assaulting the enemy's right, the order having been communicated to him at 10 o'clock a.m.

The valley of the Antietam . . . near this bridge is narrow, with high banks. On the right of the stream the bank is wooded, and commands the approaches both to the bridge and the ford. The steep slopes of the banks were lined with rifle-pits and breastworks of rails and stones. These, together with the woods, were filled with the enemy's infantry, while their batteries completely commanded and enfiladed the bridge and ford and their approaches.

The advance of the troops brought on an obstinate and sanguinary contest, and, from the great natural advantages of the position, it was nearly 1 o'clock before the heights on the right bank were carried. At about 3 o'clock p.m. the corps again advanced, and with success, the right driving the enemy before it and pushing on nearly to Sharpsburg, while the left, after a hard encounter, also compelled the enemy to retire. . . . The enemy here, however, were speedily re-enforced, and with overwhelming masses. New batteries of their artillery also were brought up and opened. It became evident that our force was not sufficient to enable the advance to reach the town, and the order was given to retire to the cover of the hill which was taken from the enemy earlier in the afternoon. This movement was effected without confusion. . . . General Burnside had sent to me for re-enforcements late in the afternoon, but the condition of things on the right was not such as to enable me to afford them. [O.R., XIX, Part 1, p. 31.]

Report of Brig. Gen. Jacob D. Cox, USA, Commanding IX Corps

About 7 o'clock orders were received from General Burnside to move forward the corps to the ridge nearest the Antietam, and hold it, in readiness to cross the stream, carrying the bridge and the heights above it by assault. The command was moved forward in column as it had been formed the previous night, and promptly took position as directed, and the light artillery [5 batteries] was ordered to cover the movement. . . . Willcox's division was also brought up and held as a reserve.

About 9 o'clock the order was received to cross the stream. Immediately the Eleventh Connecticut Infantry . . . was detailed from Rodman's division to deploy as skirmishers and drive the enemy from the head of the bridge. The column on the right (Crook's brigade, of the Kanawha Division, supported by Sturgis' division) was ordered to march under cover of the Eleventh Connecticut, and attempt to carry the bridge by assault, deploying to right and left as soon as the bridge should be carried, and taking the heights above it. The column on the left (Rodman's division, supported by Ewing's brigade, of the Kanawha Division) was ordered to cross, if possible, by a ford about one third of a mile below the bridge, take the heights above it, and join the column crossing the bridge. . . .

In accordance with the order . . . the Eleventh Connecticut advanced to the stream and warmly engaged the enemy across it. Crook's brigade in moving forward was brought under so lively an infantry fire, as well as that of artillery, that it was forced to halt and open fire in return, and Sturgis' division, passing by the rear, came first to the bridge, and was ordered to cross under protection of the artillery fire. General Sturgis ordered forward the Second Maryland and Sixth New Hampshire, which charged at double-quick with fixed bayonets, but the concentrated fire upon the bridge forced them to fall back. After repeated brave efforts these regiments were withdrawn, and the Fifty-first New York and Fifty-first Pennsylvania, from the same division, were ordered up. [*O.R.*, XIX, Part 1, pp. 424–25.]

Report of Brig. Gen. Samuel D. Sturgis, USA, Commanding Second Division, IX Corps

The bridge was strongly defended . . . and the approaches to it exposed to a murderous fire from behind breastworks. The importance of carrying it without delay was impressed upon me by General Burnside, and I went in person to the vicinity of the bridge, and ordered the Second Maryland . . . and . . . Sixth New Hampshire, to move over at a double-quick and with bayonets fixed. They made a handsome effort to execute this order, but the fire was so heavy on them before they could reach the bridge that they were forced to give way and fall back.

Meantime orders arrived from General Burnside to carry the bridge at all hazards. I then selected the Fifty-first New York and Fifty-first Pennsylvania from the Second Brigade and directed them to charge with the bayonet. They started on their mission of death full of enthusiasm, and taking a route less exposed than the regiments which had made the effort before them, rushed at a double-quick over the slope leading to the bridge and over the bridge itself with an impetuosity which the enemy could not resist, and the Stars and Stripes were planted on the opposite bank at 1 o'clock p.m., amid the most enthusiastic cheering from every part of the field from where they could be seen. Having crossed the bridge, the Second Brigade filed to the right, the First Brigade to the left, and both moved up and occupied the high grounds at once, throwing out skirmishers on all sides, who soon became hotly engaged, yet held their ground, though with considerable loss on both sides.

The enemy had by this time been re-enforced, and had their batteries placed on still higher ground, and within 500 or 600 yards of our position, and all concentrated on it. Too weak to advance, we could only lie down and await re-enforcements, and here the troops displayed their heroism more, if possible, than on any former occasion, for the enemy opened with canister and grape, shell and railroad iron, and the vehicles of destruction fell like hail among them, killing and wounding large numbers and fairly covering us with dust, yet not a man left his place except to carry off his wounded comrade. [*O.R.*, XIX, Part 1, p. 444.]

The *Official Records* contain no reports from any of the regiments involved in efforts to storm the bridge. For vivid details it is necessary to resort to regimental histories written by survivors.

NAGLE'S ATTEMPT: *The Narrative of the Sixth New Hampshire First Brigade, Second Division, IX Corps*

The two regiments were formed in a field below where the road came down to the creek, and some sixty or seventy rods below the bridge. Here they were directly under the fire of the concealed enemy. The remainder of the brigade lay still farther down the stream, under cover of fences and corn-fields, too far away to support promptly the attacking column composed of . . . two small regiments . . . each numbering only about one hundred and fifty men.

The order of General Sturgis was to charge at once, so the

regiments formed in line by the flank, side by side. They fixed bayonets, and, moving at the double-quick, passed through a narrow opening in a strong chestnut fence—which there was no time to remove—and charged in the most gallant manner directly up the road to the bridge. As the attacking party, led by Colonel Griffin [6th New Hampshire], debouched from the field into the road, the rebels, from their intrenched position, redoubled the fury of their fire, sweeping the head of the column with murderous effect. Of the first hundred men who passed through the opening in the fence, at least nine tenths were either killed or wounded. Such sweeping destruction checked, of course, the advancing column, but the men sheltered themselves behind logs, fences, and whatever other cover they could find, and bravely held the ground already gained. [Captain Lyman Jackman, *History of the Sixth New Hampshire Regiment in the War for the Union,* Concord, New Hampshire: Republican Press Association, 1891, pp. 103–4.]

FERRERO'S ATTACK: *The Narrative of the 51st Pennsylvania, Second Brigade, Second Division, IX Corps*

As soon as [Brigadier General] Ferrero received the orders he vaulted into his saddle and commanded, "Attention, second brigade!" Quick as a flash the brigade was in line. He then rode up in front of the colors of the 51st Pennsylvania Volunteers and spoke to the men. . . . "It is General Burnside's special request that the two 51sts take that bridge. Will you do it?" The request was unlooked for, and the men had not had time to think of it, when Corporal Lewis Patterson, of Co. I, although a temperate man, exclaimed: "Will you give us our whiskey, Colonel, if we take it?" Col. Ferrero turned suddenly around to the corporal and replied, "Yes, by G—, you shall all have as much as you want, if you take the bridge . . . if . . . I have to send to New York to get it, and pay for it out of my own private purse. . . ."

After a few words in private by the regimental and brigade commanders, the 51st P. V. led the advance. Marching by the flank out to the road that went across the bridge, it turned its back to the bridge and proceeded in the opposite direction from the objective point up the road to the top of the hill. All this time the regiment was receiving volley after volley of musketry, grape and shell from the rebel forces, on the opposite side of the creek. On reaching the top of the hill the regiment received orders. As each company clears the fence the command is "by company into line," and as the companies

filed left through and over the fence, they complied with the order.
. . . After the right of the regiment reached a clump of bushes on the
top of the hill, the command to charge was given by Colonel
Hartranft.

In this field and a short distance from the base of the hill . . . a
stone wall ran parallel with the creek, and close to its edge, ending
abruptly at the abutment of the bridge. As the regiments made the
charge, the company commanders discovered that it would be an
impossibility for the two regiments to charge in a body across such an
exceedingly narrow structure; they therefore changed their course
from the entrance of the bridge to the stone wall along the creek.
After reaching it they laid under cover of the wall and opened a
terrific fire of musketry on the enemy, who were snugly ensconced in
their rude but substantial breastworks, in quarry holes, behind high
ranks of cordwood, logs, stone piles, etc., making it rather too hot a
place for the enemy to be in, and too close for further resistance.
They began to withdraw from their position. . . . The distance now
between the opposing forces was only the width of the creek and a
narrow wagon road on the enemy's side. . . .

Captain Allebaugh, who commanded Co. C (the color company), now resolved that the time had come to take the bridge, and
the regiment prepared for the final struggle. . . . Colonel Hartranft
gave the final orders. . . . As the regiment made the charge, Captain
Allebaugh led his company at double-quick towards a gateway leading out of the field into the road that crossed the bridge, but on
nearing the gate his company became the target of the concentrated
fire of the enemy. . . . His first lieutenant was struck down and his
men were falling at every step. He soon perceived his perilous situation and . . . made a short detour from the gate to the abutment of
the bridge, and rushed across the bridge—only himself, the three
color bearers, one color-guard and his first sergeant. . . . These six
were the first to cross the bridge, but the remainder of the regiment
followed close on their footsteps and so choked up the entrance to it
that a halt was necessarily made on the stone structure.

The enemy now deserted their works and scattered and scam-
pered over the hills like a huge drove of scared sheep. . . . The
stubbornly contested bridge was ours. . . . The ground from the
entrance on the road to the end of the bridge was strewn with the
heroic dead and wounded, the whole thing not occupying above
twelve minutes after leaving the wall, yet in that time no less than
twenty-nine were killed outright, and ninety-six wounded. . . . [The

51st New York lost 87 additional casualties.]

A short time elapsed after the bridge was taken before any other troops came forward to reinforce the two heroic regiments; during which time the 51st Pennsylvania stacked arms on a line parallel with the creek and about 10 feet from it. A few fires were then kindled by the men for the purpose of making a cup of coffee. . . . [Thomas H. Parker, *History of the 41st Regiment of Pennsylvania Volunteers*, Philadelphia: King and Baird, Printers, 1869, pp. 232–39.]

Report of Brig. Gen. Robert Toombs, CSA, Commanding Brigade, Jones' Division, Longstreet's Corps

Between 9 and 10 o'clock the enemy made his first attempt to carry the bridge by a rapid assault, and was repulsed with great slaughter, and at irregular intervals, up to about 1 o'clock, made four other attempts . . . all of which were gallantly met and successfully repulsed by the Twentieth and Second Georgia. . . . After these repeated disastrous repulses, the enemy, despairing of wresting the bridge from the grasp of its heroic defenders . . . turned his attention to the [lower] fords . . . and commenced moving fresh troops in that direction by his left flank. The old road, by the upper of the two fords . . . led over a hill on my right and in my rear, which completely commanded my position and all ingress and egress to and from it below the bridge. . . . This approach could have been very successfully defended by a comparatively small force, and it was for this purpose that I so . . . urgently asked the aid of a regiment on the day of the battle, not having another man available for that purpose.

Not being able to get any re-enforcements for the defense of these two fords, and seeing that the enemy was moving upon them to cross, thus enabling him to attack my small force in front, right flank, and rear, and my two regiments having been constantly engaged from early in the morning up to 1 o'clock with a vastly superior force of the enemy, aided by three heavy batteries, the commanding officer . . . of the Second having been killed in the action, and the only remaining field officer . . . being painfully wounded, and fully one-half of this regiment being killed or wounded, and the Twentieth having also suffered severely . . . and the ammunition in both regiments being nearly exhausted, and *Eubank's* battery having been withdrawn to the rear nearly two hours before, I deemed it my duty . . . to withdraw my command and place it in the position designated by you opposite the two lower fords, some half a mile to the right and front of your line of battle. [*O.R.*, XIX, Part 1, p. 890.]

Now walk up the path to the left of the far side of the bridge toward the heights, following the sign to the McKinley monument. You may want to pause here to read the inscription and contemplate the origins of battlefield immortality.

Then follow the dirt trail leading south, away from the parking area. This is the "old road" mentioned in Toombs' report. Proceed about 100 yards, until you approach the top of the hill and can find a break in the brush on your right that will allow you to look across the fields to the west. Note on the distant ridge a prominent green water-tower and the obelisk-shaped Zouave monument a bit to its right and on a closer ridgeline.

STOP 14-B, BURNSIDE'S ADVANCE

Having seized the bridge, the Ninth Corps moved forward to about this line and deployed in preparation for its assault on Sharpsburg. Rodman's division, coming toward you from Snavely's ford, would have deployed on the reverse slope in the fields immediately west of your position.

Keep in mind that neither officers nor men had any notion of the terrain on the other side of the ridge or "crest," as General Cox described it, to your west, or of what awaited them when the time came to advance. Nor would they have known that *A. P. Hill's* division was approaching the battlefield from Harper's Ferry and soon would be in position to advance in force against the Union left flank.

Report of Brig. Gen. Jacob D. Cox, USA, Commanding Ninth Army Corps, continued

Meanwhile General Rodman's division and the First Brigade of the Kanawha Division, under Colonel Scammon, had succeeded in crossing at the [Snavely] ford below, after a sharp engagement and under a heavy musketry and artillery fire, and successfully took the position assigned at the left of the line of the crest above the bridge. . . .

The stubbornly contested fight at the bridge having almost exhausted the ammunition and greatly fatigued the troops engaged, I sent a request to General Burnside that Willcox's division, which had been held in reserve on the left bank, might be sent over and take its place on the right front, putting Sturgis' division in reserve at the head of the bridge. This was immediately ordered by General Burnside, and General Willcox came promptly forward with his command. During the interval the enemy kept up an incessant cannonade, and, having the exact range of the valley and the ravines, his shells came in very fast, annoying us a good deal and causing numerous casualties, notwithstanding the men were kept lying on the ground near the crests of the hill while the changes in the line and the partially new formation after the arrival of Willcox's division were being made.

At about 3 o'clock, the necessary changes . . . having been completed, the order to advance was received from General Burnside, and the whole force, except Sturgis' division, was put in motion. General Willcox on the right, his whole division in line and supported by Colonel Crook, was ordered to move on Sharpsburg, which lay about a mile distant to the right of our front. General Rodman, supported by Colonel Scammon, was ordered to move in the same direction, first dislodging the enemy from his front, and then changing direction to the right, bringing his command *en échelon* on the left of General Willcox. The advance was partly covered by Simmonds', Muhlenberg's, Clark's, and Cook's batteries, the other batteries of the corps being in part out of ammunition, and part being necessarily kept in position on the commanding ground on the left bank of the stream.

The troops moved forward in perfect order and with great enthusiasm. On the right, General Willcox and Colonel Crook quickly repulsed the enemy and drove back their artillery, pushing victoriously forward nearly to the village. On the left, General Rodman and Colonel Scammon likewise advanced rapidly, driving the rebels before them.

The enemy, however, were manifestly in much greater force than ours, and massed their troops heavily on the extreme left. This necessarily made the line of march of our left wing diverge from the course intended, and opened a gap between it and the right, which it was necessary to fill up by the troops of the second line. Batteries were accumulated against us upon the semi-circular ridge in advance, and the advancing line was subject to a most trying and destructive cross-fire of artillery. The enemy now brought up still more fresh troops upon the left, and while General Rodman was making disposition to meet them by a change of front of a part of his command, he fell, desperately wounded by a ball through his breast. The loss of their commander at a critical period caused confusion in a portion of the division on the extreme left.

The Second Brigade of this division, Colonel Harland commanding, was forced to retire after an obstinate contest, in which they suffered terribly.

Colonel Scammon, of the Kanawha Division, being ordered to make dispositions of the brigade with him to oppose the rebel force on the left, caused the Twelfth and Twenty-third Ohio Regiments to execute a perpendicular change of front, which was done with precision and success, the other regiment of the brigade (Thirtieth Ohio) maintaining its proper front. The whole line was now engaged, the supports being brought to the front, except the reserve division of General Sturgis at the bridge. This was now ordered up, and came promptly, though much exhausted and weakened by its previous exertions. . . .

The mass of the enemy on the left still continued to increase; new batteries were constantly being opened upon us, and it was manifest the corps would, without re-enforcements, be unable to reach the village . . . since the movement could not be made to the right whilst the enemy exhibited such force in front of the extreme left, and the attack both to the right and left at once would necessarily separate the wings to such an extent as to imperil the whole movement unwarrantably.

The attack having already had the effect of a most powerful diversion in favor of the center and right of the army, which by this means had been able to make decided and successful advances, and no supports being at the time available for our exhausted corps, I ordered the troops withdrawn from the exposed ground in front to the cover of the curved hill above the bridge, which had been taken from the enemy earlier in the afternoon. This movement was effected shortly before dark, in perfect order and with admirable coolness and decision. . . .

The bravery and soldierly conduct of the men was most striking . . . when it is considered that for several days they had been marching and fighting, with scarcely any rest, by night or day, and the rapidity of the movement had prevented their having any regular supplies of food, the supply train being delayed at the rear by the advance of other troops. . . . I must [express] . . . my great satisfaction with the manner in which all the subordinate commands of the corps were handled. The movements were accurate as those of a parade, and the systematic order with which they were executed made the spectacle in the heat of the battle a grand and imposing one. . . . The casualties in the corps during the day were 2,222, of which . . . 123 [are] missing. [*O.R.*, XIX, Part 1, pp. 425–27.]

Walk back to your car and retrace your route to the overpass. At the STOP sign there, go straight ahead. Pull over into the turnout near the guns on your left.

STOP 15, JONES' DEFENSE

From here you can better appreciate the way that the Confederates utilized the terrain to compensate for lack of numbers. *Maj. Gen. D. R. Jones*, who commanded six brigades comprising about 2,430 men, was responsible for the defense of this sector. Initially *Walker's* division was deployed on the extreme Confederate right, supporting two batteries on hills slightly south and to the east of the farm at the southern end of this park road (Branch Avenue), but *Walker* had been ordered by *Lee* to move to the West Woods "soon after 9 a.m." to support *Jackson*. *Jones'* command was further reduced on the right when *Garnett's* brigade was detached to the front of Sharpsburg to support several batteries of artillery posted on the high ground on both sides of the Boonsboro pike. Thus when the IX Corps had crossed the Antietam and was deploying for its final assault, *Jones* had only the brigades of *Toombs, Kemper, Drayton*, and *Jenkins [Walker]* with which to defend the line from Sharpsburg to Snavely's ford.

Initially no Confederate infantry or artillery occupied this position. Two batteries were posted a short distance east of the Otto Lane that runs along the ridge some 400 yards to your left, in support of *Toombs'* regiments overlooking the Burnside bridge, and a third fired on the bridge from the field just east of Stop 14 B. The remaining three brigades at *Jones'* disposal and his only artillery that had not been left behind, *Brown's* battery, were deployed on the high ground some 500–600 yards to your right.

When Burnside's troops seized the bridge, the Confederate batteries east of your present position were withdrawn. *Brown's* battery was first moved forward to the high ground 150 yards behind the Otto house and then withdrawn to the higher ground about 50 yards to your right. Upon the advance of Willcox's division the battery was pulled back about 450 yards to anchor the right flank of *Drayton's* and *Kemper's* men, behind an adjacent stone wall.

By 4:20 p.m. this position had been overrun by Welsh's brigade and two of Crook's regiments in support hugged the other side of the stone wall. When *A. P. Hill's* division struck Burnside's left flank, these regiments filed off to the right and withdrew down the Burnside bridge road.

Report of Maj. Gen. D. R. Jones, CSA, Commanding Division, Longstreet's Corps, Army of Northern Virginia

Daylight of September 17 gave the signal for a terrific cannonade. . . . The heavy masses in my front – repulsed again and again in their attempts to force the passage of the bridge by the two regiments . . . comprising 403 men, assisted by artillery I had placed in position on the heights – were unable to effect a crossing. . . . The gallant Second and Twentieth [Georgia] having repulsed five separate assaults and exhausted their last round of ammunition, fell back, leaving the bridge to the enemy. Meanwhile *General A. P. Hill* had come up on my right and was effecting a junction with my line, several of his batteries already in position assisting mine in firing on the enemy, now swarming over the bridge.

Undeterred, except momentarily, by this fire, the enemy advanced in enormous masses to the assault of the heights. Sweeping up to the crest, they were mowed down by *Brown's* battery, the heroic commander of which had been wounded but a few moments before. They overcame the tough resistance offered by the feeble forces opposed to them, and gained the heights [to your right], capturing *McIntosh's* battery, of *General Hill's* command. *Kemper* and *Drayton* were driven back through the town. The Fifteenth South Carolina, *Colonel De Saussure*, fell back very slowly and in order, forming the nucleus on which the brigade rallied. *Jenkins'* brigade held its own, and from their position in the orchard [northeast of the Stone Mill] poured a destructive fire on the enemy. *General Toombs*, whom I had sent for, arriving from the right with a portion of his brigade, and part of the Eleventh Georgia Regiment, was ordered to charge the enemy. This he did most gallantly, supported by *Archer's* brigade, of *Hill's* command, delivering fire at less than 50 yards, dashing at the enemy with the bayonet, forcing him from the crest, and following him down the hill. *McIntosh's* battery was retaken, and, assisted by other pieces which were now brought up to the edge of the crest, a terrific fire was opened on the lines of the enemy between the slope and the creek, which, finally breaking them, caused a confused retreat to the bridge. Night had now come on, putting an end to the conflict, and leaving my command in the possession of the ground we had held in the morning, with the exception of the mere bridge. [*O.R.*, XIX, Part 1, pp. 886–87.]

Report of Col. Joseph Walker, CSA, Commanding Jenkins' Brigade, Jones' Division, Longstreet's Corps

This brigade . . . took position in line of battle on an eminence in front of the town [the National Cemetery] and to the right of the turnpike. By order of *General Jones*, it moved late in the evening [of the 15th] across a ravine to the right, with *Kemper's*, *Garnett's*, and *Drayton's* brigades, where it remained under a heavy fire of shot and shell until 3 o'clock in the evening of the 17th, when it moved back, by order of *General Jones*, and occupied its first position in support of *Moody's* battery and a company of the Washington Artillery, both from Louisiana.

Here the brigade endured a terrific fire of shot and shell for some half hour, when, the ammunition of the artillery having been exhausted, it advanced some 400 yards to an apple orchard, under a heavy fire of artillery and small-arms. Perceiving the enemy in force in several positions, from any of which we were assailable, I threw out the First, Fifth, and Sixth Regiments South Carolina Volunteers to oppose him on the left, and the Palmetto Sharpshooters and the Second Regiment Rifles South Carolina Volunteers to meet him in the center and on the right. From this position we continued to pour a destructive fire into the ranks of the enemy, at short range, until he recoiled and retreated out of sight among the timber on Antietam Creek.

At this juncture, perceiving that the enemy had advanced three heavy columns some 400 yards in rear of the brigade and to the right across a ravine leading up from the creek, and was steadily driving back the brigades of *Generals Kemper* and *Drayton*, I moved this brigade into line parallel with the turnpike and ravine and near to the latter, and opened a destructive enfilade fire upon the enemy, which assisted materially in driving back his columns. Changing the front of the brigade again toward Antietam Creek, and at right angles to the turnpike and ravine, I threw forward a line of skirmishers to a fence near the timber on the creek, and bivouacked for the night. This position the brigade, alone and unsupported, held during the 18th, burying the dead and caring for the wounded, the skirmishers the meanwhile keeping up a brisk fire upon the enemy. [*O.R.*, XIX, Part 1, p. 907.]

STOP 16
A.P. Hill's Attack. Situation about 4:30 PM.

Approximate Scale 1″ = 1666′

Continue to follow Branch Avenue south and then west until you come to a STOP sign at a "T" intersection. Turn right and pull over immediately beside the guns.

As you drive along Branch Avenue, note the terrain to your left. From Stop 14-B there would have been no way to anticipate the compartmentalized terrain, which breaks up attack formations and offers numerous advantages to the defense. Each slight ridge represented an obstacle to be overcome and increased exposure to enemy fire.

In addition to a succession of lesser crests that must be negotiated, units on the Union left had also to pass through a 40 acre cornfield that lay pretty much in a hollow. Here they were attacked downhill by *Hill's* right brigade under *Gregg*, which immediately stopped all forward progress of Harland's brigade, on the left of Rodman's line, except for his right regiment, the 8th Connecticut, and made it impossible for Rodman to reinforce his other brigade, which had fought its way to the Monument that you see on the skyline to your right.

As you drive along Branch Avenue you will also see a farm on a comparatively level ridge directly ahead. This was where *Gregg's* brigade, followed by *Branch*, of *A. P. Hill's* division, deployed to strike Rodman's left flank in the 40 acre cornfield.

The old cornfield is to your left as you approach the right-hand turn on Branch Avenue. The low area now dotted with cedars was where Harland's brigade was stopped in its tracks.

STOP 16, A. P. HILL'S ATTACK

Having borne the heaviest part of the fighting at Harpers Ferry, *Maj. Gen. A. P. Hill's* division was left behind to parole about 11,000 prisoners and dispose of public property, including some 13,000 small arms, 73 guns and about 200 wagons. At 6:30 a.m. on the 17th he received *Lee's* order to move at once to Sharpsburg. Leaving one brigade behind to complete the removal of captured property, *Hill* had the rest of his division in motion within the hour and by 2:30 p.m. the head of his column had completed the 17 mile march and appeared along the Millers Sawmill road [which joins the Harpers Ferry Road about 200 yards behind you] and the adjoining fields to the north.

Report of Maj. Gen. A. P. Hill, CSA, Commanding Division, Jackson's Corps, Army of Northern Virginia

Reporting in person to *General Lee*, he directed me to take position on our right. *Brig. Gen. D. R. Jones*, commanding our right, gave me such information as my ignorance of the ground made necessary.

My troops were rapidly thrown into position, *Pender* and *Brockenbrough* on the extreme right, looking to a road which crossed the Antietam near its mouth, *Branch*, *Gregg*, and *Archer* extending to the left and connecting with *D. R. Jones'* division. *McIntosh's* battery had been sent forward to strengthen *Jones'* right, weakened by troops withdrawn to our left and center. *Braxton's* battery . . . was placed upon a commanding point on *Gregg's* right; *Crenshaw* and *Pegram* on a hill to my left [your present position], which gave them a wide field of fire.

My troops were not in a moment too soon. The enemy had already advanced in three lines, had broken through *Jones'* division, captured *McIntosh's* battery, and were in the full tide of success. With a yell of defiance, *Archer* charged them, retook *McIntosh's* guns, and drove them back pell-mell. *Branch* and *Gregg*, with their old veterans, sternly held their ground, and, pouring in destructive volleys, the tide of the enemy surged back, and, breaking in confusion, passed out of sight. During this attack, *Pender's* brigade was moved from my right to the center, but the enemy were driven back without actively engaging his brigade. The three brigades of my division actively engaged did not number over 2,000 men, and these, with the help of my splendid batteries, drove back Burnside's corps of 15,000 men.

The Confederacy has to mourn the loss of a gallant soldier and accomplished gentleman, who fell in this battle at the head of his brigade — *Brig. Gen. L. O'B. Branch*, of North Carolina. He was my senior brigadier, and one to whom I could have entrusted the command of the division, with all confidence. . . . My loss was 63 killed, 283 wounded; total, 346. [*O.R.*, XIX, Part 1, p. 981.]

Report of Brig. Gen. James H. Lane, CSA, Twenty-eight North Carolina, Commanding Branch's Brigade, A. P. Hill's Division, Jackson's Corps

We left Harper's Ferry on September 17, and, after a very rapid and fatiguing march, recrossed the Potomac and reached Sharpsburg in time to participate in the fight. The entire brigade was ordered to the right, and, on reaching the field, the twenty-eighth was detached by *General A. P. Hill*, in person, and sent on the road to the left leading to Sharpsburg to repel the enemy's skirmishers, who were advancing through a field of corn. The rest of the brigade moved nearly at right angles to our line, and on the enemy's flank. The Thirty-third, Seventh, and Thirty-seventh [North Carolina] were the regiments principally engaged. They fought well, and assisted in driving back three separate and distinct columns of the enemy. The Eighteenth was not actively engaged. I was ordered about sunset, to rejoin the brigade, and on doing so ascertained that *General Branch* had been killed. It was after sunset when I assumed command of the brigade. I found the Seventh, Thirty-seventh, and Thirty-third posted behind a stone fence, and the Eighteenth sheltered in a hollow in rear. I ordered the Twenty-eighth to the left of the line, but the order was delivered to the Eighteenth, which was posted to the left behind a rail fence, a portion of it being broken back to guard against a flank movement. The Twenty-eighth was posted to the left of the Seventh, in the opening caused by the withdrawal of a few Georgia troops.

Although annoyed by the enemy's sharpshooters, we held our position until ordered to fall back, on the night of the 18th. [*O.R.*, XIX, Part 1, pp. 985–86.]

Report of Brig. Gen. Samuel McGowan, CSA, Commanding Gregg's Brigade, A. P. Hill's Division, Jackson's Corps

We made a forced march up the river, crossed the river at Boteler's Ford, a short distance below Shepherdstown, and arrived on the field of Sharpsburg in the afternoon . . . reaching the actual presence of the enemy at 3:40 p.m., which was not a moment too soon. . . . The general line of our army seemed to be in front of the town . . . facing east, with its right flank stretching toward the Potomac. The enemy were in front along the line of the Antietam River.

We came upon the field on the extreme right of our line, perhaps 2 miles from the Potomac. It was seen at once that a large force of the enemy (said to be Burnside's division) were in the act of sweeping down the Antietam and around our right, with the object, manifestly, of cutting off our army from the Potomac. The Light Division came from the proper direction and at the right moment to meet this column and drive it back across the Antietam.

Gregg's brigade was placed in position on the right. The Fourteenth South Carolina Volunteers . . . being the leading regiment, was thrown out to hold a position on the extreme right, being the point of our line nearest the Potomac. The enemy, checked in his flank movement, never got so far to our right, and consequently that regiment was not actively engaged. The First, Twelfth, and Thirteenth South Carolina Volunteers formed in line of battle, and were directed to enter the field to the left of the Fourteenth and drive back the enemy. This line advanced to the top of a hill in a [40 acre] cornfield, and there engaged the enemy, who appeared advancing in force upon the opposite hill, and held a fence in the ravine between the hills. They checked at once the advance of the enemy. *Colonel Edwards* [13th South Carolina], on the left, took up a strong position behind a stone fence and held it. *Colonel Barnes* [12th South Carolina] advanced down the hill, and with a charge gallantly drove the enemy from the fence in front. He was, however, in a few moments flanked by a large body on the right and had to retire his regiment a short distance up the hill, the enemy immediately reoccupying the fence. *Colonel Barnes* soon returned to the attack, and upon the same ground charged with his fine regiment three times, and the last time drove them from the fence and up the hill beyond, with great slaughter.

In the mean time *Colonel Hamilton* [1st South Carolina], feeling a heavy pressure upon his right, obliqued his regiment in that direction and gallantly drove them, clearing the front and at the same time covering the right of *Colonel Barnes*. A heavy body now appeared on the right of *Colonel Hamilton*, and *Captain Perrin*, commanding *Orr's* Rifles, was sent out to sweep the field in that direction. He led his regiment up a hill, discovered the enemy in the hollow beyond, dispersed them at once, and held the position, which was somewhat in advance of the general line. Thus, the columns which were enveloping the right of our army were driven back at all points, and, at the last moment, Sharpsburg made a victory for the Confederate arms. [*O.R.*, XIX, Part 1, pp. 987–88.]

Continue your tour. At 0.25 mile, just as you reach the first house on your right, you will see an asphalt walk leading to the HAWKINS' ZOUAVE MONUMENT. Park at the turnout. At the time of the battle, a stone fence lined both sides of the road from near this point to the edge of Sharpsburg. This was the final Confederate defensive position.

Dismount and walk along the National Park path on your right to the monument. When the path takes a sharp turn to the left, STOP and consult the text. You should be facing east.

STOP 17, THE HIGH WATER MARK

You are now at the 'high-water mark' of the battle of Antietam. The leading elements of Burnside's attack carried to the monuments that you see to your left, forcing remnants of the brigades of *Drayton*, *Kemper*, and *Toombs* back to the road where you left your car. In the field a short distance to your right, *McIntosh's* battery fought desperately against heavy odds.

STOP 17-A

Report of Lieut. Col. R. L. Walker, CSA, Commanding Artillery Battalion, A. P. Hill's Division, Jackson's Corps

My command arrived upon the field at about 3 p.m., and went immediately into action. *Captain McIntosh* took position to the right and in rear of *General Toombs'* brigade. . . . Here he was hotly encountered by several batteries of the enemy, to whom he responded vigorously until his attention was attracted by the steady and formidable advance of the enemy's infantry upon his position, the infantry on the left not supporting him. The enemy continued to advance, in defiance of his rapid and effective fire, until within 60 yards of his guns, when *Captain McIntosh* was forced to withdraw his men, horses, and limbers. By this time *General Archer's* brigade had formed in line of battle to the rear of the battery, and, before the enemy reached the guns, charged and drove them back in great confusion. [*O.R.*, XIX, Part 1, p. 984.]

In the 1890's, while the US Army was trying to establish, identify, and mark the battle lines at various stages in the conflict, thousands of veterans of both armies participated in the process, either by visiting the site with the US Commissioners responsible for developing the battlefield, or through correspondence. The recollections of a young artilleryman trying to help determine 34 years after the event where his battery had been overrun while trying to repel Burnside's final attack is as detailed as if it had been written shortly after the battle.

Narrative of J. L. Napier, CSA, Pee Dee South Carolina Artillery (McIntosh's Battery), A. P. Hill's Division, Jackson's Corps

Blenheim, S.C., Nov. 30, 1896.

Col. D. G. McIntosh
Dear Col:-

I have been requested as a member of the Pee Dee Artillery . . . to answer a letter of inquiry that you wrote. . . . The battle of Sharpsburg is as vividly before my mind as though it occurred but yesterday. If you remember we left Harpers Ferry at 9 a.m. and by a forced march were carried to the battle field. . . . between 3 and 4 p.m. Just before entering the fight, the 12 pound Howitzer . . . and all the Caissons were pulled out to the left of the road and were not carried into the fight. . . . The Napoleon and two rifle guns were carried forward (the Napoleon in front) at a trot and put in position to the right of a large farm house [on Millers Sawmill Road]. From the forced march the line had straggled badly. When we reached the position to the right of the house, *Jake Blake* was the only other member of our gun detachment (the Napoleon) that was up; *Blake* and *Lieutenant Zimmerman* unlimbered the gun, *Blake* cut the fuse, I carried the charge and *Zimmerman* rammed it home.

By this time the rest of the detachment were up. The gun was trained on a column of Federal Soldiers about 3 or 400 yards away who were moving rapidly to the left. The Napoleon gun fired 2 shots and one of the rifle guns 1 shot from this position. If you remember, *Captain Adams* of *Gen. A. P. Hill's* staff came up at a gallop and ordered you to report to *Gen. Kemper* on the left of the "corn field" which was on the left of the house we were on the right of. The guns were limbered up, Cannoneers mounted and we were carried at a gallop.

When we reached the corn field we found a plank fence and I think there was a ditch on both sides of it. I know there was one on the side next to the road and we had to go about a 100 yards and enter the field at a bridge and gate. Just as we reached the gate a Battery of 4 guns came out and we had to wait for them to get out before we could enter. If you remember, just at this time one of the men said to you "Captain, see those men are leaving there, we had better not go in;" your reply was "I am ordered to go in there and go to fighting." After entering the field we obliqued to the right and the gun I belonged to took position about 50 yards from the cornfield, the rifles on the left. I remember very distinctly we had only 21 men all told, including the officers, with the guns in this fight.

Well, to go on with the details. On taking position we saw a few men, not more than a 100, to the left and in our front, huddled together behind a rail fence firing for all they were worth. In less than a minute after we took position the enemy captured these men, I was told it was *Kemper's* brigade, or what was left of them. We found the enemy about 2 or 300 yards from our front swarming up the hill like Pharaoh's Locusts. Their column extended further to the right than we could see and about 200 yards to our left. The guns began firing double charges of canister; there was a large U.S. flag just in front of the left gun at which our fire was directed. It was shot down 3 times when the enemy stopped and laid down. The flag staff was stuck apparently in the ground and remained flying for a few moments when it was shot down again and we saw it no more.

In the meantime *Toombs'* Georgia Brigade came up at the double quick and formed in the ditch at the fence about 100 yards in our rear. The enemy began their advance again and came to within 50 or 75 yards of our guns when you ordered the men to leave the guns and save themselves. Very near all the horses were killed and there was not enough of them to pull the guns off anyway. *Bill Gilchrist* carried his limber out past the gap where we entered with only 2 horses, with the right forefoot shot off the off horse; the others were left with their teams dead . . .

As soon as we got behind *Toombs'* men they began firing. We were ordered to go to *Hall's* gun and caissons, you remaining with *Toombs* and *Kemper, Drayton* with you. After firing a few minutes *Toombs* charged and you sent *Drayton* after us. The men were mounted on the gun and caissons and carried back at a gallop. When we reached the field again the enemy were about 400 yards away; the Howitzer joined the other guns in firing on them.

If I remember correctly a gun battery of the enemy took position about 400 yards from us and a little to our right and began shelling us. It was this battery which killed *Baxter Rollins* and wounded *Cooper* and *Coates*. I think most of the damage sustained by us was from this Battery. At dark we were moved to the rear, I think, about a mile.

The next morning we were sent back and took position a little to the left of where we fought the day before. Someone, I think it was you, counted the dead bodies and found 40 lying around their flag staff which was shot in two. . . . Just in front of where we took position was a ravine in which there was a wounded Union soldier. When asked, he said he was wounded by the Battery they were trying to capture. His thigh was broken. He said their loss was very heavy. He also said we had been charged by 3 New York Brigades who had just arrived on the field.

I am certain we checked the enemy long enough for *Toombs* to fill up the gap in which there were no other Confederate soldiers— how long the gap was I do not know. If you had not carried our guns forward and checked the enemy they would have broken through *Lee's* lines at that point. . . . I always thought we were of more service to *Gen. Lee's* army at this battle than at any other during the war. I believe the stand we made saved the army; we will never get credit for it I know, but I believe it is so all the same. . . .

I have written you a rambling account of the drama that we took part in at Sharpsburg and I have written a good many minor details thinking they might freshen your memory. You were a mature man at that time, I was a boy. My mind I guess was plastic and retained these things better, or perhaps I was worse scared than you and they were firmly fixed by fright. I am certain the incidents I give you are correct.

With many kind wishes for your future welfare, I am,
Your friend and comrade,
J. L. Napier

[J. L. Napier to Col. D. G. McIntosh, Nov. 30, 1896, Antietam Studies, Record Group 94. National Archives.]

Report of Brig. Gen. James J. Archer, CSA, Commanding Brigade, A. P. Hill's Division, Jackson's Corps

The next morning after the capture of Harper's Ferry, being too unwell for duty, I turned over the command of the Brigade to *Colonel Turney* (First Tennessee), under whom . . . it marched to the battle-field of Sharpsburg, while I followed in an ambulance. This was a long and fatiguing march; many of the men fell, exhausted from the march, by the way, so that when the four regiments of my brigade reached the battle-field there were only 350 men. I resumed command just as the brigade was forming into line on the ground assigned to it by *General Hill*, on the extreme left of his division, but not in sight of any of its other brigades. Marching by flank, right in front, along the Sharpsburg road, the brigade was halted and faced to the right, forming line of battle faced by the rear rank. *General Toombs* was in line on the same road about 300 yards to my left, with open ground in front.

In front of my position was a narrow corn-field about 100 yards wide, then a plowed field about 300 yards wide, on the opposite side of which was a stone fence. I moved forward, under a scattering musket fire, through the tall corn to the edge of the plowed field, when I found only the right regiment (the Fourteenth Tennesee) with me, the others having fallen back to the road. Some one had called out, "Fall back," which was mistaken for an order from me. I re-formed the line as rapidly as possible, and again moved forward against the enemy, posted in force behind the stone fence. In passing over the short distance of 250 yards from the corn-field, I lost nearly one-third of my already greatly reduced command, but it rushed forward alone at double-quick, giving the enemy but little time to estimate its small numbers, and drove him from his strong position. By this time it was nearly sunset. *General Branch's* brigade came down about thirty minutes after I reached the wall, and formed some 30 paces to my rear, when *General Branch* was killed, and *Colonel Lane*, assuming command of his brigade, moved it down to my left. [*O.R.*, XIX, Part 1, pp. 1000–1001.]

The Union regiment in front of *McIntosh's* battery at this location was in all probability the 8th Connecticut, which veered to its right [your left] in the small ravine in front of you to avoid the fire of *McIntosh's* guns and finally reached the plateau on your left, the position being marked by the nearer of the two monuments you can see there. The other two regiments of Harland's brigade never made it out of the 40 acre cornfield, where they were hit on the left flank by *Gregg's* brigade, *A. P. Hill's* division, losing 285 casualities of whom only 2 were listed as 'missing.' One of these regiments, the 16th Connecticut, had only been in service three weeks. These regiments were driven back to the ridge behind the cornfield, leaving the 8th Connecticut entirely unprotected on its left flank.

Report of Maj. J. Edward Ward, USA, Eighth Connecticut Infantry, Second Brigade, Third Division, IX Corps, Army of the Potomac.

About 4 o'clock p.m. [we] were ordered to advance to the support of General Willcox, on our right, who had been repulsed. We did so, and held our position far in advance, until ordered to retire by General Rodman, but not until we had lost over 50 percent of our regiment. The fire from artillery and musketry was very severe, the regiment receiving fire in front and on both flanks. The conduct of both officers and men was all that could be asked for. . . . I will notice particularly the conduct of Private Charles Walker, of Company D, who brought the national colors off the field after the sergeant and every corporal of the color-guard were either killed or wounded. Our loss was 34 killed, 139 wounded, and 21 missing; total, 194. [*O.R.*, XIX, Part 1, p. 455.]

STOP 17-B

Now follow the path to the imposing 9th New York (Hawkins' Zouaves) Monument. The 9th was one of three regiments in Fairchild's brigade, Rodman's division.

Report of Col. Harrison S. Fairchild, USA, 89th New York Infantry, Commanding First Brigade, Third Division, IX Corps.

The brigade . . . formed line of battle on the crest of the hill [Stop 14-B] . . . [and] remained firm in its position for nearly an hour, until ordered to advance. General Rodman then ordered us to advance to the support of General Sturgis' command. We continued to advance to the opposite hill under a tremendous fire from the enemy's batteries up steep embankments. Arriving near a stone fence, the enemy—a brigade composed of South Carolina and Georgia regiments [*Toombs'* brigade and probably *Drayton's*, which contained one regiment from South Carolina]—opened on us with musketry. After returning their fire, I immediately ordered a charge, with the whole brigade gallantly responded to, moving with alacrity and steadiness.

Arriving at the fence, behind which the enemy were awaiting us, receiving their fire, losing large numbers of our men, we charged over the fence, dislodging them and driving them from their position down the hill toward the village, a stand of regimental colors belonging to a South Carolina regiment being taken by Private Thomas Hare . . . Eighty-ninth New York Volunteers, who was afterward killed. We continued to pursue the enemy down the hill.

Discovering that they were massing fresh troops on our left, I went back, and requested General Rodman to bring up rapidly the Second Brigade [Harland] to our support, which he did, they engaging the enemy, he soon afterward falling badly wounded. It was then discovered that the enemy were moving up from the corn-field on our left to flank us, and I ordered the brigade to retire about 250 yards to the rear of the position we now held, which movement was executed in good order and without confusion. The large force advancing on our left flank compelled us to retire from the position, which we could have held had we been properly supported. We remained in this position until we were positively ordered to withdraw from the field, the officers and men regretting such a necessity. Thus ended one of the hardest contested battles of the day. [*O.R.*, XIX, Part 1, p. 451.]

The *Official Records* contains no report of this action from any of Fairchild's three regiments, which suffered 455 casualties among them. The heaviest hit was the 9th New York: the history of this regiment, written four years later, contains a stirring account of their charge to the crest of the hill.

Narrative of the 9th New York, First Brigade, Third Division, IX Corps

Eagerly did the men spring to their feet, and the alacrity with which they obeyed the order "First Brigade! Forward!" indicated the anxiety they had experienced to be delivered from the wearing suspense they were kept in all day.

As they reached the top of the [first] hill, they were openly exposed to the full sweep of the rebel batteries in front; and as they pushed on they left their fallen comrades by the score upon the ground. But no enemy was yet to be seen, and another elevation was before them. Fences and other obstructions were to be surmounted, and many fell in the various attitudes of climbing. When they had approached the second hill, they trampled over several brigades lying under protection of its favorable elevation. It seemed a secure place, none of the rebel batteries being able to reach it with their shell. Would the 9th seek its cover? The thought might have suggested a refuge in such an hour of peril as a secure retreat for . . . cowards.

The regiment hurried on, and soon reached the top of the second hill [a short distance *east* of Branch Avenue], where again they were forced to face the tornado of shot and shell, now augmented by a battery the rebels had placed far to the right, cutting the Union troops with a severe enfilading fire. The Zouaves . . . impetuously pressed onward. . . . Men fell at every step, but still "Forward!" was the shout preceding their war cry. . . . They passed down the descent that made a slight vale, and soon obtained the slope of the other hill, where a halt was ordered to gain a moment's breath for the final . . . struggle. . . . As far back as they could see, the track of the regiment was strewn with the slain . . .

The command "Forward!" was again given, and the 9th, in line with the whole division, once more advanced, ascending the third elevation which was but a gentle rise upon the main portion of the heights. Up to this time they had received the fire of artillery only . . . but as they arrived near the top of the ascent, several brigades of rebel infantry, which were posted behind the stone walls opened at once a galling storm of bullets upon them. . . . From the ranks of the 9th alone there fell, in the space of a few minutes, about 200 men killed and wounded. The walls in front fairly bristled with the muskets of the enemy. A scene of the wildest confusion took place when the Zouaves surmounted the wall. Some of the enemy begged for mercy on the spot, while others resisted with right good will, using the bayonet, for few in such close contact could get the chance to reload their pieces . . . The Zouaves now had it all their own way . . .

The enemy . . . were now upon a hill beyond. They had been heavily reinforced by troops thrown from their left, and the two forces now did but little more than look at each other. Had the Union troops again assaulted them in their new and strong position, they would undoubtedly have met with a bloody repulse, without the assistance of those idle brigades, which should have been used on the flank; and for this reason the left of the Federal forces fell gently back into a position where their artillery could be effectively used. . . .

The 9th bivouacked at night in the face of the enemy. . . . They numbered some 350 men less than in the morning. [J. H. E. Whitney, *The Hawkins Zouaves: Ninth New. York. Volunteers, Their Battles and Marches* (New York: 1866), pp. 143–49.

Officially the 9th New York lost 235 men in the assault. *O.R.*, XIX, Part 1, p. 197.]

Narrative of the USA, Co. G, 9th New York Volunteers, First Brigade, Third Division, IX Corps

Our knapsacks were left on the ground behind us. At the word a rush was made for the fences. The line was so disordered by the time the second fence was passed that we hurried forward to a shallow undulation a few feet ahead, and lay down among the furrows to re-form, doing so by crawling up into line. A hundred feet or so ahead was a similar undulation to which we ran for a second shelter. The battery, which at first had not seemed to notice us, now, apprised of its danger, opened fire upon us. . . . [and] depressed its guns so as to shave the surface of the ground. Its fire was beginning to tell. . . .

We lay there till dusk, . . . when the fighting ceased. During that hour, while the bullets snipped the leaves from a young locust-tree growing at the edge of the hollow and powdered us with the frag-ments, we had time to speculate on many things—among others, on the impatience with which men clamor, in dull times, to be led into a fight. We heard all through the war that the army "was eager to be led against the enemy." It must have been so, for truthful correspondents said so, and editors confirmed it. But when you came to hunt for this particular itch, it was always the next regiment that had it. The truth is, when bullets are whacking against tree-trunks and solid shot are cracking skulls like egg-shells, the consuming passion in the breast of the average man is to get out of the way. Between the physical fear of going forward and the moral fear of turning back, there is a predicament of exceptional awkwardness from which a hidden hole in the ground would be a wonderfully welcome outlet. [David L. Thompson, "With Burnside at Antietam," *Battles and Leaders*, vol. II, pp. 661–62.]

By this time the men of *Toombs* brigade who had fallen back from the Burnside bridge had been joined by his other two regiments, which had been detailed on the night of September 13 to protect *Longstreet's* wagon train and had just arrived at Sharpsburg. When all had replenished their cartridge-boxes from the ammunition train, *Maj. Gen. D. R. Jones* sent the brigade back into the fight.

Report of Brig. Gen. Robert Toombs, CSA, Commanding Brigade, Jones' Division, Longstreet's Corps

I immediately put my command in motion . . . and hastened with all speed to your [*Jones'*] position. On my arrival, I found the enemy in possession of the ground I was ordered . . . to occupy on your right. He had driven off our troops, captured *McIntosh's* battery (attached to *General Drayton's* brigade), and held possession of all the ground from the corn-field on your right down to the Antietam Bridge road, including the eastern suburbs of the town of Sharpsburg, all the troops defending it having been driven back and retired to the rear. . . .

I had instantly to determine either to retreat or fight. A retreat would have left . . . Sharpsburg and *General Longstreet's* rear open to the enemy, and was inadmissible. I, therefore, with less than one-fifth of the enemy's numbers . . . rapidly formed my line of battle in the [Harpers Ferry] road within 100 paces of the enemy's lines. While forming in the road, *Captain Troup*, my aide, on my extreme left rallied a portion of *General Kemper's* brigade, who were retiring from the field, attached it to my line of battle, and led them into action with conspicuous gallantry and skill.

As soon as possible, I opened fire upon the enemy's columns, who immediately advanced in good order upon me until he approached within 60 or 80 paces, when the effectiveness of the fire threw his column in considerable disorder, upon perceiving which I immediately ordered a charge, which, being brilliantly and energetically executed by my whole line, the enemy broke in confusion and fled. *McIntosh's* battery was recaptured and our position retaken within less than thirty minutes after the commencement of this attack. . . . The enemy fled in confusion toward the . . . bridge, making two or three efforts to rally, which were soon defeated by the vigorous charges of our troops, aided by *Captain Richardson's* battery, which I ordered up immediately upon the recovery of the heights, and . . . was rapidly placed in . . . action. . . .

Our loss in this last attack was unexpectedly small. Such was the heroic vigor and rapidity of the assault upon the enemy, he was panic-stricken; his fire was wild and comparatively harmless. [*O.R.*, XIX, Part 1, pp. 891–92.]

Return to your car and continue north on the Harpers Ferry road. Drive past one stop sign and turn right at the second (East Main Street—Maryland #34). Follow this street about 0.5 mile to the NATIONAL CEMETERY. You can parallel park along the street in front of the Cemetery.

Walk through the gates to the large monument in the center of the grounds.

STOP 18, REFLECTIONS

Reading the official reports at the previous stop reminds us, in words written by a distinguished British general after visiting another Civil War battlefield, "that in the chaos of battle things may not be what they seem to be and that two people participating in the same incident may view it very differently." [Brig. Gen. Sir Julian Thompson, Royal Marines, "Personal Impressions of the Chancellorsville Battlefield."]

Here, looking at this statue—so massive and grave that it almost reminds one of Russian monuments in East Berlin—other thoughts come to mind. Not only was the United States the first government to assume responsibility for burying its war dead in government cemeteries that receive perpetual care; the Civil War memorials also represent a break in the tradition that monuments were erected only for those who had commanded troops in great battles. After this war "at battlefields, in the town parks and public squares throughout the nation, there arose memorials to the common solider or to his regiment which had fought so bravely." [Wayne Craven, *The Sculptures at Gettysburg* (Published for the Gettysburg National Military Park: Eastern Acorn Press, 1982), p. 61.]

We are reminded too that battles are fought by young soldiers—men like *Napier* of *McIntosh's* battery and Thompson of the Hawkins Zouaves—who staunchly stand by their guns while confessing fears. The modern soldier inevitably finds himself wondering how officers could induce their men to stand in the ranks or advance in formation against such withering firepower. The answer lies not in official documents but in the human soul—and in their own experience of man.

These armies learned that part of the answer, at least, was to dig for cover. Antietam was the last battle fought between these two armies where at least one side did not resort to breastworks or entrenchments to save lives. The bloodiest single day in American military history forced this change in tactics.

The battle represents a turning point in strategy as well, for it encouraged President Lincoln to issue the Emancipation Proclamation, which changed the objectives and ultimately the nature of the war. Soldiers today are taught that war is an instrument of policy. When the policy changes, inevitably strategy must be revised if the nation is to wage war successfully. And with the Emancipation Proclamation all real hope for foreign recognition or intervention on behalf of the Confederacy disappeared.

A Union veteran, a former private of the 9th Army Corps who stood at this spot "many times" after the war, shares his private thoughts: we would not express them in his words, but the sensitive visitor will share his sentiments.

Where was then the dread chaos of War is now calm Peace and rustic simplicity; where was then the scream of shot and shell, grape, the bullet and the Minie, we heard that Sunday Bob White's mellow whistle, and saw the timid hare with his constant flag of truce; where were then death and wounds, the anesthetic and the knife, we heard the church bells ringing out "Peace on Earth and Good Will to men"—and we rode into the Cemetery, dismounted, and sat on a knoll and looked across the pretty hills and mountains and then down upon the quaint town of

Sharpsburg: "Buried here 4,006." These were all Federal soldiers. . . . and the Confederates lost quite as many. . . ." [Clarence F. Cobb, "The Maryland Campaign 1862: An address delivered before the Maryland Historical Society March 12th, 1882 (Washington, D.C.: Judd and Detweiler, Printers, 1891), p. 28.]

If you wish to sit beside Private Cobb on the knoll, walk past the monument to an earthen berm laid up against the south wall of the cemetery. From this site you have a commanding view of the south part of the battlefield.

In any case, as you return to your car, walk along the east wall of the cemetery. You should be able to see the Pry House, nearly 2 miles to the north-east, where McClellan anxiously observed Burnside's final attack and repulse.

Report of Maj. Gen. George B. McClellan, USA, Commanding the Army of the Potomac, continued.

The enemy here . . . were speedily re-enforced, and with over-whelming masses. New batteries of their artillery also were brought up and opened. It became evident that our force was not sufficient to enable the advance to reach the town, and the order was given to retire to the cover of the hill which was taken from the enemy earlier in the afternoon. This movement was effected without confusion and the position maintained until the enemy retreated. General Burnside had sent to me for re-enforcements late in the afternoon, but the condition of things on the right was not such as to enable me to afford them. . . .

With the day closed this memorable battle, in which, perhaps, nearly 200,000 [120,000] men were for fourteen hours engaged in combat. We had attacked the enemy in position, driven them from their line on one flank and secured a footing within it on the other. Under the depression of previous reverses we had achieved a victory over an adversary invested with the prestige of former successes and inflated with a recent triumph. Our forces slept that night conquerors on a field won by their valor and covered with the dead and wounded of the enemy.

The night, however, presented serious questions; morning brought with it grave responsibilities. To renew the attack again on the 18th or to defer it, with the chance of the enemy's retirement after a day of suspense, were the questions. . . . A careful and anxious survey of the condition of my command, and my knowledge of the enemy's force and position, failed to impress me with any reasonable certainty of success if I renewed the attack without re-enforcing columns. A view of the shattered state of some of the corps sufficed to deter me from pressing them into immediate action, and I felt that my duty . . . forbade the risks involved in a hasty movement, which might result in the loss of what had been gained the previous day. Impelled by this consideration, I awaited the arrival of my re-enforcements. . . .

During the 18th, orders were given for a renewal of the attack at daylight on the 19th. On the night of the 18th the enemy . . . suddenly formed the design of abandoning their line. This movement they executed before daylight . . .

The early and disgraceful surrender of Harper's Ferry deprived my operations of results which would have formed a brilliant sequence to the substantial and gratifying successes already related. Had the garrison held out twenty-four hours longer, I should in all probability have captured that part of the enemy's force engaged in the attack on the Maryland Heights, while the whole garrison, some 12,000 strong, could have been drawn to re-enforce me on the day of the decisive battle. . . . I would thus have been in a position to have destroyed the rebel army. . . . Had the besieging force on the Virginia side at Harper's Ferry not been withdrawn, I would have had 35,000 or 40,000 less men to encounter at the Antietam, and must have captured or destroyed all opposed to me. As it was, I had to engage an army fresh from a recent and . . . great victory, and to reap the disadvantages of their being freshly and plentifully supplied with ammunition and supplies. . . .

In the beginning of . . . September the safety of the National Capital was seriously endangered by the presence of a victorious enemy, who soon after crossed into Maryland and then directly threatened Washington and Baltimore . . . and threatened an invasion of Pennsylvania. The army of the Union, inferior in numbers, wearied by long marches, deficient in various supplies, worn out by numerous battles . . . first covered by its movements the important cities of Washington and Baltimore, then boldly attacked the victorious enemy in their chosen strong position and drove them back, with all their superiority of numbers, into the State of Virginia, thus saving the loyal States from invasion and rudely dispelling the rebel dreams of carrying the war into our country and subsisting upon our resources. [*O.R.*, XIX, Part 1, pp. 31–33].

McClellan, it might be added, was not asked to take any part in the ceremonies when the Antietam National Cemetery was dedicated on September 17, 1867, nor was he even invited to be present! [Douglas, *I Rode with Stonewall*, p. 177.]

Report of General R. E. Lee, CSA, Commanding the Army of Northern Virginia.

It was now nearly dark, and the enemy had massed a number of batteries to sweep the approaches to the Antietam, on the opposite side of which the corps of General Porter, which had not been engaged, now appeared to dispute our advance. Our troops were much exhausted and greatly reduced in numbers by fatigue and the casualties of battle. Under these circumstances it was deemed injudicious to push our advantage further in the face of fresh troops of the enemy, much exceeding the number of our own. They were accordingly recalled and formed on the line originally held by *General Jones*. While the attack on our center was progressing, *General Jackson* had been directed to endeavor to turn the enemy's right, but found it extending nearly to the Potomac, and so strongly defended with artillery that the attempt had to be abandoned. The repulse on the right ended the engagement . . .

The arduous service in which our troops had been engaged, their great privations of rest and food, and the long marches without shoes over mountain roads had greatly reduced our ranks before the action began. These causes had compelled thousands of brave men to absent themselves, and many more had done so from unworthy motives. This great battle was fought by less than 40,000 men on our side, all of whom had undergone the greatest labors and hardships in the field and on the march. Nothing could surpass the determined valor with which they met the large army of the enemy, fully supplied and equipped, and the result reflects the highest credit on the officers and men engaged. Our artillery, though much inferior to that of the enemy in the number of guns and weight of metal, rendered most efficient and gallant service throughout the day, and contributed greatly to the repulse of the attacks on every part of the line. *General Stuart*, with the cavalry and horse artillery, performed the duty intrusted to him of guarding our left wing with great energy and courage, and rendered valuable assistance in defeating the attack on that part of the line.

On the 18th we occupied the position of the preceding day, except in the center, where our line was drawn in about 200 yards. Our ranks were increased by the arrival of a number of troops, who had not been engaged the day before, and, though still too weak to assume the offensive, we awaited without apprehension the renewal of the attack. The day passed without any demonstration on the part of the enemy, who, from the reports received, was expecting the arrival of re-enforcements. As we could not look for a material increase in strength, and the enemy's force could be largely and rapidly augmented, it was not thought prudent to wait until he should be ready again to offer battle. During the night of the 18th the army was accordingly withdrawn to the south side of the Potomac, crossing near Shepherdstown, without loss or molestation. [O.R., XIX, Part 1, pp. 150–51.]

FIELD LOGISTICS IN THE CIVIL WAR

by
Lieutenant Colonel Charles R. Shrader

The American Civil War of 1861–1865 was the first large-scale modern war involving a continent-wide theater of operations. The numbers of men and quantities of materiel involved were unprecedented as were the distances over which the opposing armies moved and had to be supported. In the first four months of the war the Union army alone expanded to twenty-seven times its pre-war strength and by 1865 over one million men were enrolled. The costs were enormous as well; expenditures for the United States Army passed $1 billion per year for the first time in 1864–1865. Moreover, the Civil War saw the increased application of recent technological advances in transportation and communications. Although tactical mobility remained limited to the pace of the foot soldier and the horse, the railroad and steamboat greatly improved strategic mobility. Similarly, battlefield communications remained limited by line of sight and range of sound, but the overall control of armies in the field was improved dramatically by widespread use of the telegraph.

The logistical problems posed by the Civil War at every level were many and varied. The intricacies of national policy, industrial and agricultural procurement and distribution, and the detailed mobilization activities of the opposing governments as well as medical service have been discussed thoroughly elsewhere and need not detain us here. Less well-known are the details of how Civil War armies were actually supplied in the field and how the efficiency of such support, or the lack of it, influenced the outcome of battles, campaigns, and even the war itself. These are the details which we shall examine here.

Organization for Logistics

Civil War armies on both sides were forced to create or expand logistical structures and to develop new procedures as well as the trained personnel needed to support widespread military operations of tremendous scale. For the North the problems were primarily ones of expansion and coordination. The South, of course, had to build an army and its necessary supporting structures from scratch. In general, the Confederates adopted the basic institutions of the pre-war United States Army and recast them in a Southern mold. In both cases the development of efficient logistical support structures for the armies in the field required time as well as tremendous effort and expense. Confusion, failure, and waste preceded the emergence of lean and effective logistical organizations, and for the army of the Confederate States the overall lack of resources almost precluded the achievement entirely.

On 1 January 1861, the Regular Army of the United States consisted of 1,108 officers and 15,259 men organized into 19 regiments: 10 infantry, 4 artillery, 2 dragoon, 2 cavalry, and one of mounted riflemen. This army in the field was distributed in six geographical departments: East, West, Texas, New Mexico, Utah, and Pacific. The military department was the basic organizational unit for administrative and logistical purposes, and the commander of each department controlled his own logistical support with no intervening level between the departmental headquarters and the supply bureaus in Washington. During the war the number of departments increased, the boundaries changed, and it was not unusual to group several geographical departments under a military "division" headquarters.

In 1861 the highest level of the Army hierarchy was occupied by President Abraham Lincoln, the Commander-in-Chief. Secretary of War Simon Cameron, who was to be replaced in January 1862 by Edwin M. Stanton, reported directly to the President and was responsible for the administration of the Army. There also existed an extra-legal General-in-Chief, Winfield Scott, who presumed to direct the field operations of the Army from his headquarters in New York City. The aged Scott was eventually replaced in turn by Generals George B. McClellan, Henry C. Halleck, and Ulysses S. Grant.

Reporting directly to the Secretary of War and responsible for various aspects of the Army's administration were the bureau chiefs or heads of staff departments: the Adjutant General, the Inspector General, the Paymaster General, the Judge Advocate General, the Chief of Engineers, and the Chief of Topographical Engineers. After the commencement of the war a Provost Marshal General was added. The logistical support of the

Army was entrusted to the heads of the four "supply" departments: the Quartermaster General, responsible for clothing and equipment, forage, animals, transportation, and housing; the Commissary General of Subsistence, responsible for rations; the Chief of Ordnance, responsible for weapons, ammunition, and miscellaneous related equipment including accoutrements; and the Surgeon General, responsible for medical supplies and for evacuation, treatment, and hospitalization of the wounded.

The division of authority and responsibility among the Secretary of War, the Assistant Secretaries of War, and the General-in-Chief was never

clearly spelled-out, and the supply departments functioned independently and without effective central coordination throughout the Civil War. President Lincoln and Secretary of War Stanton did set up an Army Board, headed by retired Major General Ethan Allen Hitchcock, to coordinate military policy and provide military advice. However, the Army Board achieved little in the way of coordinated planning, and there was only the vaguest correlation of strategy and logistics until General Ulysses S. Grant assumed command of all Union armies in March 1864.

Both the passage of time and the new, strenuous, and urgent demands of the Civil War brought new men to the fore in the supply departments. Quartermaster General Thomas Sidney Jesup died in June 1860 after 48 years at his post. The next senior man in the department had been on duty since 1819 and was passed over in favor of Lieutenant Colonel Joseph E. Johnston. However, Johnston resigned in April 1861 and went on to become one of the senior Confederate generals. Major Ebenezer S. Sibley then served as Acting Quartermaster General until the appointment in May 1861 of Brigadier General Montgomery C. Meigs who served as Quartermaster General for the remainder of the war.

The other bureaus also changed heads at the beginning of the war — and several times during its course. The aged Commissary General of Subsistence, Colonel George Gibson, died in September 1861. He was replaced by Colonel, later Brigadier General, Joseph P. Taylor who served until his death in June 1864. Taylor was followed by Brigadier General Amos B. Eaton. In the Ordnance Department Brigadier General James W. Ripley replaced ten-year veteran Colonel Henry K. Craig as Chief of Ordnance in April 1861. Ripley was replaced by Brigadier General George D. Ramsay in September 1863, and Ramsay was replaced in turn by Brigadier General Alexander B. Dyer in September 1864. The Surgeon General, Colonel Thomas Lawson, had held his position for 25 years before his death in May 1861. He was succeeded for eleven months by Colonel Clement A. Finley who was replaced in April 1862 by Brigadier General William A. Hammond. Hammond was courtmartialled on a minor charge and dismissed from the Army in August 1864, being succeeded for the last months of the war by Brigadier General Joseph K. Barnes.

The Confederate army developed a similar bureau system with a Quartermaster General, Commissary General of Subsistence, Chief of Ordnance, and Surgeon General responsible for the main logistical functions. The Confederates added a Chief, Niter and Mining Bureau, to oversee the production of raw materials needed for munitions. The lack of central coordination and political infighting was worse among Confederate leaders than with their Northern counterparts. President Jefferson Davis, a succession of Secretaries of War, the supply department chiefs, and commanders in the field were seldom in accord on even the most basic issues. Their lack of cooperation and effective planning as well as often faulty execution was all the more serious in view of the precarious logistical situation of the South.

The Confederate supply departments had to be created from whole cloth and suffered throughout the war from a serious lack of experienced personnel. At the top the bureau chiefs were, in general, as capable and energetic as their Union counterparts. In some cases they had served in logistical positions in the pre-war United States Army. Colonel Abraham C. Myers, for example, was serving as Chief Quartermaster of the Southern Department at the time of his resignation from the United States Army in January 1861: two months later he became Quartermaster General of the Confederate States Army. Myers was replaced in August 1863 by Colonel Alexander R. Lawton. The eccentric Lucius Bellinger Northrup resigned his cavalry commission in the United States Army in January 1861 and was named Acting Commissary General of Subsistence for the Confederate States Army in March 1861. Colonel Josiah Gorgas, who had served in the United States Army Ordnance Department, was named Chief of the Bureau of Ordnance in April 1861 and was perhaps the most effective of the Confederate bureau chiefs, serving for the duration of the war. Major Isaac St. John was named Chief of the Niter and Mining Bureau upon its creation in April 1861 and served in that position until he was called upon to relieve Colonel Northrup as Commissary General in February 1865. The Confederate Surgeon General was Samuel P. Moore.

The supply departments of both armies remained seriously undermanned throughout the war, both at their headquarters and in the field. Field operations came to absorb the greatest numbers of available personnel. Before the war the supply departments had very few officers and noncommissioned officers in the field with troop units. The officers of the various supply departments were to be found almost exclusively in staff positions in Washington, at the permanent depots, or at the headquarters of the several geographical departments into which the Army was organized. The rank of these men was relatively low. Until 1864 most quartermaster, ordnance, and subsistence depots were commanded by captains who, despite their modest rank and meagre pay, had tremendous resources of men, money, and material under their control. There were a few exceptions, notably Colonel Daniel H. Rucker at the Washington Quartermaster Depot and Colonel George D. Ramsay at the Washington Arsenal.

The allocation of logistical personnel in troop units of the Union army varied depending upon the type, level, and size of the unit and whether it was a Regular Army or Volunteer organization. Infantry companies consisted of 82–100 men at full strength and were not authorized any logistical personnel, except that after 6 September 1862 Volunteer units were authorized a wagoner. Cavalry companies or troops ranged from 79–105 men and were authorized, in the Regular Army, two farriers, one saddler, one wagoner, and a company quartermaster sergeant. Volunteer units added a commissary sergeant and two teamsters. Artillery batteries, both Regular and Volunteer, had 80–156 men and were authorized 2–6 artificers, a wagoner, and a battery quartermaster sergeant.

Infantry and cavalry units of the Regular Army were sometimes organized into battalions of four to eight companies. Infantry battalions were authorized a lieutenant as battalion quartermaster and commissary, a quartermaster sergeant, a commissary sergeant, and a hospital steward. Cavalry battalions were authorized the same personnel plus a saddler sergeant and a veterinary sergeant. Volunteer units did not follow the battalion organization and many Regular units dropped it as well.

Regular Army infantry regiments had ten companies and were authorized a lieutenant as regimental quartermaster/commissary. Volunteer infantry regiments were authorized a lieutenant as regimental quartermaster/commissary, a quartermaster sergeant, a commissary sergeant, a hospital steward, a surgeon, and two assistant surgeons. Regular and Volunteer cavalry regiments were authorized the same logistical personnel as their infantry counterparts, except that in Volunteer cavalry regiments one assistant surgeon was replaced by an additional hospital steward and there were added another lieutenant as regimental commissary, a saddler sergeant, and a chief farrier or blacksmith. Artillery regiments seldom operated as a unit, but each Regular and Volunteer artillery regiment of 8–12 batteries was authorized a lieutenant as regimental quartermaster/commissary, a quartermaster sergeant, a commissary sergeant, and a hospital steward. Most regiments were also authorized an ordnance sergeant who performed minor repairs on weapons and issued ammunition. In addition, units of regimental size and larger almost always had a line officer on the staff of the commander who served as the unit ordnance officer.

Above regimental level no distinction was made as to Regular or Volunteer units and the allocation of support personnel was the same for both infantry and cavalry units. After 11 July 1862 brigades were authorized a captain as assistant quartermaster and another captain as assistant commissary of subsistence. From the beginning of the war each division normally had a quartermaster, commissary, and ordnance officer as members of the commander's staff. However, it was not until 4 July 1864 that divisions were legally authorized a quartermaster in the temporary grade of major, and division commissaries of subsistence in the temporary grade of major were not authorized until 3 March 1865. The Militia Act of 17 July 1862 empowered the President to organize army corps and authorized one lieutenant colonel as Chief Quartermaster and another as Chief Commissary of Subsistence. At Army level a Chief Quartermaster was authorized in the temporary grade of colonel and after 3 March 1865 a Chief Commissary of Subsistence in the temporary grade of colonel was also authorized. In the absence of legal authorization the necessary functions were frequently performed by an officer detailed as aide-de-camp on the staff of the commanding general.

Most unit logistical work was accomplished at regimental level. The regimental quartermaster was normally a line lieutenant nominated by the regimental commander. His duties included submitting requisitions for all quartermaster supplies and transport; accounting for all regimental quartermaster property including tentage, camp equipment, extra clothing, wagons, forage, and animals; issuing supplies; and managing the regimental trains. The regimental commissary, also an officer detailed from the line, requisitioned, accounted for, and issued rations. The regimental ordnance officer requisitioned arms, ammunition, and other ordnance stores, accounted for such items, and issued them to the troops. He also managed the movement of the unit ammunition train.

In theory, logistical staff positions at headquarters above regimental level were filled by a fully qualified officer of the supply department concerned. However, experienced manpower was perpetually in short supply and many authorized positions were filled by officers and non-commissioned officers drawn from line units or simply left vacant, the duties being performed by someone in addition to their own. Such was frequently the case in the Confederate army which had little time to build a cadre of professional logistical personnel. In both armies inexperience and ignorance of logistical principles and departmental procedures on the part of newly assigned quartermasters, commissaries, and ordnance officers generally reduced their effectiveness.

Although logistical staff officers were authorized, no provision was made in either army for soldiers to actually carry out the work. Specialized Quartermaster, Subsistence, or Ordnance units did not exist. There were some soldiers trained for quartermaster, commissary, ordnance, veterinary, and medical tasks as well as some signalmen and a few battalions of engineers, but for the most part both armies were forced to rely on hired civilians or line soldiers temporarily detached from their regiments to perform essential support duties. The urgent need for reliable support personnel usually overrode objections that the effectiveness of combat units was seriously diminished by the assignment of soldiers to other duties, and many line soldiers were so utilized.

The problem of finding sufficient men, either military or civilian, to perform necessary logistical tasks became acute as the Civil War armies expanded. One source of reliable service personnel for the Union Army was found in the large number of Negro "contrabands" (freed or runaway slaves) created in contested areas. Employed for 40–50 cents and one ration per day, they relieved soldiers and unreliable civilians from duties as teamsters, laborers, hostlers, ambulance drivers, and construction workers and often performed such duties better. However, there were never enough such workers. Of course, the Confederate armies made extensive use of Negro labor in various capacities without the necessity of payment to the individual. Requisitions upon slave owners for laborers was often necessary, but was considered onerous and decreased the amount of labor available for agricultural and other important purposes.

The obvious solution to the problem of finding adequate numbers of reliable support workers without drawing down combat units was to enlist and train men in units organized specifically to perform logistical missions. Just such a corps had been recommended by Assistant Quartermaster General Trueman Cross during the Mexican War. The dynamic of modern warfare was leading inevitably in that direction, and the Civil War did see the formation of some such special units. The most successful of these units was the Railroad Construction Corps created in the Union Army under the direction of Brigadier General Hermann Haupt.

The Soldier's Load

The usual load for the Union soldier in the field was about 45 pounds, including a rifle-musket and bayonet weighing 14 lbs. and 60 rounds of ammunition (40 rounds in the regulation cartridge boxes and another 20 rounds in pockets or knapsack) weighing 6 lbs. Three to eight days' of "marching" or "short" rations weighing 4–12 lbs. were carried in the haversack or knapsack. In addition, each soldier generally carried a canteen (4 lbs.), a blanket or overcoat (5 lbs.), and a shelter half (1.5 lbs.). Some soldiers also carried a rubberized poncho or ground sheet. Mess gear (knife, fork, spoon, cup, plate, and sometimes a small skillet), extra clothing, and a few personal items such as a razor, mirror, "housewife" (sewing kit), letters, notebook and pencil, Bible, and miscellaneous items were carried in the knapsack. The loaded knapsack usually weighed more than 20 lbs. and was habitually discarded when going into action. The Confederate soldier was usually less well-equipped and carried what little he had in the characteristic blanket roll slung over the shoulder. Veterans in both armies soon learned what items they could do without and carried only the bare minimum.

American soldiers on both sides were notorious for their lack of supply discipline. Every Civil War theater of operations was littered with discarded blankets, overcoats, knapsacks, and other equipment jettisoned by the troops on long marches, hot summer days, or before going into battle. Losses of knapsacks and other non-essential equipment were found after some battles to be as high as 50 per cent. Such profligacy early in the war provoked Brigadier General Irvin McDowell to comment: "I believe a French army of half the size of ours could be supplied with what we waste."

Arms and Ammunition

The supply of weapons, ammunition, and related equipment was a logistical problem of considerable magnitude for both sides in the Civil War. Arms and ammunition were produced in government arsenals, contracted from domestic producers, and imported from abroad. There were eventually 28 government arsenals, foundries, and armories in the North, producing weapons and ammunition. Between 1861 and 1866 Federal arsenals produced 7,892 pieces of artillery and some four million stand of small arms. Federal artillery fired some five million rounds during the course of the war, about four rounds per gun per day.

The Confederate ordnance establishment expanded quickly and eventually over 20 depots, laboratories, factories, armories, and arsenals supplied Confederate needs. However, only two factories produced heavy ordnance: the Etowah works near Atlanta and the Tredegar Iron Works in Richmond. Due to a lack of domestic production facilities the Confederates relied heavily on imports and on the capture of arms and ammunition from Union forces. At the beginning of the war the Confederates seized from Federal arsenals in the South about 159,000 small arms of all types, 429 cannon, and some 4.5 million rounds of small arms ammunition as well as the gun-making machinery of the Federal arsenal at Harper's Ferry. Confederate armaments production was significantly less than that of the Union over the course of the war and Confederate leaders faced a constant struggle to meet the voracious demand for ammunition which amounted to some 36 million rounds of small arms ammunition and

300,000 rounds of field artillery ammunition per year.

Ammunition was shipped from arsenals and factories to ordnance depots and from there to railheads and advanced depots near the forces in the field. From advanced depots issues were made on the "supply point" distribution system. Unit ordnance officers requisitioned ammunition, loaded it on unit ordnance trains, and transported it to forward positions. When an artillery battery or infantry regiment needed ammunition, the commander ordered the ammunition wagons (sometimes pack-mules) to come up from the trains area as near as available cover and concealment would permit and the men then carried the ammunition forward to the guns or distributed cartridges to the infantry. Artillery units out of ammunition or with guns destroyed were usually pulled off the line to replenish the caissons and receive replacement weapons from the artillery reserve park. A ready supply of small arms ammunition usually accompanied the unit baggage train. Brigade and division ordnance trains marched under the direction of the unit ordnance officer who was expected to know the kind and caliber of ammunition in each wagon of his train so that there would be no delay in issues. Reserve ammunition was transported in the corps trains.

There was no universal standard for the amount of ammunition carried in the unit ordnance trains. Each commander prescribed the allowances he saw fit, and the quantities varied from campaign to campaign or even from battle to battle. The most common "basic load" for the infantry of the Union army in 1862 was 200 rounds per man. The soldier carried 40 rounds in his cartridge boxes and another 20 in his pockets and knapsack. The brigade or division ordnance train carried about 40 rounds per man and the corps ordnance train carried another 100. Cavalrymen usually carried 40 rounds for the carbine and 20 rounds of pistol ammunition.

For artillery the "basic load" varied with the type of gun. The standard ammunition chest for the 12-pounder held 32 rounds; that for the 3-inch ordnance rifle and the 10-pounder Parrott held 50. Each gun was accompanied by two limbers and a caisson. One ammunition chest was mounted on each limber and two chests were mounted on the caisson. Thus, there were four chests per gun, making 128 rounds for each 12-pounder or 200 rounds for each 3-inch ordnance rifle or 10-pounder Parrott. In 1862 the ordnance trains usually carried a supply of artillery ammunition equal to that carried in the ammunition chests of all the batteries. Thus, the "basic load" for the 12-pounder was 256 rounds and for the 3-inch ordnance rifle and 10-pounder Parrott 400 rounds. There was a standard proportion of each type of artillery ammunition (solid shot, shell, spherical case/shrapnel, or canister) to be carried, but in practice it varied according to the type of action anticipated or the whim of the commander, canister being generally favored in many cases.

Subsistence

The supply of subsistence for the Union army presented few major problems beyond those associated with greatly increased requirements and wide-spread military operations. For the Confederacy, however, despite adequate agricultural production, subsistence for the armies in the field remained a major problem throughout the war, primarily because of financial, manpower, and transportation deficiencies rather than any absolute lack of supplies.

United States troops were generally well-fed. The official 1861 Army ration [per para 1191, Revised United States Army Regulations of 1861] included:

20 oz. of salt or fresh beef or 12 oz. of pork or bacon
18 oz. of flour or 20 oz. of corn meal
1.6 oz. of rice or .64 oz. of beans or 1.5 oz. of dried potatoes
1.6 oz. of green coffee or .24 oz. of tea
2.4 oz. of sugar
.54 oz. of salt
.32 gill of vinegar

Peas, hominy, or fresh potatoes could be substituted, and bread, either soft or hard, was provided when possible in lieu of flour. Desiccated compressed potatoes or desiccated compressed mixed vegetables could be substituted for the beans, peas, rice, hominy, or fresh potatoes at fixed rates. In 1862 the ration scale was increased slightly and more dried vegetables were authorized. For planning purposes the weight of one ration was calculated as 3 lbs.

The normal "short" or "marching" ration for the Union army consisted of 1 lb. of hard bread (the famous "hardtack"), ¾ lbs. of salt pork or ¼ lbs. of fresh meat, 1 oz. of coffee, 3 oz. of sugar, and salt. Soldiers on the march were issued from 3–8 days "marching" rations which were carried by the men in haversacks and knapsacks or on the unit baggage trains.

Although satisfactory as to bulk, the army ration did not provide an entirely adequate diet by today's nutritional standards. It was woefully deficient in anti-scorbutics, particularly fresh fruits and vegetables, and to prevent scurvy Union troops were sometimes issued small quantities of onions, dried apples or peaches, pickles, or sauerkraut. Canned and dehydrated foods had been introduced in 1857, but "desecrated vegetables and consecrated milk" found little acceptance, the desiccated vegetables being as often smoked as eaten. Army rations were supplemented by foraging, packages (even barrels!) from home, and purchases from sutlers' stores.

The Confederate ration was basically the same as the Union ration, but with slightly more sugar and less meat, coffee, vinegar and salt. Molasses was issued when available. However, the official ration was almost never issued in full, and for the Army of Northern Virginia the meat portion was usually issued at half or three-quarters scale and coffee was seldom available unless captured from Union stores or exchanged "through the lines" for tobacco or sugar. Confederate soldiers were often compelled to live off the land, and during the Maryland campaign of 1862 they subsisted largely on green corn and apples.

Commissary purchases were made on the market by low-bid contract in the major cities and producing areas by the officers in charge of subsistence depots. Flour and some other commodities were procured closer to the troops when possible. Cattle were contracted for delivery at specified points and major beef depots were maintained at Washington (on the grounds of the then unfinished Washington Monument), Alexandria (VA), and Louisville. Depot commissaries received in bulk and repacked for shipment to the field. The Subsistence Department developed a highly effective system of base, advanced, and temporary depots, and cattle were moved "on the hoof" in the immediate rear of the active armies.

Unit commissary officers requisitioned rations based on unit strength reports. Ration items were picked up by the unit trains at the nearest railhead or subsistence depot and delivered to forward locations where they were issued to the troops. Cattle were slaughtered by butchers at brigade level and issued on the day before expected consumption. There were no trained cooks assigned to units. Soldiers took care of their own cooking in small "mess" groups or suffered the culinary efforts of their fellow soldiers detailed to mess duty on a company basis. Improper preparation of the ration was a major contributory factor in disease and discomfort among soldiers, and the lack of clean, potable water was often a greater problem than spoiled or improperly prepared food.

Clothing and Camp Equipment

Due to the rapid expansion at the beginning of the war both armies experienced great difficulties in obtaining adequate supplies of serviceable clothing and equipment. The Union army quickly brought the problem under control, but Confederate quartermasters continued to have difficulty throughout the war in providing sufficient clothing and other material, due primarily to a lack of domestic production and raw materials and the effectiveness of the Union blockade.

The standard annual issue of clothing for United States troops included: 2 caps, 1 hat, 2 dress coats, 3 pairs of trousers, 3 flannel shirts, 3 pairs of flannel drawers, 4 pairs of stockings, and 4 pairs of bootees. An overcoat was issued every fifth year and a blanket every third year. Artillerymen and cavalrymen were issued jackets instead of coats and boots instead of bootees. The annual clothing allowance amounted to $42.

Officially, the Confederate soldier was equally well-clothed. The standard issue of clothing on an annual basis for the Regular soldier of the Confederate States Army included: 2 blue flannel shirts, 8 pairs of gray flannel trousers, 6 red flannel undershirts, 8 pairs of cotton drawers, 6 pairs of woolen stockings, 4 pairs of boots, 2 blankets, 2 leather stocks, and 2 caps. The total cost of the Confederate clothing issue was $26.95. Volunteers supplying their own uniforms received an allowance of $21.00. In practice, the Confederate Quartermaster General was seldom able to supply the required items and Confederate soldiers wore whatever came to hand, the home-dyed "butternut" jacket and trousers being characteristic items.

Shoes were an especially important item. Confederate soldiers were frequently without them and it was not unknown for Union soldiers to suffer from want of adequate footgear. The severe straggling in the Army of Northern Virginia during the Maryland campaign of 1862 can be attributed in part to the lack of shoes. Between 12 September and 25 October 1862 Union quartermasters issued over 100,000 pairs of shoes and boots to soldiers of the Army of the Potomac.

For the first three years of the war the quartermaster purchasing system for the Union Army was decentralized. Depot quartermasters purchased by low-bid contract or, in emergencies, by "open market purchase" for the areas/armies for which they were responsible. In July 1864 a more centralized purchasing system was initiated and all contracts had to be forwarded to the Quartermaster General's office in Washington for approval. Payments were then made only at the direction of the division chief in Washington after receipt of an inspector's certificate. In an emergency, the chief quartermaster of an army or detached unit could procure supplies directly. From time to time both the Union and Confederate armies found it necessary to requisition supplies from citizens. Both armies did so reluctantly and carefully, paying in cash or vouchers for all goods taken. The Confederate quartermasters and commissaries were more frequently reduced to this expedient due to a lack of adequate supplies and the inadequacies of the Confederate railroads.

Both the Union and Confederate Quartermaster's Departments operated a number of depots located in major cities. Schuykill Arsenal in Philadelphia was the chief depot and manufacturing center for United States Army clothing. Other major quartermaster depots for the Union Army were located in Boston, New York, Baltimore, Washington, Cincinnati, Louisville, St. Louis, Chicago, New Orleans, and San Francisco. The Confederate Quartermaster General's Department was reorganized in the spring of 1863 with 11 purchasing districts (generally drawn along state lines) and a number of depots located near the areas of operations. Major Confederate quartermaster depots were located at Richmond, Staunton, Raleigh, Atlanta, Columbus (GA), Huntsville, Montgomery, Jackson (MS), Little Rock, Alexandria (LA), and San Antonio. Advanced and temporary quartermaster depots were established as needed to support active operations.

Clothing and other supplies were manufactured in-house or delivered in bulk to the major quartermaster depots, then reshipped to units in the field based on requisitions received from unit quartermasters. In some cases items were shipped direct from the factory to the field. Unit quartermasters received supplies at advanced depots or railheads, moved them to the units, and issued them. Company commanders were held responsible for the condition of their men's clothing and accoutrements and unit quartermasters were accountable for the unit's tentage and other camp equipment.

Tents were a major item of camp equippage for both sides but were often dispensed with during active operations in the field. No textile was in shorter supply during the Civil War than the canvas duck needed for tents, and tentage required large amounts of transportation. Frequently it was found necessary to issue strict limitations of the tentage permitted to be carried on active operations. The pre-war Sibley tent, patterned on the Indian tepee of the Western plains, held 20 men. Two wagons were required to haul a company's allocation of such tentage. Early in the war the Union army introduced the so-called shelter half, or *tente d'Abri*, used by the French army. This became famous as the "pup tent", so-called because witty soldiers lay in the tent, stuck their heads out, and barked like dogs. The shelter half carried by the individual soldier was extremely versatile and could be used as a sleeping bag or as a lean-to. When buttoned with others it could form a two-man tent or larger structure. The shelter half still in use in the United States Army today is of the same basic pattern.

Horses and Mules

The supply of draft and riding animals was a responsibility of the Quartermaster General's Department in both armies. Horses and mules were the primary motive power for transport in the field and were used up on a grand scale. Between 1 September and 15 October 1862, the Army of the Potomac alone was issued over 10,000 horses. The leaner Confederate army as a whole consumed an average of 20,000 draft and artillery horses per year, only 5,000 of which were lost on active service, the remainder being lost through disease, starvation, abandonment, or sale. Once deprived of the major breeding areas in Tennessee, Kentucky, and Texas the Confederate army used up animals faster than they could be replaced by natural increase. Consequently, the Confederates were forced early on to exercise some central control over animal procurement and distribution. This function was performed by Major A.H. Cole, Inspector General of Field Transportation in the office of the Confederate Quartermaster General.

For the Union army there was no centralized procurement of animals at the beginning of the war and middlemen and brokers added to the cost with criminal collusion and deception. However, by the end of the war an efficient system for purchase, inspection, and distribution of horses and mules had evolved. Colonel Daniel H. Rucker, commander of the Washington Quartermaster Depot, developed a system of having cavalry officers purchase small lots of riding horses direct from owners in the stock-raising areas for shipment to remount depots. On 28 July 1863, the Cavalry Bureau was created and made responsible for organizing and equipping cavalry forces and for providing remounts. Colonel James A. Ekin was made Chief Quartermaster of the Cavalry Bureau. The remount depot at Gisboro' in the District of Columbia was the principal eastern remount depot. It was supplemented by depots at Greenville (VA), Harrisburg, and Wilmington (DE). St. Louis and Nashville served the Union armies in the western theaters, the Nashville depot alone handling some 500 animal purchases per day in the first nine months of 1864.

Forage

Given the number of animals required by Civil War armies for riding and draft purposes, the quantities of forage required were enormous. Each horse required daily 14 lbs. of hay and 12 lbs. of grain (oats, corn or barley). Each mule required 14 lbs. of hay and 9 lbs. of grain. No other commodity was so bulky or so difficult to transport.

Forage requirements represented a major portion of all transportation requirements. Pope's Army of Virginia in the summer of 1862 required 25,000 forage rations per day, 150 tons or over 18 railroad car loads of grain alone. In the winter of 1861–1862 the Army of the Potomac, then encamped around Washington and including some 15,000 horses and mules, had an extraordinary daily forage requirement of nearly 400 tons. In the winter of 1863–1864 the same Union army consumed some 37,000 bushels of grain and 1,150 tons of hay daily. The requirement for the entire United States Army at that time was some 2.5 million bushels of grain and 50,000 tons of hay per month.

The Confederate army had proportionate requirements, but suffered chronic shortages in the field due to a defective distribution system aggravated by frequent refusal of the Southern railroads to ship bulky forage. The two main Confederate field armies (the Army of Tennessee and the Army of Northern Virginia) required over 5,300 bushels of grain daily, the equivalent of 21 railroad carloads. The Army of Northern Virginia experienced particularly acute forage shortages in northern Virginia as early as May 1862, and such shortages had a direct effect on operations, weakening the animals and reducing the already strained transportation resources of Lee's army.

Transportation

The size and consequent daily resupply requirements of the field armies in the Civil War imposed enormous demands for transportation. For example, the Army of the Potomac on 1 October 1862 was composed of 127,818 men, 22,493 horses, and 10,392 mules plus 321 guns of mixed types. Some simple calculations using the standard planning factors give the Army of the Potomac's daily resupply requirement as 191.7 tons of rations, 411.9 tons of forage, and 63.9 tons of small arms ammunition, a total of 667.5 tons. Assuming that forage and rations for five days and full ammunition loads were carried, the trains would have included 290.6 tons of artillery ammunition, 894.7 tons of small arms ammunition, 958.6 tons of rations, and 2,059.6 tons of forage, for a total in the trains of 4,203.5 tons, or the equivalent of 3,503 wagon loads at 2,400 lbs. per wagon. Of course, these figures do not include the transportation required for necessary replacement weapons, clothing, camp equipment, or medical supplies. Nor do they include the wagons necessary for the movement of troop, officer, and headquarters baggage and tentage, forage for officers' horses, or sutler's stores. Of course, the total requirement was not uploaded all at one time, nor could it be; Chief Quartermaster Ingalls reported only 3,219 wagons and 315 ambulances on hand as of 1 October. In any event it is clear that a Civil War army, whether on the move or stationary, required an enormous amount of transport to maintain itself, and the support of multiple armies in the field on both sides during the Civil War was a gigantic undertaking involving all modes of transportation.

1. Water Transport

Both ocean and river transport were used extensively by both sides during the war. Union control of the Mississippi River and its tributaries as well as Eastern and Gulf coastal waters naturally limited the free use of water transport by the Confederates, but this relatively cheap and efficient means was employed whenever possible. The Quartermaster General's Department of both armies was responsible for obtaining and controlling waterborne transport. In the case of the Union army this function was partially vested in 1861–1862 in a General Agent of the War Department (later Assistant Secretary of War), John Tucker.

The Union army was able to move large numbers of men, animals, and supplies by sea. The most spectacular water movement of the Union army was the transportation by sea of the Army of the Potomac from Washington to Fort Monroe at the beginning of the Peninsula Campaign in March 1862. The move dwarfed anything done before and was not equalled during the war. With only a little over 5 weeks for planning and preparation General Agent Tucker, assisted by officers of the Quartermaster's Department, obtained some 400 vessels (113 steamers, 188 schooners, and 88 barges) and moved an army of 121,500 men, 14,592 animals, 44 batteries of artillery, and associated wagons, ammunition, and other equipment from Perryville (MD), Alexandria, and Washington to Fort Monroe with the loss of only eight mules and nine barges, the cargoes of which were saved. The embarkation began at Alexandria on 17 March and the movement was completed by 6 April. The army was subsequently resupplied by sea from Alexandria, Washington, Annapolis, New York, and Baltimore.

Steamboats and barges operating on major rivers were also important, especially in the western theater. The ordinary Ohio River steamer, carrying both passengers and freight, could lift 500 tons. Thus, one steamer could support 70,000 men and 20,000 animals for one day. In the East the older canal systems also played a role. The Chesapeake and Ohio Canal, for example, was used to support the Army of the Potomac in the fall of 1862 after Antietam.

2. Wagon Transport

The equipment and organization of wagon trains in both armies were the result of long experience on the western plains. Throughout the war commanders on both sides fought a constant battle to keep down the size of their wagon trains, particularly the regimental and headquarters baggage trains, and thereby improve the tactical mobility of their forces. In fact the size of trains, in the Union army at least, did decrease with each subsequent campaign. However, as General Halleck observed in November 1862: "Once accustomed to a certain amount of transport, an army is unwilling to do without the luxuries which it supplies in the field," and adherence to the limitations prescribed was frequently lax.

The standard 6-mule Army wagon in good condition could haul 4,000 lbs. on good roads in the best season of the year. However, such conditions were seldom found. The Army of the Potomac on the Peninsula seldom found it possible to exceed 2,000 lbs. per wagon. The usual wagon load was about 2,400 lbs. including forage for the team. Lack of sufficient draft animals sometimes occasioned the use of 4-horse or 4-mule teams which could haul only about 1,800 lbs. The Confederates commonly used the smaller teams due to the scarcity of suitable draft animals. Ambulances, 2-horse wagons, spring wagons, and other conveyances were sometimes used as well. The standard Army wagon cost $125 and with six horses or mules at roughly $125 each the total cost came to about $900. Maintenance, including forage for the team, cost about $3 per day. By contrast, a railroad car cost $500, carried eight tons, and had relatively little upkeep.

Mules were preferred over horses as draft animals due to their lower cost, better endurance, and smaller forage requirement. American mule breeding was world famous, and British General Sir Evelyn Wood later recommended both the American mule and the American Wilson wagon for use in South Africa. The Union army used pack trains only to a limited extent in the main theaters during the Civil War. Pack-mules were tested by the Union army in the spring of 1863, particularly for ammunition trains, but the results were unsatisfactory. It was found that while a 6-mule team and wagon could haul 25 boxes of ammunition and forage for the team, six mules could pack only 12 boxes plus forage. The pack-mules could carry only 200–250 lbs. each, required more experienced handlers, and wore out quickly. However, for much of the war each corps in the Army of the Potomac carried 200 packsaddles (the *aparejo*) in the train and wagon mules were used, if necessary.

The rate of march of wagon trains varied from 12–24 miles per day depending on road conditions. Since ideal conditions were seldom found, the maximum of 24 miles per day was seldom achieved. The trains of the Army of the Potomac took over 24 hours to move the three miles from Malvern Hill to Harrison's Landing in the mud and rain of 2–3 July 1862. Each 6-mule team and wagon occupied a space of roughly 12 yards, thus a column of 800 wagons occupied road space of about 6–8 miles at normal interval in single column at an easy gait. A pack train of 25 mules took up about 75 yards at close interval.

Although there was no standard authorization for supply trains in 1862, both the Union Army of the Potomac and the Confederate Army of Northern Virginia issued orders restricting the allowance for baggage trains. General Order No. 153, Headquarters, Army of the Potomac, issued on 10 August 1862 while the army was still at Harrison's Landing, limited baggage trains to:

4 wagons for each corps headquarters
3 wagons for each division or brigade headquarters
6 wagons for each full regiment of infantry
3 wagons for each squadron of cavalry or battery of artillery

The allowances were to be reduced to correspond with the actual number of men present for duty and excess wagons were to be turned in. Officers' baggage was limited to blankets, a small valise or carpetbag, and a reasonable mess kit. The order also prescribed that the regimental and battery wagons were to be used to carry forage, cooking utensils, hospital stores, small rations, and officers' baggage. One wagon per regiment was reserved exclusively for hospital stores and one wagon for grain for officers' horses. [O.R. XI, part 3, pp. 365–366]

Shortly after the battle of Antietam General Lee restated the allowances which he personally had fixed for the Army of Northern Virginia:

3 4-horse wagons for each division headquarters
2 4-horse wagons for each brigade headquarters
1 4-horse wagon for each regimental headquarters
1 4-horse wagon for each regiment's medical stores
1 4-horse wagon for each regiment's ammunition
1 4-horse wagon for every 100 men per regiment for baggage, camp equipment, rations, etc. [O.R. XIX, part 2, p. 641]

Other commanders at other times and places prescribed similar allowances.

While the size of supply trains, as distinct from unit baggage trains, varied according to the size of the force supported and the situation, there was a constant effort to keep the total number of wagons and teams as low as possible. Success was often measured by comparison with Napoleon's ideal ratio of 12.5 wagons per 1,000 men. General Grant generally allowed only 19 wagons for every 1,000 men on the march. General Sherman was noted for travelling light and moving fast, but he left Atlanta in November 1864 on the famous "March to the Sea" with 40 wagons for every 1,000 men of his command. The supposedly sluggish Army of the Potomac under General McClellan generally did better. At Harrison's Landing in July 1862 there were 26 wagons for every 1,000 men; at Antietam in September, 29 per 1,000; and at Warrenton in early November only 25 per 1,000.

The Confederates generally operated with a lower ratio of wagons to men, out of necessity rather than choice. Stonewall Jackson in the Shenandoah Valley in the spring of 1862 had only 7 wagons per 1,000 men. His opponents were not nearly so efficient; at the end of May 1862 Major General Nathaniel P. Banks reported 500 wagons for a force of only 5,500 men, a ratio of a whopping 91 wagons for every 1,000 men. Of course, Banks was no Napoleon either!

As the war went on the organization and operation of wagon trains became systematized and fairly efficient. Unit quartermasters were responsible for the unit baggage trains, which generally moved right behind the unit on the march with the unit's ready reserve of small arms ammunition marching first for ready access. The unit of organization for the supply trains of subsistence, ordnance, and forage was by division. The division quartermaster controlled the division's general supply trains and the division ordnance officer controlled the ammunition train. Division trains were sometimes grouped and moved by corps. During movements of the general supply trains the usual order of march was for the wagons containing small arms ammunition to come first followed by the wagons containing artillery ammunition, subsistence, and forage in that order. Sutlers' wagons brought up the rear. The wagons of the division and corps supply trains were also used to move supplies from advanced depots and railheads to smaller temporary dumps or train areas in the immediate proximity of the troops. During active operations the trains were guarded by cavalry or reserve infantry units detailed for that purpose.

By way of example, Confederate Major General D.H. Hill's division supply train (for about 5,800 men) immediately after Antietam consisted of 52 wagons: 22 for ammunition, 20 for subsistence, and 10 for forage. Hill also had a small baggage train of two wagons for each brigade headquarters and 6 wagons per regiment. In contrast, the supply train of the Union XII Corps (two divisions; 13,450 men) at Chancellorsville in April 1863 consisted of 192 wagons: 49 for small arms ammunition, 20 for artillery ammunition, and the remaining 123 for rations, forage, and general supplies. In addition there was a baggage train of 155 wagons.

Brigadier General Rufus Ingalls, Chief Quartermaster of the Army of the Potomac, and later of all the Federal armies operating against Richmond, was perhaps the most competent field quartermaster of the war on either side. Taking charge of the bloated and confused trains of the Army of the Potomac on the Peninsula, he streamlined and organized them into an efficient and effective logistical tool. He eventually developed a system for marking each wagon in unit baggage trains with the corps badge, division color, and number of the brigade to which it belonged. He also caused general supply wagons to be marked to indicate their contents, whether infantry or artillery ammunition, grain or hay, or one of the various types of ration items. As soon as a wagon was unloaded, it was sent back to the nearest depot for another load of the same commodity. General Grant praised the efficiency of the quartermaster corps of the Army of the Potomac in 1864, and Ingalls was the officer primarily responsible. In September 1863, Ingalls explained some of the principles by which he operated:

> In a forward movement our trains are never in the way of the troops; on the contrary each corps has its train which follows it on the march, and which forms its indispensible, movable magazine of supplies. Wagon trains should never be permitted to approach within the range of the battlefields. They should be parked in safe and convenient places out of risk, and well guarded. Troops should go forward to battle lightly loaded, and without wagons except for extra ammunition. If they are successful, the trains can be brought up very quickly; if defeated, they will find an unobstructed road, and will get back to their wagons soon enough. [Annual Report, Brigadier General Rufus Ingalls, Chief Quartermaster, Army of the Potomac, for the Fiscal Year ending 30 June, 1863]

3. Railroad Transport

In August 1861 General McClellan wrote to President Lincoln that, ". . .the construction of railroads has introduced a new and very important element into war. . ." The Civil War was indeed the first major conflict in which the railroad played a significant part, and an efficient railroad system proved a decisive advantage for the North. Even with a relatively large system to maintain the North successfully overcame the problems of properly coordinating and maintaining its rail lines even in areas of active operations, although congestion in forward areas, detention of cars, and interference by field commanders with train movements decreased effectiveness.

The coordination and maintenance of a far more limited rail system was never successfully achieved by the South. Of 30,000 miles of railroad in the United States in 1860, only 9,000 lay in the future Confederacy and most of that ran North-South, feeding the Gulf and the Ohio River. There were no through connections between Virginia and the Deep South, the political and financial conditions of railroad construction in the South having dictated short, independent lines of varying gauge and broken at the cities. The South also possessed few railroad construction and repair resources. Nor were the existing facilities and resources used to their maximum extent. Confederate leaders were never able to summon the political courage needed to impose centralized control of the independent, and often recalcitrant, railroad owners. Inadequate railroads and the lack of means to improve them were important factors in the defeat of the Confederacy.

By contrast, on 31 January 1862 the President of the United States was authorized by law to take possession of and to operate any railroad as needed for the conduct of the war. Although President Lincoln formally took possession of all railroads in the United States on 25 May 1862, the Federal government never exercised its control option except in the conquered areas of the South, although Secretary of War Stanton did direct Brigadier General Hermann Haupt to seize and operate the inefficient Cumberland Valley Railroad in September 1862. Furthermore, on 11 February 1862 President Lincoln had appointed Colonel Daniel C. McCallum to head the Military Rail Road Service under the Quartermaster General, thereby centralizing the supervision and management of military rail operations.

To keep the Military Rail Road Service in operation in the face of active Confederate regular and guerilla forces a Railroad Construction Corps was formed and placed under the skilled direction of the noted railroad builder Hermann Haupt. Originally composed of only 300 soldiers, the Corps later grew to a mixed force of over 10,000 soldiers and civilians organized into standard units under military command and discipline. It was used to rebuild or repair track and bridges damaged by combat operations or guerilla action and eventually built or repaired some 1,769 miles of military railroad as well as wharves and other facilities at depots and along the lines of communication.

In early October 1863 the Orange and Alexandria Railroad was thoroughly destroyed by the rebels from Manassas Junction almost to Brandy Station, a distance of 22 miles. Haupt and his men repaired the line, including a 625 foot bridge over the Rappahannock River, in only 19 working hours. Their most spectacular achievement, however, occurred during Sherman's advance to Atlanta. The Etowah Bridge over the Etowah and Chattahoochie Rivers between Chattanooga and Atlanta— 625 feet long and 75 feet high—was rebuilt by 600 men of the Railroad Construction Corps in only six days. The organization's fame was justly deserved and prompted the often repeated declaration of Confederates that "'ol Sherman carries a spare railroad tunnel along with him."

Despite their success both the Military Rail Road Service and the Railroad Construction Corps were disbanded promptly at the end of the war. While not "pure" corps of enlisted combat service support specialists, both were in many respects the forerunners of the specialized men and units which the rapidly changing nature of war would require in the future.

Good management and a good system of repair permitted spectacularly successful railroad movements by the Union army. The usefulness of the railroad for emergency resupply was amply demonstrated during the Maryland Campaign of 1862, and the Union victory at Gettysburg in 1863 can be ascribed in part to the effective use of the railroads for bringing up men and supplies. The most dramatic Union rail movement occurred in the autumn of 1863 with the shift of the XI and XII Corps under Major General Joseph Hooker from the Army of the Potomac in Virginia to the Army of the Cumberland near Chattanooga. The move began on the afternoon of 25 September 1863 with trains routed from Washington via Jeffersonville (IN), Louisville, Nashville, and Chattanooga. They began to arrive on the evening of 30 September at Bridgeport, Alabama. Some 23,300 men, 10 batteries of artillery, 100 cars of baggage, and the associated animals and other equipment covered 1,192 miles in eleven and one-half days.

A Few Remarks on the Maryland Campaign of 1862

In many respects the Maryland campaign of 1862 is an ideal operation to examine from a logistical point of view. The campaign had logistical objectives and its outcome was in large part determined by the logistical strengths and weaknesses of the opposing sides. Conducted soon after the strenuous Peninsula campaign and the defeat of the Union army at Second Manassas, the Maryland campaign exhibits the logistical system of the Union army in the process of gelling and that of the Confederate army before it became unglued. Both sides faced serious specific problems of supply and transport. In addition, from the Union point of view at least, every possible mode of transportation was involved. Unfortunately, only a few highlights can be mentioned here.

When the Confederate Army of Northern Virginia crossed into Maryland in early September 1862 at least two of Lee's objectives were logistical in nature: to obtain supplies from a "liberated" Maryland and to cut the main east-west railway lines in Maryland and Pennsylvania thereby dividing the North. But Lee recognized that his army was in poor shape for such an undertaking. To President Jefferson Davis on 3 September he wrote: "The Army is not properly equipped for an invasion of an enemy's territory. It lacks much of the material of war, is feeble in transport, the animals being much reduced, and the men are poorly provided with clothing, and, in thousands of instances, are destitute of shoes." [*O.R.* XIX, part 2, pp. 590–591]

The Confederate logistical problem was made more serious by the distance from the proposed area of operations to the base in Richmond. Under even ideal conditions Confederate railroads were scarcely to be relied on, and at the time of the climactic battle at Sharpsburg Lee's army had only one railhead on the Virginia Central at Staunton, 150 miles away. Advanced depots were established at Winchester and Staunton, but limited wagon transport made it imperative that Lee's men live off the country, particularly at the beginning of the campaign.

Arms and ammunition were of particular concern and the capture of Harper's Ferry on 15 September was a windfall for the Confederates. Nearly 12,000 stand of small arms, 73 pieces of artillery, 200 wagons, and large quantities of horses, mules, rations, ammunition, and other supplies fell into Confederate hands, too late, however, to influence the battle at Sharpsburg on 17 September. In any event Lee's ordnance officer, Lieutenant Colonel E.P. Alexander, managed to ensure that sufficient supplies of ammunition were available, even with the loss of Longstreet's trains to Union cavalrymen on the Hagerstown Pike on the night of 14 September.

Lee's hopes of obtaining significant supplies in Maryland were disappointed, and the day of battle found many Confederate soldiers exhausted from the marching and suffering from lack of food. Many did not make it to the battlefield at all, the want of shoes contributing to an enormous number of stragglers which, according to Major General D.H. Hill, reduced Lee's effective force to less than 30,000 men. Hill also noted:

It is true that hunger and exhaustion had nearly unfitted these brave men for battle. Our wagons had been sent off across the river on Sunday, and for three days the men had been sustaining life on green corn and such cattle as they could kill in the fields. In charging through an apple orchard [Piper's] at the Yankees, with the immediate prospect of death before them, I noticed men eagerly devouring apples. [*O.R.* XIX, part 1, p. 1025]

Despite their poor condition the Confederate veterans of the Army of Northern Virginia acquitted themselves with honor.

On 17 September the main Confederate supply route crossed the Potomac near Sharpsburg by way of Blackford's (Boteler's) Ford. The Confederate trains were positioned during the battle in and around the western edge of the town of Sharpsburg, some being retained on the western bank of the Potomac. On the night of 18 September the entire Army of Northern Virginia with all its equipment recrossed the Potomac and moved slowly up the Shenandoah Valley toward the advanced depot at Winchester, looking to fight again another day.

At the beginning of October Lee broke up the depot of Winchester and moved his base still farther up the Valley to Staunton. Despite the best efforts of the Confederate quartermasters the army ended the campaign as it had begun, poorly clad and without shoes. On 7 November Lee wrote to Secretary of War George W. Randolph: "It has been snowing all day, and I fear that our men, with insufficient clothing, blankets, and shoes, will suffer much, and our ranks be proportionately diminished." [*O.R.* XIX, part 2, p. 702] Such was perpetually the case with the supply of the Confederate armies in the field.

The Army of the Potomac had a definite logistical advantage as it began the pursuit of Lee in early September. Although significant quantities of supplies and transport were lost at Second Manassas and Harper's Ferry, the reserves of the Union Army were plentiful and the means existed to move them to where they were needed. From the Union point of view the area of operations was also well-served by transportation lines. The wagon haul from Washington to the Antietam was less than 100 miles over generally excellent roads. The Baltimore and Ohio Railroad served both Frederick and, after its recapture, Harper's Ferry, while the less efficient Cumberland Valley line terminated at Hagerstown. Thus, relatively good rail connections to both north and south were available no farther than 10–20 miles from the battlefield of Antietam. In addition, the Chesapeake and Ohio Canal was navigable as far up as Poolesville.

On 7 September McClellan established his camp at Rockville, Maryland, 14 miles from Washington. Union regiments and batteries mauled at Second Manassas or recently arrived from the Peninsula pushed through Washington during the first days of September without, as Colonel Daniel H. Rucker, commander of the Washington Quartermaster Depot, later wrote:

> . . . waiting for the supplies so urgently required, merely stopping while *in transitu* to draw such articles as were absolutely indispensable, and to turn in the almost worthless material with which they were encumbered. All were in haste, and for a few days the offices of the depot were thronged with division, brigade, and regimental quartermasters, each anxious that his particular wants should be first supplied and insisting upon the extreme urgency of the necessities of that portion of the army for which he was to provide, apparently forgetting that all shared the same ill-fortune. [*O.R.* LI, part 1, p. 1096]

At Rockville the troops were reorganized and re-equipped while McClellan tried to determine Lee's movements and intentions. Although all of the unit baggage trains had not yet arrived from the Peninsula, Lieutenant Colonel Rufus Ingalls, Chief Quartermaster of the Army of the Potomac, did a masterful job of organizing the available transport and found sufficient wagons and teams to supply the Army's needs.

On 11 September the Army of the Potomac moved north from Rockville on a course via Frederick which brought it to the battlefield of South Mountain on 14 September. Having driven the Confederates back across the Antietam Creek, McClellan failed to press Lee's forces on 15 September and wasted the following day probing for the enemy through a heavy fog and reorganizing his forces. His ordnance officer, First Lieutenant Francis J. Shunk, spent the day of 16 September redistributing and hurrying up ammunition. The next day, 17 September 1862, saw the bloodiest day in American military history as McClellan's army crossed Antietam Creek and attempted to dislodge Lee's forces from their defensive positions on the high ground before Sharpsburg. Unlike their Confederate counterparts, the Union soldiers arrived on the battlefield of Antietam well-fed and well-equipped, and they too fought with distinction.

The Union long-range guns in position near the Pry House did good work suppressing the fire of Confederate batteries and supporting the attacks of Union forces, the 20-pounder Parrott batteries using up their available ammunition. In a singular demonstration of the value of the railroad as a means of supporting an army in the field 2,500 rounds of 20-pounder Parrott ammunition were rushed by special four-car train from the Washington Arsenal to Hagerstown in less than 18 hours, arriving shortly after noon on 18 September. Subsequently, the railroads were the primary method by which supplies were moved to the Army of the Potomac from Washington, Alexandria, Baltimore, New York, and other northern cities.

During the battle the Union supply trains were staged on the Boonsboro Pike near Keedysville and were protected by Fitz-John Porter's V Corps. They remained there for some time afterward. Advanced quartermaster and subsistence depots were established four miles south of Frederick on the east bank of the Monocacy River until the railroad bridge there was repaired on 22 September, then were moved into Frederick itself. Advanced depots were also opened at Hagerstown, at Harper's Ferry after its recapture and also, late in the campaign, at Berlin, Maryland. No advanced ordnance depot was established, all ammunition for the Army of the Potomac being supplied direct from the Washington Arsenal by wagon or by rail to railheads at Frederick, Hagerstown, and Harper's Ferry.

In the six weeks after the battle of Antietam McClellan, despite his advantage in men and materiel and the orders, pleas, and prayers of Abraham Lincoln, failed to aggressively pursue the Army of Northern Virginia. The Union army sat idle near Sharpsburg reporting a totally unexpected shortage of clothing, shoes, and camp equippage and a serious lack of serviceable horses brought on by overwork and an unexplained disease. Only rations, under the control of Chief Commissary Colonel Henry F. Clarke, appear to have been plentiful. When prodded to move forward, General McClellan replied, with some justification, that he was not in a position to do so until his forces were better equipped. When the Army of the Potomac finally was ordered to cross the Potomac in pursuit of Lee on 6 October, Chief Quartermaster Ingalls reported that the:

> . . . army was wholly deficient in cavalry and a large part of our troops were in want of shoes, blankets, and other indispensable articles of clothing, notwithstanding all the efforts that had been made since the battle of Antietam, and even prior to that date, to refit the Army with clothing as well as horses. [O.R. XIX, part 1, p. 74]

The supply departments in Washington and the quartermasters and commissaries with the army in the field worked together feverishly to supply McClellan's wants. Between 12 September and 25 October Union quartermasters issued to soldiers of the Army of the Potomac over 100,000 pairs of shoes and boots as well as some 93,000 pairs of trousers, 120,000 pairs of stockings, 97,700 pairs of drawers, 10,000 blankets, and 33,100 shelter halves. Between 1 September and 15 October more than 10,000 horses were issued. Quartermaster General Meigs balked at only one item. On 29 October he telegraphed Ingalls: "Horse-covers are not an article of supply under the regulations, and I doubt very much the propriety of encumbering our already overloaded cavalry with one thousand heavy horse-covers to a regiment." [*O.R.* XIX, part 2, p. 504]

Except in the case of horses and mules, the problem was not so much insufficient supply as it was congestion on the railroads, especially the inefficient Cumberland Valley line to Hagerstown. Brigadier General Hermann Haupt was directed by the Secretary of War on 18 September to do what he could to facilitate the movement of military supplies over the available lines. For the next month the energetic Haupt coordinated with quartermasters and railroad officials, personally directed traffic and the unloading of cars, and generally succeeded in bringing order out of the chaos created by massive and urgent rail movements.

By the time the Army of the Potomac began its move south into Virginia in early November the lessons learned by commanders and staff officers were at last beginning to pay off. The shift of the Army's line of communication to the Manassas Gap and Orange and Alexandria Railroads south of Washington proceeded rapidly and without the confusion which had marked the beginning of the campaign in Maryland. The relief of General McClellan by Major General Ambrose E. Burnside on 7 November brought the Maryland campaign of 1862 to an end. Unlike the Army of Northern Virginia, the Army of the Potomac ended the campaign in much better shape logistically than it had begun it. Effective procedures and experienced logistical leaders had evolved and henceforth the support of the Army of the Potomac would only continue to improve. The confusion attendant with all active operations would, of course, never be entirely eliminated, but Ingalls, Clarke, Shunk, and the other logisticians would never again be daunted by the magnitude and complexity of their task, if indeed they ever had been.

McClellan's failure to pursue the Army of Northern Virginia aggressively after Antietam and to destroy it once and for all has been a much debated topic. McClellan was no doubt a hesitant and overcautious commander, but the degree to which his caution was induced by real constraints of logistics, as opposed to exaggerated fears of the strength and ability of his opponent, has never been accurately measured. It is obvious that the Army of the Potomac faced serious problems of supply in the month after Antietam. The want of clothing and equipment occasioned by overloaded rail lines, coupled with a serious lack of serviceable horses, was certainly good reason for postponing an all-out advance. But in the last analysis these relatively minor problems may not have been sufficient reasons for failing to pursue the Confederates, who, after all, were suffering from crippling defects in both supply and transportation. In any event McClellan should have recognized that his relatively superior logistical situation gave him an advantage which his opponent simply did not enjoy—an advantage which might even have decided any further engagements between the Union and Confederate forces in northern Virginia in the fall of 1862 in favor of the Union cause.

Conclusion

Superior Union army logistics, or rather defective Confederate logistics, came close to deciding the contest at Antietam. The irascible Confederate Major General D.H. Hill opined that the battle of Sharpsburg would have been a glorious victory for the South but for three causes: 1. the separation of Confederate forces; 2. the bad handling of Confederate artillery; and 3:

> "the enormous straggling. The battle was fought with less than 30,000 men. Had all our stragglers been up, McClellan's army would have been completely crushed or annihilated. Doubtless the want of shoes, the want of food, and physical exhaustion had kept many brave men from being with the army; but thousands of thieving poltroons had kept away from sheer cowardice." [*O.R.* XIX, part 1, p. 1026]

In short, the outcome of the Maryland campaign of 1862 turned in large part on the strengths and weaknesses of the logistical system supporting each of the opponents. For the Army of Northern Virginia the major defect was an inadequate quantity of food, clothing, and other equipment compounded by scarce and inefficient transport. On the other hand, the Army of the Potomac did not face an actual want of supplies, and such difficulties as existed during the campaign can be attributed primarily to problems of managing the transportation of enormous amounts of supplies by railroad. But perhaps the real advantage for the Union army during the Maryland campaign and throughout the war was a corps of energetic and innovative logisticians working to overcome the many and complex problems of supporting a modern army in the field.

While the tactical and strategic lessons of the American Civil War were generally ignored by European military experts, the great development of logistical support for the American armies in the field did attract considerable attention in the late nineteenth century. Many European military commentators recognized the difficulties and achievements of Union and Confederate logisticians. Only more recently have we ourselves come to understand that the supplying of Civil War armies was as great a task as their enlistment and maneuver and that it brought forward men who in their own areas of expertise were the equals of Grant, Sherman, and Lee.

Bibliographical Note

The reader interested in matters of national policy, industrial production and procurement, mobilization, and the organization for logistics at the highest level may refer with profit to such works as Fred A. Shannon's two volume *The Organization and Administration of the Union Army, 1861–1865* (Cleveland, 1928), A. Howard Meneely's *The War Department, 1861: A Study in Mobilization and Administration* (New York, 1928), Marvin A. Kreidberg and Merton G. Henry's *History of Military Mobilization in the United States Army, 1775–1945* (Washington, 1955), and Richard D. Goff's *Confederate Supply* (Durham, 1969).

Almost nothing of consequence has been written about the actual logistical support of Civil War armies in the field. A few chapters of Erna Risch's *Quartermaster Support of the Army: A History of the Corps, 1775–1939* (Washington, 1962), and of James A. Houston's *The Sinews of War: Army Logistics, 1775–1953* (Washington, 1966) are useful, but the details must be mined laboriously from the pertinent volumes of the multi-volume *Official Records of the War of the Rebellion*. Even then the researcher finds all too little on the Confederate side. Many of the reports of Union quartermasters, commissaries, and ordnance officers appear in the *O.R.*, but the corresponding Confederate reports are few and far between.

ORDER OF BATTLE
UNITED STATES ARMY

Organization of the Army of the Potomac, Maj. Gen. George B. McClellan, U.S. Army, commanding, September 14–17, 1862.

*On September 14 the right wing of the army, consisting of the First and Ninth Corps, was commanded by Major-General Burnside; the center, composed of the Second and Twelfth Corps, by Major-General Sumner; and the left wing, comprising the Sixth Corps and Couch's division (Fourth Corps), by Major-General Franklin.

FIRST ARMY CORPS (Maj. Gen. Joseph Hooker)
(Brig. Gen. George G. Meade)

First Division (Brig. Gen. Rufus King)
(Brig. Gen. John P. Hatch)
(Brig. Gen. Abner Doubleday)

First Brigade (Col. Walter Phelps, Jr.)
22d New York
24th New York
30th New York
84th New York (14th Militia)
2d U.S. Sharpshooters

Second Brigade (Brig. Gen. Abner Doubleday)
(Col. William P. Wainwright)
(Lieut. Col. J. William Hofmann)
7th Indiana
76th New York
95th New York
56th Pennsylvania

Third Brigade (Brig. Gen. Marsena R. Patrick)
21st New York
23d New York
35th New York
80th New York (20th Militia)

Fourth Brigade (Brig. Gen. John Gibbon)
19th Indiana
2d Wisconsin
6th Wisconsin
7th Wisconsin

Artillery (Capt. J. Albert Monroe)
New Hampshire Light, First Battery
1st Rhode Island Light, Battery D
1st New York Light, Battery L
4th United States, Battery B

Second Division (Brig. Gen. James B. Ricketts)

First Brigade (Brig. Gen. Abram Duryea)
  97th New York
  104th New York
  105th New York
  107th Pennsylvania

Second Brigade (Col. William A. Christian
  (Col. Peter Lyle)
  26th New York
  94th New York
  88th Pennsylvania
  90th Pennsylvania

Third Brigade (Brig. Gen. George L. Hartsuff)
  (Col. Richard Coulter)
  12th Massachusetts
  13th Massachusetts
  83d New York (9th Militia)
  11th Pennsylvania

Artillery
  1st Pennsylvania Light, Battery F
  Pennsylvania Light, Battery C

Third Division (Brig. Gen. George G. Meade)
(Brig. Gen. Truman Seymour)

First Brigade (Brig. Gen. Truman Seymour)
  (Col. R. Biddle Roberts)
  1st Pennsylvania Reserves
  2d Pennsylvania Reserves
  5th Pennsylvania Reserves
  6th Pennsylvania Reserves
  13th Pennsylvania Reserves (1st Rifles)

Second Brigade (Col. Albert L. Magilton)
  3d Pennsylvania Reserves
  4th Pennsylvania Reserves
  7th Pennsylvania Reserves
  8th Pennsylvania Reserves

Third Brigade (Col. Thomas F. Gallagher)
  (Lieut. Col. Robert Anderson)
  9th Pennsylvania Reserves
  10th Pennsylvania Reserves
  11th Pennsylvania Reserves
  12th Pennsylvania Reserves

Artillery
  1st Pennsylvania Light, Battery A
  1st Pennsylvania Light, Battery B
  5th United States, Battery C

SECOND ARMY CORPS (Maj. Gen. Edwin V. Sumner)

First Division (Maj. Gen. Israel B. Richardson)
(Brig. Gen. John C. Caldwell)
(Brig. Gen. Winfield S. Hancock)

First Brigade (Brig. Gen. John C. Caldwell)
- 5th New Hampshire
- 7th New York
- 61st New York
- 64th New York
- 81st Pennsylvania

Second Brigade (Brig. Gen. Thomas F. Meagher)
- (Col. John Burke)
- 29th Massachusetts
- 63d New York
- 69th New York
- 88th New York

Third Brigade (Col. John R. Brooke)
- 2d Delaware
- 52d New York
- 57th New York
- 66th New York
- 53d Pennsylvania

Artillery
- 1st New York Light, Battery B
- 4th U.S., Batteries A and C

Second Division (Maj. Gen. John Sedgwick)
(Brig. Gen. Oliver O. Howard)

First Brigade (Brig. Gen. Willis A. Gorman)
- 15th Massachusetts
- 1st Minnesota
- 34th New York
- 82d New York (2d Militia)
- Massachusetts Sharpshooters, First Company
- Minnesota Sharpshooters, Second Company

Second Brigade (Brig. Gen. Oliver O. Howard)
- (Col. Joshua T. Owen)
- (Col. De Witt C. Baxter)
- 69th Pennsylvania
- 71st Pennsylvania
- 72d Pennsylvania
- 106th Pennsylvania

Third Brigade (Brig. Gen. Napoleon J. T. Dana)
- (Col. Norman J. Hall)
- 19th Massachusetts
- 20th Massachusetts
- 7th Michigan
- 42d New York
- 59th New York

Artillery
- 1st Rhode Island Light, Battery A
- 1st United States, Battery I

Third Division (Brig. Gen. William H. French)

First Brigade (Brig. Gen. Nathan Kimball)
  14th Indiana
  8th Ohio
  132d Pennsylvania
  7th West Virginia

Second Brigade (Col. Dwight Morris)
  14th Connecticut
  108th New York
  130th Pennsylvania

Third Brigade (Brig. Gen. Max Weber)
  (Col. John W. Andrews)
  1st Delaware
  5th Maryland
  4th New York

Unattached Artillery
  1st New York Light, Battery G
  1st Rhode Island Light, Battery B
  1st Rhode Island Light, Battery G

FOURTH ARMY CORPS

First Division (Maj. Gen. Darius N. Couch)

First Brigade (Brig. Gen. Charles Devens, Jr.)
  7th Massachusetts
  10th Massachusetts
  36th New York
  2d Rhode Island

Second Brigade (Brig. Gen. Albion P. Howe)
  62d New York
  93d Pennsylvania
  98th Pennsylvania
  102d Pennsylvania
  139th Pennsylvania

Third Brigade (Brig. Gen. John Cochrane)
  65th New York
  67th New York
  122d New York
  23d Pennsylvania
  61st Pennsylvania
  82d Pennsylvania

Artillery
  New York Light, Third Battery
  1st Pennsylvania Light, Battery C
  1st Pennsylvania Light, Battery D
  2d United States, Battery G

FIFTH ARMY CORPS (Maj. Gen. Fitz John Porter)

First Division (Maj. Gen. George W. Morell)

First Brigade (Col. James Barnes)
2D MAINE
18th Massachusetts
22d Massachusetts
1st Michigan
13th New York
25th New York
118th Pennsylvania
Massachusetts Sharpshooters, Second
Company

Second Brigade (Brig. Gen. Charles Griffin)
2d District of Columbia
9th Massachusetts
32d Massachusetts
4th Michigan
14th New York
62d Pennsylvania

Third Brigade (Col. T. B. W. Stockton)
20th Maine
16th Michigan
12th New York
17th New York
44th New York
83d Pennsylvania
Michigan Sharpshooters, Brady's
company

Artillery
Massachusetts Light, Battery C
1st Rhode Island Light, Battery C
5th United States, Battery D

Sharpshooters
1st United States

Second Division (Brig. Gen. George Sykes)

First Brigade (Lieut. Col. Robert C. Buchanan)
3d United States
4th United States
12th United States, First Battalion
12th United States, Second Battalion
14th United States, First Battalion
14th United States, Second Battalion

Second Brigade (Maj. Charles S. Lovell)
1st and 6th United States
2d and 10th United States
11th United States
17th United States

Third Brigade (Col. Gouverneur K. Warren)
5th New York
10th New York

Artillery
1st United States, Batteries E and G
5th United States, Battery I
5th United States, Battery K

Artillery Reserve (Lieut. Col. William Hays)
1st Battalion New York Light, Battery A
1st Battalion New York Light, Battery B
1st Battalion New York Light, Battery C
1st Battalion New York Light, Battery D
New York Light, Fifth Battery
1st United States, Battery K
4th United States, Battery G

SIXTH ARMY CORPS (Maj. Gen. William B. Franklin)

First Division (Maj. Gen. Henry W. Slocum)

First Brigade (Col. Alfred T. A. Torbert)
1st New Jersey
2d New Jersey
3d New Jersey
4th New Jersey

Second Brigade (Col. Joseph J. Bartlett)
5th Maine
16th New York
27th New York
96th Pennsylvania

Third Brigade (Brig. Gen. John Newton)
18th New York
31st New York
32d New York
95th Pennsylvania

Artillery (Capt. Emory Upton)
Maryland Light, Battery A
Massachusetts Light, Battery A
New Jersey Light, Battery A
2d United States, Battery D

Second Division (Maj. Gen. William F. Smith)

First Brigade (Brig. Gen. Winfield S. Hancock)
(Col. Amasa Cobb)
6th Maine
43d New York
49th Pennsylvania
137th Pennsylvania
5th Wisconsin

Second Brigade (Brig. Gen. W. T. H. Brooks)
2d Vermont
3d Vermont
4th Vermont
5th Vermont
6th Vermont

Third Brigade (Col. William H. Irwin)
7th Maine
20th New York
33d New York
49th New York
77th New York

Artillery (Capt. Romeyn B. Ayres)
Maryland Light, Battery B
New York Light, 1st Battery
5th United States, Battery F

NINTH ARMY CORPS (Maj. Gen. Ambrose E. Burnside)
(Maj. Gen. Jesse L. Reno)
(Brig. Gen. Jacob D. Cox)

First Division (Brig. Gen. Orlando B. Willcox)

First Brigade (Col. Benjamin C. Christ)
28th Massachusetts
17th Michigan
79th New York
50th Pennsylvania
*Transferred from First Brigade
September 16

Second Brigade (Col. Thomas Welsh)
8th Michigan*
46th New York
45th Pennsylvania
100th Pennsylvania

Artillery
Massachusetts Light, Eighth Battery
2d United States, Battery E

Second Division (Brig. Gen. Samuel D. Sturgis)

First Brigade (Brig. Gen. James Nagle)
2d Maryland
6th New Hampshire
9th New Hampshire
48th Pennsylvania

Second Brigade (Brig. Gen. Edward Ferrero)
21st Massachusetts
35th Massachusetts
51st New York
51st Pennsylvania

Artillery
Pennsylvania Light, Battery D
4th United States, Battery E

Third Division (Brig. Gen. Isaac P. Rodman)

First Brigade (Col. Harrison S. Fairchild)
9th New York
89th New York
103d New York

Second Brigade (Col. Edward Harland)
8th Connecticut
11th Connecticut
16th Connecticut
4th Rhode Island

Artillery
5th United States, Battery A

Kanawha Division (Brig. Gen. Jacob D. Cox)
(Col. Eliakim P. Scammon)

First Brigade (Col. Eliakim P. Scammon)
(Col. Hugh Ewing)
12th Ohio
23d Ohio
30th Ohio
Ohio Light Artillery, First Battery
Gilmore's company West Virginia
Cavalry
Harrison's company West Virginia
Cavalry

Second Brigade (Col. George Crook)
11th Ohio
28th Ohio
36th Ohio
Schambeck's company Chicago Dragoons
Kentucky Light Artillery, Simmonds'
battery

Unattached
6th New York Cavalry (eight companies)
Ohio Cavalry, Third Independent Company
3d U.S. Artillery, Batteries L and M

TWELFTH ARMY CORPS (Maj. Gen. Joseph K. F. Mansfield)
(Brig. Gen. Alpheus S. Williams)

First Division (Brig. Gen. Alpheus S. Williams)
(Brig. Gen. Samuel W. Crawford)
(Brig. Gen. George H. Gordon)

First Brigade (Brig. Gen. Samuel W.
Crawford)
(Col. Joseph F. Knipe)
10th Maine
28th New York
46th Pennsylvania
124th Pennsylvania
125th Pennsylvania
128th Pennsylvania

Third Brigade (Brig. Gen. George H.
Gordon)
(Col. Thomas H. Ruger)
27th Indiana
2d Massachusetts and Pennsylvania
Zouaves d'Afrique
13th New Jersey
107th New York
3d Wisconsin

Second Division (Brig. Gen. George S. Greene)

First Brigade (Lieut. Col. Hector
Tyndale)
(Maj. Orrin J. Crane)
5th Ohio
7th Ohio
66th Ohio
28th Pennsylvania

Second Brigade (Col. Henry J.
Stainrook)
3d Maryland
102d New York
111th Pennsylvania

Third Brigade (Col. William B. Goodrich)
    (Lieut. Col. Jonathan Austin)
    3d Delaware
    Purnell Legion, Maryland
    60th New York
    78th New York

    Artillery (Capt. Clermont L. Best)
        Maine Light, 4th Battery
        Maine Light, 6th Battery
        1st New York Light, Battery M
        New York Light, 10th Battery
        Pennsylvania Light, Battery E
        Pennsylvania Light, Battery F
        4th United States, Battery F

CAVALRY DIVISION (Brig. Gen. Alfred Pleasonton)

First Brigade (Maj. Charles J. Whiting)
    5th United States
    6th United States

Second Brigade (Col. John F. Farnsworth)
    8th Illinois
    3d Indiana
    1st Massachusetts
    8th Pennsylvania

Third Brigade (Col. Richard H. Rush)
    4th Pennsylvania
    6th Pennsylvania

Fourth Brigade (Col. Andrew T. McReynolds)
    1st New York
    12th Pennsylvania

Fifth Brigade (Col. Benjamin F. Davis)
    8th New York
    3d Pennsylvania

Artillery
    2d United States, Battery A
    2d United States, Batteries B and L
    2d United States, Battery M
    3d United States, Batteries C and G

Unattached
    15th Pennsylvania Cavalry (detachment),
        Col. William Palmer

Organization of the Army of Northern Virginia, General Robert E. Lee, commanding, during the Maryland Campaign

LONGSTREET'S CORPS (Maj. Gen. James Longstreet)

McLaws' Division (Maj. Gen. Lafayette McLaws)

Kershaw's Brigade (Brig. Gen. J. B. Kershaw)
    2d South Carolina
    3d South Carolina
    7th South Carolina
    8th South Carolina

Semmes' Brigade (Brig. Gen. Paul J. Semmes)
    10th Georgia
    53d Georgia
    15th Virginia
    32d Virginia

Cobb's Brigade (Brig. Gen. Howell Cobb)
    (Lieut. Col. C. C. Sanders)
    (Lieut. Col. William MacRae)
    16th Georgia
    24th Georgia
    Cobb's (Georgia) Legion
    15th North Carolina

Barksdale's Brigade (Brig. Gen. William Barksdale)
    13th Mississippi
    17th Mississippi
    18th Mississippi
    21st Mississippi

Artillery (Maj. S. P. Hamilton)
(Col. H. C. Cabell)
Manly's (North Carolina) battery
Pulaski (Georgia) Artillery
Richmond (Fayette) Artillery
Richmond Howitzers (1st company)
Troup (Georgia) Artillery

Anderson's Division (Maj. Gen. Richard H. Anderson)

Wilcox's Brigade (Col. Alfred Cumming)
    8th Alabama
    9th Alabama
    10th Alabama
    11th Alabama

Armistead's Brigade (Brig. Gen. Lewis A. Armistead)
    (Col. J. G. Hodges)
    9th Virginia
    14th Virginia
    38th Virginia
    53d Virginia
    57th Virginia

Mahone's Brigade (Col. William A. Parham)
    6th Virginia
    12th Virginia
    16th Virginia
    41st Virginia
    61st Virginia

Pryor's Brigade (Brig. Gen. Roger A. Pryor)
    14th Alabama
    2d Florida
    8th Florida
    3d Virginia

Featherston's Brigade (Brig. Gen.
Winfield S. Featherston)
    (Col. Carnot Posey)
  12th Mississippi
  16th Mississippi
  19th Mississippi
  2d Mississippi Battalion

Wright's Brigade (Brig. Gen. A. R.
Wright)
  44th Alabama
  3d Georgia
  22d Georgia
  48th Georgia

Artillery (Maj. John S. Saunders)
  Donaldsonville (Louisiana) Artillery (Maurin's battery)
  Huger's (Virginia) battery
  Moorman's (Virginia) battery
  Thompson's (Grimes') (Virginia) battery

Jones' Division (Brig. Gen. David R. Jones)

Toombs' Brigade (Brig. Gen. Robert
Toombs)
    (Col. Henry L. Benning)
  2d Georgia
  15th Georgia
  17th Georgia
  20th Georgia

Drayton's Brigade (Brig. Gen. Thomas F.
Drayton)
  50th Georgia
  51st Georgia
  15th South Carolina

Kemper's Brigade (Brig. Gen. J. L.
Kemper)
  1st Virginia
  7th Virginia
  11th Virginia
  17th Virginia
  24th Virginia

Anderson's Brigade (Col. George T.
Anderson)
  1st Georgia (Regulars)
  7th Georgia
  8th Georgia
  9th Georgia
  11th Georgia

Artillery
  Wise (Virginia) Artillery (J. S. Brown's battery)

Pickett's Brigade (Col. Eppa Hunton)
    (Brig. Gen. R. B. Garnett)
  8th Virginia
  18th Virginia
  19th Virginia
  28th Virginia
  56th Virginia

Jenkins' Brigade (Col. Joseph Walker)
  1st South Carolina
  2d South Carolina Rifles
  5th South Carolina
  6th South Carolina
  4th South Carolina Battalion
  Palmetto (South Carolina) Sharp-
    shooters

Walker's Division (Brig. Gen. John G. Walker)

Walker's Brigade (Col. Van H. Manning)
(Col. E. D. Hall)
- 3d Arkansas
- 27th North Carolina
- 46th North Carolina
- 48th North Carolina
- 30th Virginia
- French's (Virginia) battery

Ransom's Brigade (Brig. Gen. Robert Ransom, Jr.)
- 24th North Carolina
- 25th North Carolina
- 35th North Carolina
- 49th North Carolina
- Branch's Field Artillery (Virginia)

Hood's Division (Brig. Gen. John B. Hood)

Hood's Brigade (Col. W. T. Wofford)
- 18th Georgia
- Hampton (South Carolina) Legion
- 1st Texas
- 4th Texas
- 5th Texas

Law's Brigade (Col. E. M. Law)
- 4th Alabama
- 2d Mississippi
- 11th Mississippi
- 6th North Carolina

Artillery (Maj. B. W. Frobel)
- German Artillery (South Carolina)
- Palmetto Artillery (South Carolina)
- Rowan Artillery (North Carolina)

Evans' Brigade (Brig. Gen. Nathan G. Evans)
- (Col. P. F. Stevens)
- 17th South Carolina
- 18th South Carolina
- 22d South Carolina
- 23d South Carolina
- Holcombe (South Carolina) Legion
- Macbeth (South Carolina) Artillery

ARTILLERY

Washington (Louisiana) Artillery (Col. J. B. Walton)
- 1st Company
- 2d Company
- 3d Company
- 4th Company

Lee's Battalion (Col. S. D. Lee)
- Ashland (Virginia) Artillery
- Bedford (Virginia) Artillery
- Brooks (South Carolina) Artillery
- Eubank's (Virginia) battery
- Madison (Louisiana) Light Artillery
- Parker's (Virginia) battery

JACKSON'S CORPS (Maj. Gen. Thomas J. Jackson)

Ewell's Division (Brig. Gen. A. R. Lawton)
(Brig. Gen. Jubal A. Early)

Lawton's Brigade (Col. M. Douglass)
(Maj. J. H. Lowe)
(Col. John H. Lamar)
13th Georgia
26th Georgia
31st Georgia
38th Georgia
60th Georgia
61st Georgia

Trimble's Brigade (Col. James A. Walker)
15th Alabama
12th Georgia
21st Georgia
21st North Carolina
1st North Carolina Battalion

Early's Brigade (Brig. Gen. Jubal A. Early)
(Col. William Smith)
13th Virginia
25th Virginia
31st Virginia
44th Virginia
49th Virginia
52d Virginia
58th Virginia

Hay's Brigade (Brig. Gen. Harry T. Hays)
5th Louisiana
6th Louisiana
7th Louisiana
8th Louisiana
14th Louisiana

Artillery (Maj. A. R. Courtney)
Chesapeake (Maryland) Artillery
Courtney (Virginia) Artillery
Johnson's (Virginia) battery
Louisiana Guard Artillery
First Maryland Battery
Staunton (Virginia) Artillery

Hill's Light Division (Maj. Gen. Ambrose P. Hill)

Branch's Brigade (Brig. Gen. L. O'B. Branch)
(Col. James H. Lane)
7th North Carolina
18th North Carolina
28th North Carolina
33d North Carolina
37th North Carolina

Archer's Brigade (Brig. Gen. J. J. Archer)
(Col. Peter Turney)
5th Alabama Battalion
19th Georgia
1st Tennessee (Provisional Army)
7th Tennessee
14th Tennessee

Gregg's Brigade (Brig. Gen. Maxcy Gregg)
1st South Carolina (Provisional Army)
1st South Carolina Rifles
12th South Carolina
13th South Carolina
14th South Carolina

Pender's Brigade (Brig. Gen. William D. Pender)
(Col. R. H. Brewer)
16th North Carolina
22d North Carolina
34th North Carolina
38th North Carolina

Field's Brigade (Colonel Brockenbrough)
40th Virginia
47th Virginia
55th Virginia
22d Virginia Battalion

Thomas' Brigade (Col. Edward L. Thomas)
14th Georgia
35th Georgia
45th Georgia
49th Georgia

Artillery (Maj. R. L. Walker)
Crenshaw's (Virginia) battery
Fredericksburg (Virginia) Artillery
Letcher (Virginia) Artillery
Pee Dee (South Carolina) Artillery
Purcell (Virginia) Artillery

Jackson's Division (Brig. Gen. John R. Jones)
(Brig. Gen. W. E. Starke)
(Col. A. J. Grigsby)

Winder's Brigade (Col. A. J. Grigsby)
(Lieut. Col. R. D. Gardner)
(Maj. H. J. Williams)
2d Virginia
4th Virginia
5th Virginia
27th Virginia
33d Virginia

Jones' Brigade (Col. B. T. Johnson)
(Brig. Gen. J. R. Jones)
(Capt. J. E. Penn)
(Capt. A. C. Page)
(Capt. R. W. Withers)
21st Virginia
42d Virginia
48th Virginia
1st Virginia Battalion

Taliaferro's Brigade (Col. E. T. H. Warren)
(Col. J. W. Jackson)
(Col. J. L. Sheffield)
47th Alabama
48th Alabama
10th Virginia
23d Virginia
37th Virginia

Starke's Brigade (Brig. Gen. William E. Starke)
(Col. L. A. Stafford)
(Col. E. Pendleton)
1st Louisiana
2d Louisiana
9th Louisiana
10th Louisiana
15th Louisiana
Coppens' (Louisiana) battalion

Artillery (Maj. L. M. Shumaker)
Alleghany (Virginia) Artillery
Brockenbrough's (Maryland) battery
Danville (Virginia) Artillery
Hampden (Virginia) Artillery
Lee (Virginia) Battery
Rockbridge (Virginia) Artillery

Hill's Division (Maj. Gen. Daniel H. Hill)

Ripley's Brigade (Brig. Gen. Roswell S. Ripley)
(Col. George Doles)
4th Georgia
44th Georgia
1st North Carolina
3d North Carolina

Garland's Brigade (Brig. Gen. Samuel Garland, Jr.)
(Col. D. K. McRae)
5th North Carolina
12th North Carolina
13th North Carolina
20th North Carolina
23d North Carolina

Rodes' Brigade (Brig. Gen. R. E. Rodes)
3d Alabama
5th Alabama
6th Alabama
12th Alabama
26th alabama

Anderson's Brigade (Brig. Gen. George B. Anderson)
(Col. R. T. Bennett)
2d North Carolina
4th North Carolina
14th North Carolina
30th North Carolina

Colquitt's Brigade (Col. A. H. Colquitt)
13th Alabama
6th Georgia
23d Georgia
27th Georgia
28th Georgia

Artillery (Major Pierson)
Hardaway's (Alabama) battery
Jeff. Davis (Alabama) Artillery
Jones' (Virginia) battery
King William (Virginia) Artillery

RESERVE ARTILLERY (Brig. Gen. William N. Pendleton)

Brown's Battalion (Col. J. Thompson Brown)
Powhatan Artillery
Richmond Howitzers, 2d company
Richmond Howitzers, 3d company
Salem Artillery
Williamsburg Artillery

Jones' Battalion (Maj. H. P. Jones)
Morris (Virginia) Artillery
Orange (Virginia) Artillery
Turner's (Virginia) battery
Wimbish's (Virginia) battery

Cutts' Battalion (Lieut. Col. A. S. Cutts)
Blackshears' (Georgia) battery
Irwin (Georgia) Artillery
Lloyd's (North Carolina) battery
Patterson's (Georgia) battery
Ross's (Georgia) battery

Nelson's Battalion (Maj. William Nelson)
Amherst (Virginia) Artillery
Fluvanna (Virginia) Artillery
Huckstep's (Virginia) battery
Johnson's (Virginia) battery
Milledge (Georgia) Artillery

Miscellaneous
Cutshaw's (Virginia) battery
Dixie (Virginia) Artillery
Magruder (Virginia) Artillery
Rice's (Virginia) battery

CAVALRY (Maj. Gen. James E. B. Stuart)

Hampton's Brigade (Brig. Gen. Wade Hampton)
1st North Carolina
2d South Carolina
10th Virginia
Cobb's (Georgia) Legion
Jeff. Davis Legion

Lee's Brigade (Brig. Gen. Fitz. Lee)
1st Virginia
3d Virginia
4th Virginia
5th Virginia
9th Virginia

Robertson's Brigade (Brig. Gen. B. H. Robertson)
(Col. Thomas T. Munford)
2d Virginia
6th Virginia
7th Virginia
12th Virginia
17th Virginia Battalion

HORSE ARTILLERY (Capt. John Pelham)

Chew's (Virginia) battery
Hart's (South Carolina) battery
Pelham's (Virginia) battery

APPENDIX III
RECAPITULATION OF CASUALTIES

Estimates of numbers engaged in the battles of the Maryland Campaign vary, and statistics on killed, wounded, captured and missing are incomplete. Participants attempted to fill gaps as they wrote their official reports, and historians have tried to refine the data. The tabulation that follows is drawn from the *Official Record*, Vol. XIX, Pt. 1, pp. 189–20, 810–13, and from Thomas L. Livermore, *Numbers and Losses in the Civil War in America, 1861–1865* (New York: Houghton, Mifflin and Company, 1901).

UNION ARMIES
Battles of South Mountain
September 14, 1862
Total Engaged 28,480

	Killed	Wounded	Captured or Missing	Aggregate
I Corps	170	720	43	933
VI Corps	115	416	2	533
IX Corps	158	670	30	858
Cavalry Brigade	0	1	0	1
Total	443	1,807	75	2,325

Harpers Ferry
September 13–15, 1862
Total Engaged 14,200

	Killed	Wounded	Captured or Missing	Aggregate
Composite Garrison	44	173	12,520	12,737

Antietam
September 16–17, 1862
Total Engaged 87,100

	Killed	Wounded	Captured or Missing	Aggregate
I Corps	348	2,016	255	2,619
II Corps	860	3,801	548	5,209
V Corps	21	107	2	130
VI Corps	70	355	33	438
IX Corps	432	1,741	120	2,293
XII Corps	274	1,384	85	1,743
Couch's Division	0	9	0	9
Cavalry Division	5	23	0	28
Total	2,010	9,416	1,043	12,469

Boteler's Ford
September 19–20, 1862

	Killed	Wounded	Captured or Missing	Aggregate
V Corps	70	148	128	346

ARMY OF NORTHERN VIRGINIA
Total Killed and Wounded*
September 14–20, 1862
Total Engaged 51,800

	Killed	Wounded	Aggregate
Jackson's Corps	725	3,842	4,567
Longstreet's Corps	795	4,621	5,416
Evans' Independent Brigade	47	262	309
Total	1,567	8,725	10,292

*Livermore estimated Confederate "Captured or Missing" to be approximately 2,000. Confederate returns in the *Official Records* do not address this category of losses and may underestimate killed and wounded.

INDEX

Legend for Maps

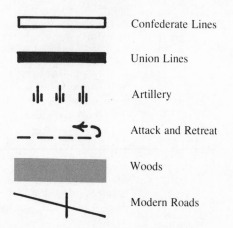

Confederate Lines

Union Lines

Artillery

Attack and Retreat

Woods

Modern Roads

Scale is variable—See notations on maps